Praise for *Data Mesh*

Zhamak impressively addresses what any data-driven company needs to implement data mesh at the culture, organizational, architectural, and technical levels to deliver value at scale sustainably. Anyone who works in data must have this book on their shelf and read it a couple of times. Like a good movie, they will discover new subtleties over and over again.

—Andy Petrella, Founder of Kensu

In this book, Zhamak provides the nuance and detail that turns data mesh from a compelling idea into a viable strategy for putting data to work inside complex organizations.

—Chris Ford, Head of Technology, Thoughtworks Spain

With *Data Mesh*, Zhamak was able to bring together the technical and organizational design practices that helped engineering organizations scale and package them in a way that makes sense for the data and analytics space.

—Danilo Sato, Head of Data & AI for UK/Europe Thoughtworks

Data Mesh is a new concept, and data practitioners need to learn when and how to implement it. Zhamak's new book provides a good balance of theory and practice that can guide engineers on their path and enable them to make good design choices. The detailed approach in the book makes this new concept clear and useful. The best part, though, are the diagrams—sometimes a picture is worth more than 1,000 words.

—Gwen Shapira, Cofounder and CPO at Nile Platform;
Author of Kafka: The Definitive Guide

Data Mesh
Delivering Data-Driven Value at Scale

Zhamak Dehghani

Beijing · Boston · Farnham · Sebastopol · Tokyo

Data Mesh

by Zhamak Dehghani

Published by O'Reilly Media, Inc., 1005 Gravenstein Highway North, Sebastopol, CA 95472.

O'Reilly books may be purchased for educational, business, or sales promotional use. Online editions are also available for most titles (*http://oreilly.com*). For more information, contact our corporate/institutional sales department: 800-998-9938 or *corporate@oreilly.com*.

Acquisitions Editor: Melissa Duffield
Development Editor: Gary O'Brien
Production Editor: Beth Kelly
Copyeditor: Charles Roumeliotis
Proofreader: Kim Wimpsett

Indexer: Potomac Indexing, LLC
Interior Designer: David Futato
Cover Designer: Karen Montgomery
Illustrator: Kate Dullea

March 2022:   First Edition

Revision History for the First Edition
2022-03-08:   First Release
2022-07-15:   Second Release

See *http://oreilly.com/catalog/errata.csp?isbn=9781492092391* for release details.

978-1-098-11276-9

[LSI]

To Dad
Your light remains

Table of Contents

Part III. How to Design the Data Mesh Architecture

Part IV.   How to Design the Data Product Architecture

Foreword

I've been involved in developing software for large corporations for several decades, and managing data has always been a major architectural issue. In the early days of my career, there was a lot of enthusiasm for a single enterprise-wide data model, often stored in a single enterprise-wide database. But we soon learned that having a plethora of applications accessing a shared data store was a disaster of ad-hoc coupling. Even without that, deeper problems existed. Core ideas to an enterprise, such as a "customer," required different data models in different business units. Corporate acquisitions further muddied the waters.

As a response, wiser enterprises have decentralized their data, pushing data storage, models, and management into different business units. That way, the people who best understand the data in their domain are responsible for managing that data. They collaborate with other domains through well-defined APIs. Since these APIs can contain behavior, we have more flexibility for how that data is shared and more importantly, how we evolve data management over time.

While this has been increasingly the way to go for day-to-day operations, data analytics has remained a more centralized activity. Data warehouses aimed to provide an enterprise repository of curated critical information. But such a centralized group struggled with the work and its conflicting customers, particularly since they didn't have a good understanding of the data or the needs of its consumers. A data lake helped by popularizing access to raw data, allowing analysts to get closer to original source, but too easily became a data swamp of poor understanding and provenance.

Data mesh seeks to apply the same lessons we learned with operational data to the world of analytical data. Business unit domains become responsible for publishing analytical data through APIs the same way they do for operational data. By treating their data as a first class product, they communicate the meaning and provenance of the data, and they collaborate with their consumers. To make the work involved in this achievable, the enterprise needs to provide a platform for building and publishing these data products, together with a federated governance structure to keep it all coherent. Pervading all of this is a recognition of the importance of technical excellence so that the platforms and products can evolve swiftly as business needs change.

Data mesh is thus at heart a rather simple, perhaps obvious, application of a well-established data management principle to the world of analytical data. In practice, however, there's a great deal involved in making this work, particularly since so much vendor investment has focused on centralized models, exacerbated by not supporting the practices (such as testing, abstraction building, and refactoring) that developers of operations systems know are essential for healthy software.

Zhamak has been at the sharp end of this, advising our clients on the path forward, learning from their setbacks and triumphs, and nudging vendors into producing the tools to make it easier to build these platforms. This book collects her and her colleagues' knowledge in this early but important stage of the adoption of data meshes worldwide. I've learned a lot about these pragmatic difficulties while reviewing this book, and I'm convinced that anyone who wants their organization to best utilize their data resources will find this book charts out the best we understand of the path forward.

— Martin Fowler
Chief Scientist, Thoughtworks

Preface

Data mesh is the nudge that puts us on a new trajectory in how we approach data: how we imagine data, how we capture and share it, and how we create value from it, at scale and in the field of analytics and AI. This new trajectory moves us away from the centralization of data and its ownership toward a decentralized model. This new path embraces the complexity of our organizations, their rapid change, and their continuous growth. It aims to enable organizations to get value from data at scale, despite the messiness and organizational complexity.

Looking back through the history of our industry, we have been nudged before. The birth of Unix and its philosophy to "Write programs that do one thing and do it well. Write programs to work together ..." was perhaps the butterfly flapping its wings that set the conditions for us to tackle complexity at the heart of *software*, decades later, through distributed architecture, service-oriented design, communications through standard APIs, and autonomous domain team organization. I hope that data mesh sets the condition for a new path to tackle complexity at the heart of *data* in the field that needs it most, analytics and AI.

I formulated the thesis of data mesh in 2018, after observing common failure patterns in getting value from data in large and technologically forward companies that had made substantial investments in their data technologies. Observing their struggles to scale data management solutions and organization to meet their ambitious data aspirations led to questioning the decades-old assumptions in how we get value from data: we collect it, we centrally store it, we put a data team in charge of it, and then we unleash it on a diverse set of users and use cases. These assumptions had to be revisited.

I shared the ideas behind data mesh in an O'Reilly conference in New York around the same time. I called it "Beyond the Lake" (*https://oreil.ly/O3hbf*) as I was struggling to solve one of the hardest problems in technology, "naming things." Despite my fear of receiving harsh criticism, as I was speaking sacrilegious words of fundamentally shifting our view on data, the audience positively embraced the talk. The pains of data users—data analyst or scientist—were real; they were all struggling to get timely access to high quality and trustworthy data. The pains of data engineers were shared, stuck in the middle between data providers and data users, trying to get meaning out of data from unreliable upstreams and put it in a form that others can use, and doing all that without close contact with the business. The leaders in the audience nodded that the returns on their data and analytics solutions were middling. I left that conference feeling more confident about what could come *beyond the lake*. A few months later I missed a week-long tech advisory board meeting in China. My three-year-old daughter had broken a fever the night before the flight out of the US. I made it to the plane, hiding my desperation separating from my sick kid for a week, but I broke down as the pilot announced to the crew to secure the plane doors. I got off the plane. Now I had a week to hide and put the thoughts and experience of data mesh into words in an article called "How to Move Beyond a Monolithic Data Lake to a Distributed Data Mesh" (*https://oreil.ly/rxjiW*), kindly hosted by Martin Fowler. The article was a success and received an incredible amount of readership, as if I had just said the words that others were quietly thinking of. Three years on, this book goes into the depth of why, what, and how to realize Data Mesh.

Why I Wrote This Book and Why Now

In the handful of years since the creation of data mesh, it has received tremendous support from lead adopter companies implementing it. It has encouraged vendors to attempt to adapt their products to suit data mesh implementations. It has created a thriving learning community to share their experiences.

Despite such rapid movement, I'm perhaps writing this book a bit earlier than I would have liked. We are still in the early years of a fundamentally different approach in sharing and creating data for analytical and machine learning (ML) use cases. But our industry has the tendency to percolate new concepts and buzzwords beyond recognition. Hence, I decided to write this book to create a common foundation for future evolutions of data mesh implementations. I wanted to make sure, before we get carried away with building new technical solutions, we understand why we need to make a change, what the problems we are trying to address are, and how we are trying to do that.

This book creates a foundation of *the objectives* of data mesh, why we should bother, its *first principles*. We look at how to apply the first principles to create a high-level *architecture* and leave you with tools to *execute* its implementation and shift the *organization* and *culture*.

Who Should Read This Book

This book is written for people with a diverse set of roles and skill sets. Data mesh is a paradigm shift, and it needs the collective effort of many complementary roles and disciplines to make it a reality for any organization, from architects, practitioners and infrastructure engineers to product managers, data leaders, and executives.

Here is a quick summary of readers' personas and what they can take away from this book:

- *Analytical data users* such as data scientists and analysts should read this book to understand what data mesh enables for them and how they become part of this movement as an active member of the mesh, in turn, providing their insights and inferences as new data products are shared on the mesh.

- *Data providers*, such as application teams or data engineers, should read this book to understand how data mesh integrates the two planes of operational and analytical data and applications. They will see and how their roles move into cross-functional domain teams and what kind of architecture they will build to enable data mesh.

- *Infrastructure product owners, architects, and engineers* should read this book to understand the role and design of a self-serve data platform to create a well-integrated set of services that enable data sharing decentrally at scale and by cross-functional domain teams.

- *Data governance teams* should read this book to understand the new structure and approach to achieving governance objectives in a way that is conducive to independent domain ownership of data, removes organizational bottlenecks, and relies heavily on automation and computation. This book introduces a new role and shape for data governance.

- *Data leaders, managers, and executives* should read this book to understand the paradigm shift that is coming and learn to formulate a data strategy based on data mesh, execute its transformation, and cultivate their organization along the way.

This book is written for people with backgrounds in traditional data and analytics, and people who have been more focused on software and application delivery. Data mesh closes the gap between these two groups.

If you come from a *traditional data background*, perhaps having been a data engineer or data analyst, I encourage you to suspend your past biases. Be open to new ways of solving the problem of analytical data management and processing. Embrace computation and automation as an indispensable companion of data.

If you come from an *application development background*, software architecture or application infrastructure engineering, read this book with empathy for data and analytics. See yourself as part of the solution for sharing data and getting value from data to improve your applications. Imagine a new future where data work and application development are two complementary pieces of making your solutions successful.

How to Read This Book

I highly encourage you to start with the Prologue: Imagine Data Mesh. This short chapter helps you feel and visualize what data mesh looks like in action. It demonstrates the impact of data mesh on a day-to-day basis. It shows the principles of data mesh applied through a fictional story of a digital streaming company: Daff, Inc.

The rest of the book is structured into five parts:

Part I, "What Is Data Mesh?"
> This part introduces each of the data mesh first principles and describes their transformational impact. I do hope that everyone reads this section of the book as the content here informs all discussions around data mesh to come.

Part II, "Why Data Mesh?"
> If you are unsure that data mesh is the right choice for you, or if you want to understand what problems it solves and how it solves them, or simply influence others, read this part of the book. It compares data mesh to the past and discusses why what has got us here won't take us to the future. I encourage all readers to go through this content.

Part III, "How to Design the Data Mesh Architecture"
> This part is for all technologists, leaders, or practitioners. The chapters in this part of the book focus on the high-level architecture of data mesh components. They help you design your data mesh architecture as well as evaluate off-the-shelf technologies for alignment with data mesh.

Part IV, "How to Design the Data Product Architecture"
> This part goes into the detailed design of a core concept in data mesh, called a data product. It intends to simplify complex concepts without compromising on necessary details. It should be approachable for all roles, managers, leaders, or practitioners. However, people who will be in a technical leadership position of implementing various aspects of data mesh will get the most out of this part of the book.

Part V, "How to Get Started"
> This part is a guide for people in roles that influence the overall execution of the data strategy and organizational change. It gives actionable advice on how to

approach an evolutionary execution of a data mesh transformation, and how to make organizational design decisions around team structure, incentives, culture, and so on.

Conventions Used in This Book

The following typographical conventions are used in this book:

Italic
> Indicates new terms, URLs, email addresses, filenames, and file extensions.

Bold
> Used for data domain and data product names.

`Constant width`
> Used for program listings, as well as within paragraphs to refer to program elements such as variable or function names, databases, data types, environment variables, statements, and keywords.

`Constant width bold`
> Shows commands or other text that should be typed literally by the user.

`Constant width italic`
> Shows text that should be replaced with user-supplied values or by values determined by context.

> This element signifies a general note.

> This element indicates a warning or caution.

O'Reilly Online Learning

For almost 40 years, *O'Reilly* (*http://oreilly.com*) has provided technology and business training, knowledge, and insight to help companies succeed.

Our unique network of experts and innovators share their knowledge and expertise through books, articles, conferences, and our online learning platform. O'Reilly's online learning platform gives you on-demand access to live training courses, in-depth learning paths, interactive coding environments, and a vast collection of text and video from O'Reilly and 200+ other publishers. For more information, please visit *http://oreilly.com*.

How to Contact Us

Please address comments and questions concerning this book to the publisher:

O'Reilly Media, Inc.
1005 Gravenstein Highway North
Sebastopol, CA 95472
800-998-9938 (in the United States or Canada)
707-829-0515 (international or local)
707-829-0104 (fax)

We have a web page for this book, where we list errata, examples, and any additional information. You can access this page at *https://oreil.ly/data-mesh*.

Send email to *bookquestions@oreilly.com* to comment or ask technical questions about this book.

For more information about our books, courses, conferences, and news, see our website at *https://www.oreilly.com*.

Find us on Facebook: *https://facebook.com/oreilly*

Follow us on Twitter: *https://twitter.com/oreillymedia*

Watch us on YouTube: *https://youtube.com/oreillymedia*

Acknowledgments

I like to dedicate this book to my partner, Adrian Paoletti, and daughter, Arianna Paoletti. Without their patience and selfless love and support, this book would not exist. We missed many holidays and weekends together over the last year and half for me to finish this book. I will always be grateful for your understanding and love. I would also like to dedicate this book to my mother, Nayer Dadpay, and sister, Parisa Dehghani, whose love and encouraging words have gently nudged me through the process of completing this book. I love you all.

They say writing a book is a solitary endeavor—not in my case. I'd like to thank my thoughtful early reviewers that came along on the writing journey and generously shared their time and feedback. In no particular order, Andy Petrella, thank you for sharing your perspective of a data scientist with humility and humor. Chris Ford, thank you for your thoughtful architectural comments, often broadening my view. Mammand Zadeh, thank you for bringing the voice of an experienced yet pragmatic data infrastructure leader and always helping me connect the dots from idea to reality. Martin Fowler, thank you for illuminating the big picture, showing me the gaps, and helping me to clarify complex concepts. Danilo Sato and Sam Ramji, thank you for your guidance, wisdom, and time.

People at Thoughtworks have been part of the creation of many epoch-making movements in the tech industry: microservices, continuous delivery, agile, and the list goes on. One of the reasons behind that is that Thoughtworks leadership creates just the right conditions for distributive creativity in the pursuit of software excellence. In no particular order, Rebecca Parsons and Chris Murphy, thank you for supporting me in writing this book. I'd like to thank my past and present colleagues at Thoughtworks in no particular order: Gagan Madan, Zichuan Xiong, Neal Ford, Samia Rahman, Sina Jahangirizadeh, Ken Collier, Srikar Ayilavarapu, Sheroy Marker, Danilo Sato, Emily Gorcenski, David Colls, Erik Nagler, and many others.

I would like to thank all the people at O'Reilly who have made publishing this book possible. Among the wonderful and passionate family of O'Reilly, I'd like to call out Gary O'Brien. Gary, thank you for your continuous support and all the weekends you took away from family to review my content and answer my questions, cheering me up through the lows and the doubts and getting me back on track. Melissa Duffield, thank you for getting this book off the ground, helping me to take the first step and supporting me along with your undeniable human empathy.

Finally, I would like to thank my teacher and mentor through the writing process, Martin Fowler. Martin, thank you for guiding me every step of the way.

Prologue: Imagine Data Mesh

Imagination will often carry us to worlds that never were. But without it we go nowhere.
—Carl Sagan

Behind every successful company stand three, failed and forgotten. This is a ratio by which the failures outnumber the survivors.[1] In the age of AI, it is no curious coincidence that the ones standing and leading have cracked the code of complexity, embedded data-driven experimentation in every aspect of their business, embraced continuous change in response to rapid learnings, and partnered with machine intelligence to understand reality beyond human logic and reasoning.

Daff, Inc.,[2] a fictional global music and audio streaming company,[3] is an example of such a company. Daff has successfully delivered on its mission: "Connect artists and listeners across the globe, in an immersive artistic experience, at every moment of life." Behind Daff's mission stands the company's great expectations from data, analytics, and machine intelligence, delivered through an approach known as *data mesh*. Data mesh is the backbone of Daff's data strategy, architecture, and operating model that has given them scale and speed to experiment, learn, and adapt using data and machine learning (ML).

What I want to share with you is Daff's story after they have implemented data mesh. Through the story of Daff you will learn the essence of data mesh. You will see data mesh principles applied, its benefits demonstrated, its architecture in action, and the organizational structure, up and running.

---

1 According to the US Bureau of Labor Statistics (BLS) data (*https://oreil.ly/SrQSC*), only 25% of new businesses make it to 15 years or more. These statistics haven't changed much over time and have been fairly consistent since the 1990s.

2 The fictional company's name, "Daff," comes from the name of a Persian percussion instrument dating back more than 3,000 years ago and still played today, as a symbol for something long-lasting.

3 Daff is inspired by my experience as a listener of Spotify (*https://oreil.ly/rzLnp*). The examples of internal workings of the company and its services are all fictional.

I find the best way to introduce a complex phenomenon such as data mesh is with an example. However, it's too early in the life of data mesh to describe an example of a company with a mature data mesh, as we are currently in the process of building the first data meshes. Therefore, I'm describing a fictional organization that exhibits the characteristics I would expect to see in a few years' time. While we don't expect that reality will conform to our imagination, our vision of what we're working toward is a vital part of understanding what we are trying to achieve. To best convey this picture, I'm writing about this fictional company as I would imagine it being featured in the business press.

As I tell the story, I will leave footnotes for you to find your way to later chapters that deep dive into the facets I briefly surface here. However, my intention is for you to stay with me in the story and only fly off to the later chapters after you reach the ending of this prologue.

Data Mesh in Action

It's the year 2022.

Daff has demonstrated strong growth of its premium subscribers with a relentless focus on a user experience utilizing machine learning. The company remains one of the most loved feature-rich platforms that has used data to personalize an immersive experience, curate an expansive library of content, and reach new and rising artists. Daff has continuously evolved by adding new services and expanding into adjacent domains of streaming podcasts, videos, and organizing events. Today, Daff operates in almost every country worldwide with a growing ecosystem of local and global business collaborators, from event and art venues to workout platforms.

Over the last three years, Daff has pivoted how they manage and use analytical data to an approach called *data mesh*. Data mesh is a new approach to harnessing value from analytical data at scale that aligns data and business closer than ever.

Daff has deployed sophisticated machine learning models that continuously exploit patterns in a diverse and evolving set of data, internal and external to the organization. Daff has served its listeners with recommendations specialized to their taste, mood, time of day, and location. Using data, they have empowered artists with targeted campaigns to help them grow their reach. They have the real-time pulse of their adaptive business with business analytics, dashboards, reports, and visualization. This is just the tip of the iceberg of how Daff gets value from their data.

Let's take a walk around Daff to see how they do it.

A Culture of Data Curiosity and Experimentation

One of the most notable changes in Daff is the ubiquitous culture that dares to obsessively ask, "What if …": what if we could make a change to make things just a little bit better? There is a culture that obsessively runs experiments, observes the results, analyzes the data, makes sense of it, learns from it, and adapts.

This culture is built on a technical foundation that has just made it so easy for everyone to dare to try: try big experiments with applied machine learning or little ones just tweaking user interface features.

Daff is organized around business units that it refers to as *domains*. The **player** domain focuses on the core music player used on mobile devices, the **partnership** domain works with business partners such as exercise applications and art venues, and the **playlist** domain investigates advanced approaches for generating playlists. Each domain combines software development and broader business capabilities and is responsible for the software components that support that domain.

Walking around Daff you notice that at any point in time, there are many concurrent experiments being run by each domain to improve their applications and services. For example, **player** teams are continuously experimenting with better engagement with users. The **partnership** domain team is experimenting with data captured from a variety of external sources such as **exercise platforms**, **art venues**, etc. The **playlist** teams keep applying more advanced machine learning in curating and recommending engaging compilations. And the **artist** domain team is utilizing machine learning to discover, attract, and onboard artists who normally would have gone unnoticed.

Every domain of the business and their collaborating technology teams have a deep appreciation for meaningful, trustworthy, and secure data. Not only that, everyone has an expectation that on-demand access to data across the organization is a norm. They know their role in making that happen. They are all responsible for data and have a stake in it.

Every domain is enthusiastically applying machine learning models wherever the feature or the function of the domain can be implemented through the exploitation of past data and patterns in it. For example, the **playlist** teams are using generative machine learning models to create weird and wonderful compilations. The compilations are targeted for different activities, from running to focusing on learning. The **artist** team is exploiting multiple datasets from social media and other agencies outside of Daff to detect emerging artists and onboard, promote, and connect them with their new audience.

You can feel the enthusiasm around data usage and learning a new reality that allows for the creation and discovery of signals that would have been just noise to our human senses.[4]

Data culture before data mesh

This culture vastly contrasts what Daff was three years ago. Data collection, experimentation, and intelligence were outsourced to a separate data team. The data team was under sheer pressure. Domains did not have trust in the data, or often couldn't find the data they needed. The data team was always playing catchup, either chasing the data pipeline havoc caused by every little change in upstream applications and their databases or trying to meet the needs of the impatient domains needing a data solution yesterday. The domains themselves had taken no responsibility and interest in making data readily available, reliable, and usable. The lead time and friction to get to the right data made it incredibly difficult for domains to dare imagine new experiments.

Comparing the two experiences shows how far Daff has come in three years after their pivot to data mesh.

An Embedded Partnership with Data and ML

The data experimentation culture just seems too good to be true. To see what it looks like in practice, let's follow the story of a recent data-driven business feature Daff has worked on and follow the experience of the people involved.

Smart music playlists have been a successful feature of the Daff platform. The **music playlist** domain has worked on multiple ML models that cross-correlate data from a variety of sources to recommend better-matched playlists for listeners, depending on where they are, what they're doing, where their interest lies, and what the occasion is.

The playlist ML models exploit patterns in analytical data products from a variety of sources across the organization such as:

- Data shared by the **listener** domain, **listener profiles**, **listener social networks**, **listener locations**, etc., to understand the context and cohorts of listeners.
- Data shared by the **player** domain, **play sessions** and **play events,** to understand the behavior and preferences of listeners on their player devices.
- Data from the **music album** domain, **music tracks**, and **music profiles,** to get an understanding of the profiles and classifications of music tracks.

---

4 See Chapter 16, "Organization and Culture", for a discussion on values, culture, incentives, and responsibilities in a data mesh organization, utilizing the Daff example introduced here.

There are multiple trained machine learning models that generate smart playlists such as **monday playlists, sunday morning playlists, focus playlists,** and so on.

The **playlist** team shares these continuously improved compilations as *data products* to other teams. Data as a product is a well-established concept that refers to data shared following Daff's established data sharing standards. Data products are automatically accessible through the global data discovery tool. They share and guarantee a set of service-level objectives (SLOs), such as how often each playlist is refreshed, its accuracy, and timeliness. They have up-to-date and easy to understand documentation. In short, data products are high-quality data available to users with the right access permissions, and they are easy to understand and use.

The **player** domain team that focuses on the presentation of content to listeners across different player user interfaces—such as mobile, desktop, car, etc.—is one of the main users of the **playlist** data products. They continuously consume the latest and greatest playlists and present them to the listeners.

The **playlist** team is planning to advance their models to recommend a new variety of playlists for different sports activities, e.g., **running playlists, cycling playlists,** and so on. They need to find existing data that has information about music that listeners have liked and played during sports activities.

To get started, the **playlist** team goes to the mesh discovery portal and searches for all data products that might have something related to sports activities. Through the discovery mechanism they find that the **partnership** domain has some data related to this. The discovery tool allows the team to automatically get access to documentation, sample code, and more information about the data products. They automatically request access and get a connection to the **partnership** data products and examine sample datasets. While they find some useful data involving **joint members** (listeners who are members of partner **workout platforms**), they don't find any information about the music they listen to or like on those platforms when they run, cycle, or do yoga.

The **playlist** team gets in contact with the **partnership** data product owner. Each domain has a dedicated product owner who focuses on the data shared by that domain. Through a direct conversation they let the **partnership** team know that they need to get access to the music tracks that workout platforms play during different activities as well as the ones that their members like. This conversation leads to the prioritization of creating **partner playlists** data products.

The **partnership** business team's purpose is to create a better experience for listeners through seamless integration with partner platforms such as the **workout platforms** and sharing music. Creating **partner playlists** data products is aligned with their business objective. The **partnership** team is best positioned to create these data products. They work most closely with partner platforms and are aware of their integration APIs and the life cycle of those APIs, which directly feed the **partner playlists** data products.

Given the self-serve data infrastructure and platform capabilities that Daff has built over the course of the last three years, it is fairly simple for the **partnership** team to create new data products. They start working with one of the most popular **cycling and workout** partners and use their APIs to access the tracks their members have played and liked.

The **partnership** team uses the platform data product life cycle management tools to build the transformation logic that presents this data as a data product in multiple modes, near-real-time snapshots of delta files initially. To make the integration of **partner playlists** with other data products easier, the transformation code focuses on harmonizing the **music track ID** with the global track ID system that Daff uses across all data products. In the span of a few hours, they have the new **partner playlists** data product built and deployed to the mesh, and made available to the **playlist** teams to continue their experiment.

In this simple scenario there are a few fundamentals of data mesh principles at play: one is the decentralized *domain ownership of data*[5] to remove the gap between data users and data providers, in this case allowing the **playlist** domain to work directly with the **partnership** domain, with each team having long-term accountability for providing data, **playlists**, and **partner playlists**.

The culture and technology of treating *data as a product*[6] is the second principle of data mesh we see in action. The teams have the responsibility to provide data that is easily discoverable, understandable, accessible, and usable, known as data products. There are established roles such as data product owners in each cross-functional domain team that are responsible for data and sharing it successfully.

The feasibility of sharing new **partner playlists** data products in a span of a few hours or maybe at most a day or two and the possibility of discovering the right data and using it without friction are all dependent on the *self-serve data platform*.[7] The platform provides services to cross-functional teams for sharing and using data, and it paves the path to efficiently and securely create and share data products for that purpose. For example, automated access control, encryption of personal information by default, and registering all data products with a global discovery tool are among the platform services.

---

5 Chapter 2, "Principle of Domain Ownership", unpacks the long-term data product ownership in a data mesh organization.

6 Chapter 3, "Principle of Data as a Product", unpacks the concept of data sharing as a product across a data mesh organization.

7 Chapter 4, "Principle of the Self-Serve Data Platform", describes the purpose and characteristics of data mesh infrastructure services as a self-serve platform.

Daff depends on a well-established set of governance policies to share data confidently and effectively. For example, a collective understanding around who should own what data is an example of such a policy. In this case, the **partnership** team became the owners of **partner playlists**. They are the team closest to the source and control the relationship with the partners. They are closely aware of factors that impact partnership data. While this appeared to be a simple and organic decision, it was made based on a set of heuristics that Daff had established to govern the policy of "assigning long-term owners to data products." A federated group of domain representatives defines the policies and the data platform automates them. This is data mesh's *federated computational governance*[8] principle.

Daff has come a long way to arrive at this seamless and frictionless journey. Figure P-1 shows this peer-to-peer and decentralized collaboration.

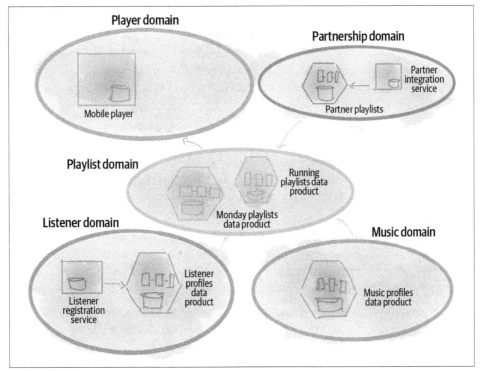

Figure P-1. Intelligent playlist creation scenario with data mesh

---

8 Chapter 5, "Principle of Federated Computational Governance", describes the operating model and approach to establishing global policies across a mesh of data products.

Data work before data mesh

The same scenario three years ago would have faced weeks of work, many points of friction and bottlenecks, and multiple handovers across multiple teams, likely resulting in poor quality data. Three years ago, the expected length of the effort and all the friction likely inhibited the initiative from starting, leaving it abandoned or in the best case costing a lot more.

Three years ago, the **playlist** team would have needed to ask a central data and AI team to prioritize building and training a new model for **sports playlists**. The data scientists within the central data and AI team would have needed to prioritize this among many other ML-based initiatives demanded across the organization. In the best-case scenario of highly prioritizing the playlists request, the data scientists would have had to go to a centralized lake or warehouse team for data and request access to the data from a centralized governance team.

This would have added another few days. Even then, after finding the data, it was likely that data scientists couldn't quite understand the data. The data would have been stale, as the **partnership** team had established many new integrations that hadn't yet made it to the central warehouse or lake. The central data scientist team likely had trust issues with the data.

After realizing that data scientists needed more music-related data from partners, the data lake team would have needed to go to a data engineering team in charge of pipelines to get the new extract, transform, load/extract, load, transform (ETL/ELT) pipelines set up to get data from partner integration APIs and get them to the warehouse or lake, yet another backlog to get stuck behind.

The centralized data engineering teams had to spend days negotiating and understanding a completely new domain, the **partnership** domain, to get the data from their application databases into the pipeline and then into the lake. They had to understand their internal databases to map internal music IDs to the global ID, among other internal application nuances. This would have taken some more time.

Without direct involvement and understanding of the business case, the **partnership** team had low incentives to prioritize high-quality partnership music integration[9] and support the data engineers' ETL pipelines. The ad hoc integrations faced days of debugging until some data flew into the lake. And the saga continues.

Daff's functionally divided organizational design and technology was simply not conducive to data-driven experimentation.[10]

---

9 Chapter 16, "Organization and Culture", describes the intrinsic motivations of teams in sharing data.

10 Chapter 8, "Before the Inflection Point", describes the nature of data teams before data mesh.

Figure P-2 shows Daff's organizational structure and architecture before data mesh. They had a modern software development architecture and organization structure as they had aligned their business and technology development teams around autonomous domains. However, their data and analytics team and architecture were functionally divided and centralized, using the monolithic architecture of the lake and warehouse.

The central data team and the monolithic architecture had become a bottleneck in response to the proliferation of data sources—inside and outside of the company—and diversity of their use cases. The data team had been under a large amount of pressure and had substantially slowed down in response to the growth of Daff. The returns of investments had now plateaued.

In short, Daff's data team structure and architecture were out of step with its aspirations and organizational growth.[11]

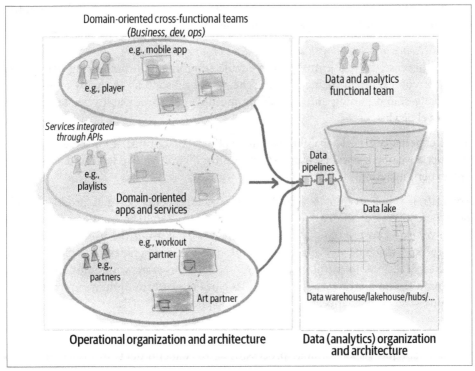

Figure P-2. Daff's organization and architecture before data mesh

---

11 Chapter 8, "Before the Inflection Point", goes into detail about the bottlenecks and inadequacies of existing architectural and organizational approaches for today's businesses.

The Invisible Platform and Policies

Post data mesh, in the sports playlist scenario I just shared with you, the experience of data users and providers almost feels magical: no friction, rapid end-to-end results, a sense of shared accountability with clear boundaries of responsibilities.

For this to be remotely possible, Daff has created a set of self-service technologies and automations that feel native to use and almost invisible.

Beneath the experience of the data providers and data users, to rapidly and autonomously share data, sits a platform composed of self-service capabilities that enable a set of key experiences:

The experience of building, deploying, monitoring, and evolving data products
> In this example, the data platform facilitated a frictionless experience to create and evolve **partner playlists** and **sports playlists** data products in a short amount of time, including integration with the source, building and testing the data transformation code, and serving the data.

The experience of working with a mesh of data products as a whole
> In this case, the platform services enable searching and discovering data products, connecting to them, querying their data, subscribing to their evolving data changes, and joining and correlating multiple data products to create new and novel playlists.

These experience-based capabilities of the platform are optimized for the users—data product developers, owners, users—to minimize their cognitive load in data sharing and experimentation.

For Daff, it is not acceptable to optimize the users' experience—data product developers and users—at the cost of machine deoptimization. The invisible part of the platform, closer to the physical layer and further away from the user, takes care of physical and machine optimizations. While the platform's experience plane—a set of cohesive services—optimizes the user experience to work with autonomous and yet connected data products, the utility plane of the platform optimizes physical and machine-level performance.[12] For example, it supports:

- Efficient polyglot storage of data products
- Efficient query and workload processing across data products
- Efficient search and indexing
- Reduced data movement

---

12 Chapter 10, "The Multiplane Data Platform Architecture", describes the different planes of the platform with further details.

The seamless experience of the **playlist** team using and correlating multiple data products sourced from different teams such as **partnerships**, **listeners**, and **music profiles** depends on a set of global standard policies governing all data products:[13]

- Standardization of data sharing APIs
- Standardization of metadata including SLOs, documentation, and data modeling language
- Standardization of shared data entity IDs

Limitless Scale with Autonomous Data Products

Data mesh meets Daff's growth aspirations with a scale-out organizational and technical structure. As you saw in the example of smart playlists, the introduction of new playlists or improving existing ones is simply a matter of adding more data products and connecting them, e.g., **running playlists**, **cycling playlists**, **workout platform X partner playlists**, **workout platform Y partner playlists**, etc. This is a scale-out architecture where you can achieve limitless scale by adding more coequal nodes and connecting them with each other. Data products are implemented as an architecture quantum, the smallest unit of an architecture that can be deployed independently and still have all the structural components to do its job.

The architecture assures that each data product implements a standard set of contracts for data access and data sharing in a way that each can connect to other data quanta on the mesh to share data and semantics. Each data product encapsulates the data transformation logic and policies that govern their data. The architecture matches the domain-oriented organizational autonomy, with a corresponding data-product-oriented distributed architecture.

Daff's standardization of data products has given it speed and scale.[14]

The Positive Network Effect

The success of Daff in using data and analytics can be summarized by the positive network effect created by peer-to-peer connectivity of domains exchanging data products as units of value. The larger the network and the more connections established, the more data that is shared between domains to generate intelligence and high-order insights, ultimately improving the business.

Daff has invested significantly to execute its data mesh strategy, making an organizational and cultural shift and creating the infrastructure and platform foundation. But

---

13 Part IV, "How to Design the Data Product Architecture", describes shared facets of data products as an architectural quantum on the mesh.

14 Chapter 11, "Design a Data Product by Affordances", describes the design and affordances of data quantum.

they have been diligent in tracking the return of their investment with measurable benefits.

Based on their measurements, externally, they have created deeper user engagement and have grown the number of active listeners by applying ML and data to improve the listeners' experience across multiple touchpoints. Internally, they have reduced the lead time to access data by removing central and middleman bottlenecks. They have reduced the risk of change of data by creating standard contracts and interfaces for discovering and sharing data products. They have reduced the waste of developing data products by adopting automated continuous delivery practices for data products. They have increased the application of data across the business measured by the amount of connectivity between their data products. They have increased the number of teams engaged in creating data-driven solutions by embedding the ownership of data in each domain and team. They reduced the cost of data ownership and end-to-end data solution creation by utilizing the platform services and focusing on the experience of data developers.

These are some of the areas of improvement that they measure against their data mesh investments.[15]

Why Transform to Data Mesh?

Let's go back to the year 2019, the year of an inflection point for Daff.[16]

Over the last few years, Daff had substantially invested in their data solutions such as data lakes and data warehousing to capture data at scale. They had built a large data and AI team under the chief data and AI officer who had been charged with organizational-wide data capture, modeling, and serving, as well as building analytical and ML solutions the business needed. The organizational structure and operating model that Daff had adopted was the industry standard at the time.

This was the year that Daff reflected and realized that their data aspirations had outgrown their ability to execute on them. The central data team and the monolithic architecture had become a bottleneck in response to the proliferation of data sources—inside and outside of the company—and diversity of their use cases. The data team was under a large amount of pressure and had substantially slowed down in response to the growth of Daff. The returns of investments had now plateaued.

They needed to change, and that was when they discovered data mesh.

---

15 See Chapter 15, "Strategy and Execution", on how to measure and monitor the progress of the data mesh execution.

16 Chapter 6, "The Inflection Point", goes into the main industry-wide drivers that demand a new approach in managing and using data, similar to the ones mentioned for Daff here.

Before embarking on data mesh, Daff looked closely at the alignment between their business—goals, organization, technical capabilities—and data mesh.

The expected outcomes of data mesh were aligned with addressing their pain points:

Rapid growth and increased complexity
They were growing fast, their business was becoming more complex, and implementing their diverse and audacious analytical aspirations was becoming slow. Data mesh is designed to get value from data and retain agility in complex and large environments.

Getting value from data at scale
They were making substantial investments on their technical foundation for data and analytics and yet the results were plateauing. Data mesh gets value from data more cost effectively by mobilizing the larger population of generalist technologists to become data developers and users.

The objectives of data mesh and the overall scope of the impact sounded promising. However, there was a question of whether this was the right choice for them, right now, given the context of Daff.

The answer to this question was promising.

Data mesh was compatible with the existing domain-oriented organizational design of Daff. It was an extension to their existing design and architecture. Data mesh built up on a decentralized model of data ownership that simply extended their existing business-aligned development teams.

In reality, the centralized data team was one of the last functionally divided teams, somewhat at odds with their current domain-oriented business and tech organizational design. Given their aspirations to make every domain data-driven and embed intelligent decision making in them, it made sense to move the ownership of data and analytics to domains. The company was already operating with business-dev-ops domain-aligned teams, so the extension of these teams with data capabilities and responsibilities seemed like a natural progression to truly democratize access and utilization of data. Naturally, governance needed to follow these organizational seams too.

They knew that as a lead adopter of data mesh, they needed to dedicate their time and resources to building the foundational technology and enabling platforms. Daff viewed itself as a software company with technology at its core, not only enabling its business but shaping and extending it. They didn't shy away from technical investments.[17]

---

17 Part V, "How to Get Started", introduces a self-assessment tool to evaluate whether data mesh is the right approach for a company or not, at the time of this writing.

Daff realized that implementing a new approach—encompassing changes to data culture, data organizational structure, data roles, data architecture, and technology—was going to be a multiyear transformation.

So, they dedicated the next three years to make the pivot to data mesh incrementally. Throughout the journey they delivered carefully selected data-driven use cases, while transforming the organization and establishing the platform and the technology.[18]

The Way Forward

Despite the business, cultural, and technical successes, Daff has a way to go. Their evolution of data mesh execution has certainly passed the phases of *exploration*, which established the ways of working and the foundational platform. They have *expanded* the mesh to many of their domains. However, to continue to *extract* value from the mesh, they need to continuously optimize and refine their approach. They need to work on domains that are laggards in becoming active members of the mesh and extend their platform capabilities to domains that work with legacy systems and don't yet work in a domain-oriented cross-functional team.

This is the expected trajectory of data mesh transformation: an evolutionary path, punctuated with repeating cycles of *explore*, *expand*, and *extract*.[19]

I hope the tale of data mesh at Daff has nudged you to keep reading past this point, in which case I will see you in the next chapter.

---

18 This would have been a long novel if I included their multiyear journey. However, if you want to read about the execution and transformation approach see Chapter 15, "Strategy and Execution", and Chapter 16, "Organization and Culture".

19 Chapter 15, "Strategy and Execution", introduces an approach to establishing data mesh in an evolutionary transformation.

PART I

What Is Data Mesh?

. . .the only simplicity to be trusted is the simplicity to be found on the far side of complexity.
—Alfred North Whitehead

When you look at the application of data mesh, like the Daff, Inc., example from the opening of the book, you get a sense of the engineering and organizational complexity required to implement it. We could probably talk about these complex and intricate pieces of data mesh implementation for a while. Instead, to understand data mesh, I like to discuss it from its *first principles*. Once we understand its basic elements, then we can assemble them from the ground up to create the implementations.

This is how I'm going to introduce data mesh to you in this part of the book, focusing on its first principles and how they interact with each other.

These principles are propositions and values that guide the behavior, structure, and evolution of its implementations. My intention for this part of the book is to create a foundation that provides a baseline for future refinements of practices and technology.

It's worth considering that this book is being written at the time when data mesh is arguably still in the *innovator* and *early adopter* phase of an innovation adoption curve.[1] It's at a phase where the venturesome *innovators* have embraced it and are already in the process of creating tools and technologies around it, and the highly respected *early adopters* are shifting their data strategy and architecture inspired by

---

1 Everett Rogers, *Diffusion of Innovations*, 5th Edition (New York: Simon & Schuster, 2003).

data mesh. Hence, it's only appropriate to include an articulation of principles and architectural style in my explanation of data mesh at this point in time and leave the specific implementation details and technology to be refined and built over time. I anticipate that any specific implementation design or tooling suggestion will be simply outdated by the time you get to read this book.

I've organized this part into five chapters. Chapter 1, "Data Mesh in a Nutshell", gives you a quick overview of its four principles and their composition into a high-level model. The following chapters each focus on one of the principles: Chapter 2, "Principle of Domain Ownership", Chapter 3, "Principle of Data as a Product"; Chapter 4, "Principle of the Self-Serve Data Platform"; and Chapter 5, "Principle of Federated Computational Governance".

The order in which the principles are introduced matter, because they build on each other. The domain-oriented distribution of data ownership and architecture is at the heart of the approach. Everything else follows from that. Data mesh is all of these principles.

I suggest that every reader who is interested in understanding or applying data mesh read this part. I hope that what this part offers informs every conversation about data mesh.

CHAPTER 1

Data Mesh in a Nutshell

"Think in simples" as my old master used to say—meaning to reduce the whole to its parts in simplest terms, getting back to first principles.
—Frank Lloyd Wright

Data mesh is a decentralized sociotechnical approach to share, access, and manage analytical data in complex and large-scale environments—within or across organizations.

Data mesh is a new approach in sourcing, managing, and accessing data for analytical use cases at scale. Let's call this class of data *analytical data*. Analytical data is used for predictive or diagnostic use cases. It is the foundation for visualizations and reports that provide insights into business. It is used to train machine learning models that augment business with data-driven intelligence. It is the essential ingredient for organizations to move from intuition and gut-driven decision making to taking actions based on observations and data-driven predictions. Analytical data is what powers the software and technology of the future. It enables a technology shift from human-designed rule-based algorithms to data-driven machine-learned models. Analytical data is becoming an increasingly critical component of the technology landscape.

The term *data* in this book, if not qualified, refers to analytical data. Analytical data serves reporting and machine learning training use cases.

The Outcomes

To get value from data at scale in complex and large-scale organizations, data mesh sets to achieve these outcomes:

- Respond gracefully to change: a business's essential complexity, volatility, and uncertainty
- Sustain agility in the face of growth
- Increase the ratio of value from data to investment[1]

The Shifts

Data mesh introduces multidimensional technical and organizational shifts from earlier analytical data management approaches.

Figure 1-1 summarizes the shifts that data mesh introduces, compared to past approaches.

Data mesh calls for a fundamental shift in the assumptions, architecture, technical solutions, and social structure of our organizations, in how we manage, use, and own analytical data:

- *Organizationally*, it shifts from centralized ownership of data by specialists who run the data platform technologies to a decentralized data ownership model pushing ownership and accountability of the data back to the business domains where data is produced from or is used.
- *Architecturally*, it shifts from collecting data in monolithic warehouses and lakes to connecting data through a distributed mesh of data products accessed through standardized protocols.
- *Technologically*, it shifts from technology solutions that treat data as a byproduct of running pipeline code to solutions that treat data and code that maintains it as one lively autonomous unit.
- *Operationally*, it shifts data governance from a top-down centralized operational model with human interventions to a federated model with computational policies embedded in the nodes on the mesh.
- *Principally*, it shifts our value system from data as an asset to be collected to data as a product to serve and delight the data users (internal and external to the organization).

---

1 Chapter 7 unpacks the expected outcomes of data mesh, with a high level of description of how it achieves those outcomes.

- *Infrastructurally*, it shifts from two sets of fragmented and point-to-point integrated infrastructure services—one for data and analytics and the other for applications and operational systems to a well-integrated set of infrastructure for both operational and data systems.

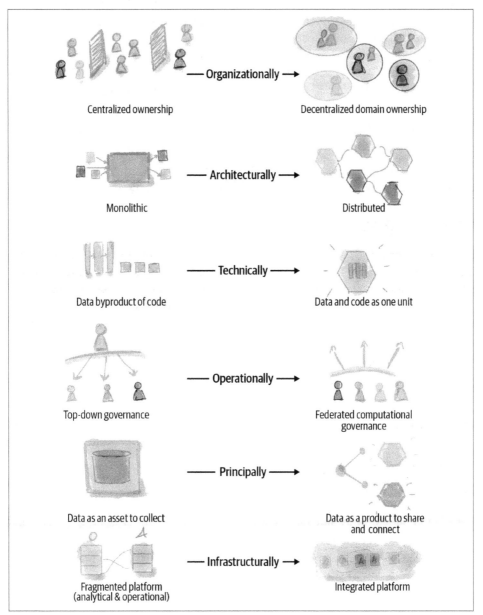

Figure 1-1. Data mesh dimensions of change

Since the introduction of data mesh in my original blog post (*https://oreil.ly/1deXz*) (kindly hosted by Martin Fowler (*https://oreil.ly/ybdAb*)), I have noticed that people have struggled to classify the concept. Is data mesh an architecture? Is it a list of principles? Is it an operating model? After all, we rely on the *classification of patterns*[2] as a major cognitive function to understand the structure of our world. Hence, I have decided to classify data mesh as a *sociotechnical* paradigm: an approach that recognizes the interactions between people and the technical architecture and solutions in complex organizations. This is an approach to data management that not only optimizes for the technical excellence of analytical data sharing solutions but also improves the experience of all people involved: data providers, users, and owners.

Data mesh can be utilized as an element of an enterprise *data strategy*, articulating the target state of both the *enterprise architecture* and an *organizational operating model* with an iterative execution model.

In the simplest form it can be described through four interacting principles. In this chapter I give a very brief definition of these principles and how they work together.

The Principles

Four simple principles can capture what underpins data mesh's logical architecture and operating model. These principles are designed to progress us toward the objectives of data mesh: increase value from data at scale, sustain agility as an organization grows, and embrace change in a complex and volatile business context.

Here is a quick summary of the principles.

Principle of Domain Ownership

Decentralize the ownership of analytical data to business domains closest to the data—either the source of the data or its main consumers. Decompose the (analytical) data logically and based on the business domain it represents, and manage the life cycle of domain-oriented data independently.

Architecturally and organizationally align business, technology, and analytical data.

The motivations of domain ownership are:

- The ability to scale out data sharing aligned with the axes of organizational growth: increased number of data sources, increased number of data consumers, and increased diversity of data use cases

---

2 Jeff Hawkins and Sandra Blakeslee (2005). *On Intelligence* (p. 165). New York: Henry Holt and Co.

- Optimization for continuous change by localizing change to the business domains

- Enabling agility by reducing cross-team synchronizations and removing centralized bottlenecks of data teams, warehouses, and lake architecture

- Increasing data business truthfulness by closing the gap between the real origin of the data, and where and when it is used for analytical use cases

- Increasing resiliency of analytics and machine learning solutions by removing complex intermediary data pipelines

Principle of Data as a Product

With this principle in place, domain-oriented data is shared as a product directly with data users—data analysts, data scientists, and so on.

Data as a product adheres to a set of usability characteristics:

- Discoverable

- Addressable

- Understandable

- Trustworthy and truthful

- Natively accessible

- Interoperable and composable

- Valuable on its own

- Secure

A data product provides a set of explicitly defined and easy to use data sharing contracts. Each data product is autonomous, and its life cycle and model are managed independently of others.

Data as a product introduces a new unit of logical architecture called *data quantum*, controlling and encapsulating all the structural components needed to share data as a product—data, metadata, code, policy, and declaration of infrastructure dependencies—autonomously.

The motivations of data as a product are to:

- Remove the possibility of creating domain-oriented data silos by changing the relationship of teams with data. Data becomes a product that teams share rather than collect and silo.

- Create a data-driven innovation culture, by streamlining the experience of discovering and using high-quality data, peer-to-peer, without friction.

- Create resilience to change with built-time and run-time isolation between data products and explicitly defined data sharing contracts so that changing one does not destabilize others.

- Get higher value from data by sharing and using data across organizational boundaries.

Principle of the Self-Serve Data Platform

This principle leads to a new generation of self-serve data platform services that empower domains' *cross-functional* teams to share data. The platform services are centered around removing friction from the end-to-end journey of data sharing, from source to consumption. The platform services manage the full life cycle of individual data products. They manage a reliable mesh of interconnected data products. They provide mesh-level experiences such as surfacing the emergent knowledge graph and lineage across the mesh. The platform streamlines the experience of data users to discover, access, and use data products. It streamlines the experience of data providers to build, deploy, and maintain data products.

The motivations of the self-serve data platform are to:

- Reduce the total cost of decentralized ownership of data.

- Abstract data management complexity and reduce the cognitive load of domain teams in managing the end-to-end life cycle of their data products.

- Mobilize a larger population of developers—technology generalists—to embark on data product development and reduce the need for specialization.

- Automate governance policies to create security and compliance standards for all data products.

Principle of Federated Computational Governance

This principle creates a data governance operating model based on a federated decision-making and accountability structure, with a team composed of domain representatives, data platform, and subject matter experts—legal, compliance, security, etc. The operating model creates an incentive and accountability structure that balances the autonomy and agility of domains, with the global interoperability of the mesh. The governance execution model heavily relies on codifying and automating the policies at a fine-grained level, for every data product, via the platform services.

The motivations of federated computational goovernance are:

- The ability to get higher-order value from aggregation and correlation of independent yet interoperable data products

- Countering the undesirable consequences of domain-oriented decentralizations: incompatibility and disconnection of domains
- Making it feasible to build in cross-cutting governance requirements such as security, privacy, legal compliance, etc., across a mesh of distributed data products
- Reducing the overhead of manual synchronization between domains and the governance function

Interplay of the Principles

I intended for the four principles to be collectively necessary and sufficient. They complement each other, and each addresses new challenges that may arise from others. Figure 1-2 shows the interplay of the principles.

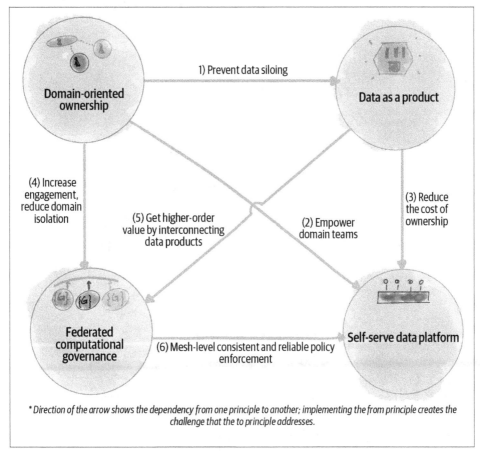

Figure 1-2. Four principles of data mesh and their interplay

For example, decentralized domain-oriented ownership of data can result in data siloing within domains, and this can be addressed by the data as a product principle that demands domains have an organizational responsibility to share their data with product-like qualities inside and outside of their domain.

Similarly, the domain ownership of data products can lead to duplicated effort, increased cost of data product ownership, and lowered data sharing productivity. In this case, the self-serve data platform empowers the cross-functional domain teams in sharing and using data products. The platform objective is to lower the domain teams' cognitive load, reduce unnecessary effort, increase domains' productivity, and lower the total cost of ownership.

Data Mesh Model at a Glance

Operationally you can imagine the principles in action as demonstrated in Figure 1-3.

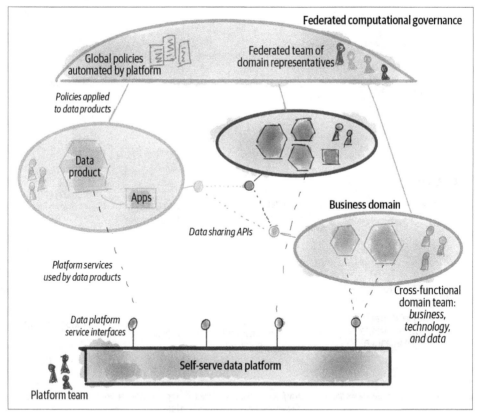

Figure 1-3. Operating model of data mesh principles

The domains with cross-functional teams are achieving the business domain's goals with digital applications and data products. Each domain shares its data and services through contracts. Data products can be composed and owned by new domains. The global policies are defined by a federated group composed of representatives of the domains. The policies along with other platform services are offered as automated capabilities.

This is a simplified operating model of data mesh.

The Data

Data mesh focuses on analytical data. It recognizes the blurry delineation of the two modes of data, introduces a new model of tight integration of the two, and yet respects the clear differences between them.

"What is operational data versus analytical data?" This has been a point of confusion for early enthusiasts of data mesh. Allow me to clarify what I mean by these terms.

Operational Data

Operational data supports running the business and keeps the current state of the business with transactional integrity. This data is captured, stored, and processed by transactions in real time, by OLTP (online transaction processing) systems.

Operational data sits in databases of microservices, applications, or systems of records that support business capabilities. It keeps the current state of the business.

Operational data modeling and storage are optimized for application or microservice logic and access patterns. It is constantly updated, with read and write access to it. Its design has to account for multiple people updating the same data at the same time in unpredictable sequences, which results in a need for transactions. The access is also about relatively in-the-moment activity.

Operational data is referred to as "data on the inside" (*https://oreil.ly/YOZhC*). It is the private data of an application or a microservice that performs CRUD (create, update, delete) operations on it. Operational data can be intentionally shared on the outside through APIs—e.g., REST, GraphQL, or events. The operational data on the outside has the same nature as the operational data on the inside: it is what we know about the business, *now*.

Operational data is recording what happens in the business, supporting decisions that are specific to the business transaction. In short, *operational data is used directly to run the business and serve the end users.*

Imagine Daff. Its **listener registration** service implements the business function of subscribing new users or unsubscribing them. The transactional database that supports the registration process and keeps the current list of subscribers is considered operational data.

Today, operational data is collected and then transformed into analytical data. Analytical data trains the machine learning models that then make their way into the operational systems as intelligent services.

Analytical Data

This is the historical, integrated, and aggregate view of data created as the byproduct of running the business. It is maintained and used by OLAP (online analytical processing) systems.

Analytical data is the temporal, historic, and often aggregated view of the facts of the business over time. It is modeled to provide retrospective or future-perspective insights. Analytical data is optimized for analytical logic—training machine learning models and creating reports and visualizations. Analytical data is part of the "data on the outside" (*https://oreil.ly/X6J5h*) category, data directly accessed by analytical consumers.

Analytical data has a sense of history. Analytical use cases require looking for comparisons and trends over time, while a lot of operational uses don't require much history.

Analytical access mode tends to include intensive reads across a large body of data, with fewer writers. The original definition of analytical data as *a nonvolatile, integrated, time-variant collection of data*[3] still remains valid.

In short, analytical data is used to *optimize* the business and user experience. This is the data that fuels the organization's AI and analytics aspirations.

For example, in the case of Daff it's important to optimize the listeners' experience with playlists recommended based on their music taste and favorite artists. The analytical data that helps train the playlist recommendation machine learning model captures all the past behavior of the listener as well as all characteristics of the music the listener has favored. This aggregated and historical view is analytical data.

Today, analytical data is stored in a data warehouse or lake.

---

3 Definition provided by William H. Inmon, known as the father of data warehousing.

The Origin

To reject one paradigm without simultaneously substituting another is to reject science
itself.

—Thomas S. Kuhn, *The Structure of Scientific Revolutions*

Thomas Kuhn, an American historian and philosopher of science, introduced the
paradigm shift in his at the time rather controversial book, *The Structure of Scientific Revolutions* (1962). He observed how science progressed in two main modes:
incremental and *revolutionary*; science progressed through long stretches of legato
normal science where the existing theories form the foundation of all further research,
followed by the occasional disruption of staccato paradigm shifts that challenged and
transcended the existing knowledge and norm. For example, the progress of science
from *Newtonian mechanics* to *quantum mechanics* is considered a paradigm shift as
scientists could no longer explain the governing laws of physics at the quantum level
with the existing theories. Kuhn recognized that a prerequisite for a paradigm shift
is identifying *anomalies*, observations that don't fit the existing norm, and entering
the phase of *crisis*, questioning the validity of the existing paradigm in solving the
new problems and observations. He also observed that people try, with increasing
desperation, to introduce unsustainable complexities into the existing solutions to
account for anomalies.

This almost perfectly fits the origin of data mesh and its principles. It came from the
recognition of anomalies—failure modes and accidental complexities that I describe
in Part I—and moments of crisis where the characteristics of the existing data solutions didn't quite fit the realities of enterprises today. We are in a moment of Khunian
crisis in the progression of our approach for data. Hence, there is a need for a new
paradigm.

I wish I could claim that data mesh principles were novel and new and I cleverly
came up with them. On the contrary, the principles of data mesh are a generalization
and adaptation of practices that have evolved over the last two decades and proved
to solve our last complexity challenge: scale of *software complexity* led by the *mass
digitization of organizations*.

These principles are the foundation of how digital organizations have solved organizational growth and complexity, while delivering unprecedented digital aspirations:
moving all of their services to the web, using mobile for every single touchpoint with
their customers, and reducing organizational synchronizations through automation
of most activities. They are an adaptation of what formulated the previous paradigm
shift in software: the microservices (*https://oreil.ly/IMENg*) and APIs revolution,

platform-based Team Topologies,[4] computational governance models such as Zero Trust Architecture,[5] and operating distributed solutions securely and across multiple clouds and hosting environments. In the last several years, these principles have been refined and adapted to the analytical data problem space.

Let's look more closely at each of the data mesh principles.

---

4 Matthew Skelton and Manual Pais (2019). *Team Topologies: Organizing Business and Technology Teams for Fast Flow*. Portland, OR: IT Revolution.

5 Scott W. Rose, Oliver Borchert, Stuart Mitchell, and Sean Connelly (2020). "Zero Trust Architecture" (*https://oreil.ly/rGEfn*), Special Publication (NIST SP), National Institute of Standards and Technology, Gaithersburg, MD.

CHAPTER 2

Principle of Domain Ownership

Data mesh, at its core, is founded in *decentralization* and *distribution of data responsibility* to people who are closest to the data. This is to support a scale-out structure and continuous and rapid change cycles.

The question is how to identify the boundaries around which the data is decomposed, how to integrate those components, and, consequently, how to distribute the responsibilities.

To find the axis of data decomposition, data mesh follows the *seams of organizational units*. It follows the lines of division of responsibility aligned with the business. It does not follow the borders set by the underlying technology solutions, such as the lake, warehouse, pipelines, etc., nor the functional lines, data team, or analytics team.

The data mesh approach is contrary to how existing data architectures are partitioned and data responsibility is divided. Chapter 8 demonstrates that traditional data architectures are partitioned around technology, e.g., data warehouses, and give data ownership to teams performing activities related to the technology, e.g., the data warehouse team, data pipeline team, etc. The traditional architectures mirror an organizational structure that centralizes the responsibility of sharing analytical data to a single data team. The previous approaches have been set up to localize the complexity and cost of dealing with a relatively new field of analytical data management within a specialized group.

The past approach in how organizations divide data responsibility is at odds with the organizational structure of modern digital businesses. Organizations today are decomposed based on their business domains. Such decomposition localizes the impact of continuous change and evolution, for the most part, to a domain. For example, Daff has divided its business (and its digital solutions enabling and shaping the business) into domains such as **podcast**, **event**, **partnership**, **listener**, etc.

Data mesh gives the data sharing responsibility to each of the business domains. Each domain becomes responsible for the data it is most familiar with: the domain that is the first-class user of this data or is in control of its point of origin. For example, the **listener** team is in charge of **listener profiles**, **listener demographics**, **listener subscription events**, and any other analytical data they have the most understanding, influence, and control of. I call this the *principle of domain ownership*.

 I have used the word *ownership* as a shorthand for *product ownership*: long-term ownership of *responsibilities* to create, model, maintain, evolve, and share data as a product to meet the needs of data users.

All the appearances of *data ownership* in this book are limited and scoped to the accountability of organizations to maintain the quality, longevity, and lawful accessibility of the data they generate in transactions with internal and external entities such as users, customers, and other organizations.

This should not be confused with data *sovereignty*, control of data by whom it is collected from. The ultimate sovereignty of data remains with the users, customers, or other organizations whose data is being captured and managed. The organizations act as *data product owners* while the individuals remain the *data owners*.

The concept of *self-sovereign data*—individuals having full control and authority over their personal data—is close and dear to my heart but outside of the scope of this work. However, I'm of the firm belief that data mesh can establish a foundation toward self-sovereign data, but that would be the topic of a different book.

I have also refrained from phrases such as *data custodianship* that carry a specific and different meaning from past data management and governance methods. This is to avoid confusion with existing data governance roles that are not compatible with data mesh.

This rather intuitive division of responsibility solves a host of problems that I will cover in depth in Chapter 7, "After the Inflection Point", but it introduces new challenges. It leads to a distributed logical data architecture—distributed architectures are scalable but are more complex to manage. It requires new ways of handling data interoperability and connectivity between domains. The future chapters and principles address these challenges.

In the following section, I unpack how to apply domain-driven design (DDD) strategies to decompose data and its ownership and introduce the transformational shifts necessary for organizations to move to domain-oriented data ownership.

A Brief Background on Domain-Driven Design

Domain-driven design is an approach to decomposition of software design (models) and team allocation, based on the seams of a business. It decomposes software based on how a business decomposes into domains, and models the software based on the language used by each business domain.

Eric Evans introduced the concept in his book *Domain-Driven Design* (*https://oreil.ly/ T5saX*) in 2003. In the time since, DDD has deeply influenced modern architectural thinking and, consequently, organizational modeling. DDD was a response to the rapid growth of software design complexity that stemmed from the digitization of businesses. As organizations grew their digital assets—backoffice applications, digital services, web and mobile technologies—and kept increasing their features, software became more complex and harder to manage. As the book's subtitle, "Tackling Complexity in the Heart of Software," specifies, we needed a new approach to software modeling and ownership.

DDD defines a *domain* as "a sphere of knowledge, influence, or activity."[1] In the Daff example, the **listener subscription** domain has the *knowledge* of what events happen during the subscription or unsubscription, what the rules governing the subscription are, what data is generated during the subscription events, and so on. The subscription domain *influences* exactly how subscriptions should be done and what data should be known and captured during the subscription process. It has a set of *activities* to perform such as onboarding listeners, triggering payments, etc. What I like to add to this description is the *outcome*. The domain has a specific business objective and an outcome it is optimizing for. The subscription domain is optimizing for the outcome of maximizing the number of subscribers and an easy onboarding process and minimizing dropouts.

Domain-driven design, and the idea of breaking software modeling based on domains, has greatly influenced the software architecture of the last decade, for example with microservices. Microservices architecture decomposes large and complex systems into distributed services built around business domain capabilities. It delivers user journeys and complex business processes through loose integration of services.

Domain-driven design has fundamentally changed how technology teams form and has led to the alignment of business and technology cross-functional teams. It has greatly influenced how organizations scale, in a way that a team can independently and autonomously own a domain capability and digital services.

---

1 Eric Evans, *Domain-Driven Design: Tackling Complexity in the Heart of Software*, (Upper Saddle River, NJ: Addison-Wesley, 2003).

I highly recommend that you familiarize yourself with DDD using resources outside of this book before applying its concepts to data. Defining DDD with enough depth to detail how it can be utilized with data mesh is outside of the scope of this book.

Applying DDD's Strategic Design to Data

Though we have adopted domain-oriented decomposition and ownership when dealing with operational systems, ideas of decomposition based on business domains have yet to penetrate the analytical data space.

So far, the closest application of DDD in data platform architecture I have seen is for source operational systems to emit their business domain events (*https://oreil.ly/ 9ENd4*) and for the monolithic data platform to ingest them. However, beyond the point of ingestion the domain team's responsibility ends, and data responsibilities are transferred to the data team. As more transformations are performed by the data team, the data becomes more removed from its original form, language, and intention. For example, Daff's **podcast** domain emits logs of podcasts being played on a short-retention log. Then downstream, a centralized data team will pick these events up and attempt to transform, aggregate, and store them as long-lived files or tables.

To apply DDD to data I suggest going back to the original scripture. In his book, Eric Evans introduces a set of complementary strategies to scale *modeling* at the enterprise level called *DDD's Strategic Design*. These strategies are designed for organizations with complex domains and many teams. DDD's Strategic Design techniques move away from the previously used modes of modeling and ownership:

Organizational-level central modeling
> Eric Evans observed that total unification of the domain models of the organization into one is neither feasible nor cost-effective. This is similar to the data warehouse approach to data modeling, with tightly dependent shared schemas. Centralized modeling leads to organizational bottlenecks for change.

Silos of internal models with limited integration
> This mode introduces cumbersome interteam communications. This is similar to data silos in different applications, connected via brittle extract, transform, load procedures (ETLs).

No intentional modeling
> This is similar to a data lake, dumping raw data into blob storage.

Instead, DDD's Strategic Design embraces modeling based on *multiple models each contextualized to a particular domain*, called a *bounded context* (*https://oreil.ly/ 2RhbM*).

A bounded context is "the delimited applicability of a particular model [that] gives team members a clear and shared understanding of what has to be consistent and what can develop independently."[2]

Additionally, DDD introduces *context mapping*, which explicitly defines the relationship between bounded contexts, the independent models.

Data mesh adopts the boundary of bounded contexts to individual data products—*data*, its *models*, and its *ownership*.

For organizations that have already adopted a microservices or domain-oriented architecture, this is a relatively simple extension. They have built services based on the domain bounded contexts. Now, they apply the same decomposition and modeling to their analytical data in each domain.

Domain data ownership is the foundation of *scale* in a complex system like enterprises today.

Let's put this in an example for Daff. There is a **media player** team that is responsible for mobile and web digital media players. The media player application emits **play events** that show how listeners interact with the player. The data is used for many downstream use cases, including improving the player application's performance and improving user engagement by reconstructing and analyzing the **listener sessions**, the longitudinal journey of discovering and listening to music.

In the absence of a data mesh implementation, the **media player** team basically dumps the play events—with whatever quality and cadence they arrive from the player devices—on some sort of a short-retention streaming infrastructure or worse in its transactional database. Then these events get picked up by the centralized data team to be put into a lake or warehouse or likely both.

Data mesh changes the behavior of the **media player** domain. It extends the responsibility of the **media player** team to providing a high-quality long-retention analytical view of the **play events**—real-time and aggregated. The **media player** team now has the end-to-end responsibility of sharing the **play events** analytical data directly with the data analysts, data scientists, or other people who are interested in the data. The **play events** analytical data is then transformed by the **listener session** domain and aggregated into a journey-based view of the listener interactions.

The **recommendation** domain uses the **listener sessions** to create new datasets—graphs to recommend music based on the play behavior of listeners' social networks.

In this example, the **listener session** domain is purely a data domain with the sole objective of providing the best representation of listeners' journeys when interacting

---

2 Evans, *Domain-Driven Design* (p. 511).

with players, augmented with unique information about listeners' profiles. In this case, the need for this data has reshaped the organization. It has created a new domain and a new long-standing team. Figure 2-1 summarizes this example.

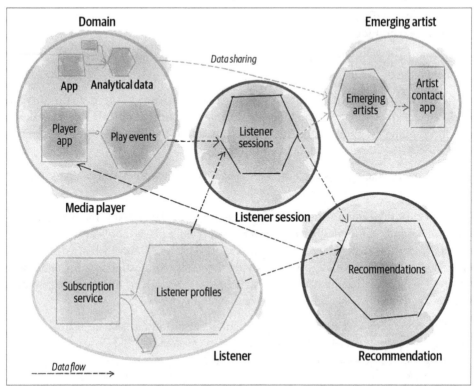

Figure 2-1. Decomposing the analytical data ownership and architecture, aligned with existing or new business domains

Domain Data Archetypes

When we map the data mesh to an organization and its domains, we discover a few different archetypes of domain-oriented analytical data. Data mesh principles don't differentiate greatly between the archetypes of domains. However, at a practical level, recognizing their characteristics helps with optimizing the implementations.

There are three archetypes of domain-oriented data:

Source-aligned domain data
   Analytical data reflecting the business facts generated by the operational systems. This is also called a *native* data product.

Aggregate domain data
   Analytical data that is an aggregate of multiple upstream domains.

Consumer-aligned domain data
> Analytical data transformed to fit the needs of one or multiple specific use cases. This is also called *fit-for-purpose* domain data.

Figure 2-2 expands on our previous example and demonstrates the archetypes of the domain-oriented data. For example, the **media player** domain serves *source-aligned* analytical data collected from the **media player** application events. The **listener session** domain serves *aggregate* data products that transform and aggregate individual listener player events into constructed sessions of interaction, augmented with more information about the listener fetched from the **listener** domain. And the **recommendation** domain data is *consumer-aligned*. It serves the specific needs of the intelligent recommendations offered by the player application.

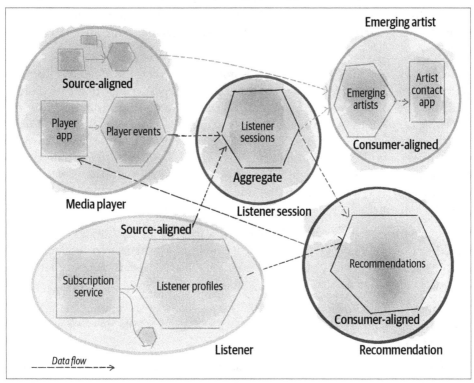

Figure 2-2. Example of domain data archetypes

Source-Aligned Domain Data

Some domains naturally align with the source, where the data originates. *Source-aligned domain data* represents the *facts and reality* of the business. It captures the data that is mapped very closely to what the operational systems of its origin, *systems of reality*, generate. In our example, facts of the business such as "how users are interacting with the media players" or "how users subscribe" lead to the creation of source-aligned domain data such as **play events**, **audio play quality streams**, and **listener profiles**. These facts are best known and generated by their corresponding operational systems. For example, the **media player** system knows best about **play events**.

In summary, data mesh assumes that domains are responsible for providing the *truths of their business domain* as source-aligned domain data.

The business facts are best presented as business domain events (*https://oreil.ly/ 9ENd4*) and can be stored and served as distributed logs of time-stamped events. In addition to timed events, source-aligned domain data often needs to be provided in easily consumable historical slices, aggregated over a time interval that closely reflects the interval of change in the business domain. For example, in the **listener** domain, a daily aggregate of the **listener profiles** is a reasonable model for analytical usage.

Note that source-aligned analytical data is not modeled or accessed directly from the source application's (private) transactional database. Exposing analytical data directly from the operational database is an antipattern. This antipattern is observed in the implementation of ETLs and application of change data capture[3] and data virtualization[4] on top of the application's database. The application database model serves a very different purpose and is often modeled for speed of performing transactions as needed by the application and its end users. The analytical data is stored and structured for ease of understanding and access for reporting, machine learning training, and nontransactional workloads.

The analytical data life cycle is different from the source application's operational database. Not every change to optimize the application database leads to analytical data changes, and not every new transformation of analytical data requires changes to its source application database.

The nature of the domain analytical data is different from the internal data that the operational systems use to do their job. Chapter 1 captures the differences between the two data types.

For these reasons, at this point in time, data mesh differentiates between the source application's operational database and its collaborating analytical data storage. While the two types of data are considered separate, they are tightly integrated and owned by the same domain team.

---

3 A technique to observe internal database operations (insert, update, delete) and externalize them as events.

4 Creating materialized views on top of an operational application database for external queries and workloads.

Source-aligned domain data is the most foundational archetype. It is expected to be permanently captured and made available. As the organization evolves, its *data-driven* and *intelligence* services can always go back to the business facts and create new aggregations or projections.

Note that source-aligned domain data closely represents the *raw data* at the point of creation and is not fitted or modeled for a particular consumer. The other domain data archetypes are.

Aggregate Domain Data

There is never a one-to-one mapping between a core concept of a business and a source system at an enterprise scale. There are often many systems that can serve parts of the data that belong to a shared business concept. Hence there might be a lot of *source-aligned data* that ultimately needs to be aggregated into a more aggregate form of a concept. For example, attributes that define "subscribers," "songs," or "artists" can be mapped from many different points of origin. For example, the **listeners** domain can have profile-related information about subscribers, while the **player** domain knows about their music preferences. There are use cases, such as marketing or sales, that demand a holistic view of the subscriber. This demands new long-standing aggregate data representing multiple facets of **listeners** that compose data from multiple source-aligned domains.

I strongly caution you against creating *ambitious aggregate domain data*—aggregate domain data that attempts to capture all facets of a particular concept, like **listener 360**, and serve many organization-wide data users. Such aggregates can become too complex and unwieldy to manage, difficult to understand and use for any particular use case, and hard to keep up-to-date. In the past, the implementation of Master Data Management (MDM)[5] has attempted to aggregate all facets of shared data assets in one place and in one model. This is a move back to single monolithic schema modeling that doesn't scale.

Data mesh proposes that end consumers compose their own *fit-for-purpose* data aggregates and resist the temptation of highly reusable and ambitious aggregates.

---

5 "Control over Master Data values and identifiers that enable consistent use, across systems, of the most accurate and timely data about essential business entities. The goals of MDM include ensuring availability of accurate, current values while reducing risks associated with ambiguous identifiers (those identified with more than one instance of an entity and those that refer to more than one entity)." DAMA International, *DAMA-DMBOK: Data Management Body of Knowledge*, 2nd Edition (p. 356). (Basking Ridge, NJ: Technics Publications, 2017).

Consumer-Aligned Domain Data

Some domains align closely with consuming use cases. Consumer-aligned domain data, and the teams that own it, aim to satisfy one or a small group of closely related use cases. For example, **recommendations** are created as fit-for-purpose data that is presented to listeners while they interact with the player app.

Engineered *features* to train machine learning models often fall into this category. For example, Daff introduces a machine learning model that analyzes the sentiment of a song, e.g., positive or negative. Then it uses this information for music recommendations and rankings. However, to perform sentiment analysis on a piece of music, data scientists need to extract a few features and additional information from the song such as "liveliness," "danceability," "acousticness," "valence," etc. Once these attributes (features) are extracted, they can be maintained and shared as consumer-aligned domain data to train the **sentiment analysis** domain or other adjacent models such as **playlist** creation.

Consumer-aligned domain data has a different nature in comparison to source-aligned domain data. It structurally goes through more changes and transforms the source domain events to structures and content that fit a particular use case.

I sometimes call this *fit-for-purpose* domain data. The notion of the consumer here refers to the applications that consume the data, or data users such as data scientists or analysts.

Transition to Domain Ownership

To me, domain-driven data ownership feels organic, a natural progression of modern organizations' digital journey. Despite that, it disputes some of the archaic rules of analytical data management. Below is a list of a few of these rules, and I'm sure you can think of others.

Push Data Ownership Upstream

Data architecture nomenclature has flourished from the source of life itself: water. Things of concepts like data lakes, lakeshore marts, dataflow, lakehouses, data pipelines, lake hydration, etc. I do admit that it's a reassuring symbol; it's soothing and simply beautiful. However, there is a dangerous notion lurking underneath it, the notion that data must flow from a source to some other place—e.g., the centralized lake—to become useful, to become meaningful, to have value, and to be worthy of consumption. There is an assumption that data upstream is less valuable or useful than data downstream.

Data mesh challenges this assumption. Data can be consumable and useful right at the source domain—the source analytical data and *not* the source operational application. I call this source-aligned domain data. It only flows from an operational system to its collaborators and adjacent analytical data products. The purifying or optimizing transformations are limited before it becomes suitable for analytical use.

Of course, at a later point downstream, source-aligned domain data can be aggregated and transformed to create a new higher order insight. I call this aggregate domain data or fit-for-purpose domain data. These downstream transformations happen within the context of downstream domains, under the domains' long-term ownership. There is no intelligent transformation that happens in the no-man's-land in-between domains, in what is today called a *data pipeline*.

Define Multiple Connected Models

Data warehousing techniques and central data governance teams have been in search of the *one canonical model* holy grail. It's a wonderful idea, one model that describes data domains and can be used to provide a shared meaning to all data users. But in reality systems are complex and continuously changing, and no one model can tame this messy life of data. Data mesh in contrast follows DDD's bounded context and context mapping for data modeling. Each domain can model its data according to its context, share this data and its models with others, and identify how one model can relate and map to others.

This means there could be multiple models of the same concept in different domains and that is OK. For example, the **artist** representation in the **payment** includes payment attributes, which is very different from the **artist** model in the **recommendation** domain, which includes the artist profile and genre. But the mesh should allow mapping an **artist** from one domain to another and be able to link artist data from one domain to the same artist in another. There are multiple ways to achieve this, including a unified identification scheme, a single ID used by all domains that include an **artist**.

Polysemes

Polysemes (https://oreil.ly/G78lb) are shared concepts across different domains. They point to the same entity, with domain-specific attributes. Polysemes represent shared core concepts in a business such as "artist," "listener," and "song."

Following DDD, data mesh allows different domains' analytical data to model a polyseme according to the bounded context of their domain. However, it allows mapping a polyseme from one domain to another, with a global identification scheme.

Embrace the Most Relevant Domain Data: Don't Expect a Single Source of Truth

Another myth circulating the data industry is the search for the single source of truth for each shared business concept, for example, one source of truth to know everything about "listeners," "playlists," "artists," etc. This is a wonderful idea. The motivations are necessary: prevent multiple copies of out-of-date data and the sprawl of untrustworthy data. But in reality it's proved costly, an impediment to scale and speed, or simply unachievable. Data mesh does not enforce the idea of one source of truth. However, it places multiple practices in place that reduces the likelihood of multiple copies of out-of-date data.

Long-term domain-oriented ownership with accountability to share discoverable, high-quality, and usable data—in multiple modes for analysts and scientists—reduces the need for copying and keeping stale data around.

Data mesh endorses reshaping and recomposition of data to create fit-for-purpose data. Data can be read from one domain and transformed and stored by another domain. For example, the **emerging artist** domain reads **play events** domain data and transforms and then stores it as **emerging artists**. This mimics the real world, as data moves around, gets copied, and gets reshaped. It's very difficult to maintain the ideology of a single source of truth under such a dynamic topology. Data mesh enables the emergence of truth, while embracing a dynamic topology for scale and speed.

As you will see in future chapters, the data mesh platform observes the mesh, prevents errors that often arise when data gets copied, and surfaces the most relevant and reliable data.

Hide the Data Pipelines as Domains' Internal Implementation

As the need for cleansing, preparing, aggregating, and sharing data remains, so does the application of a *data pipeline*, regardless of using a centralized data architecture or data mesh. The difference is that in traditional data architectures, data pipelines are first-class architectural concerns that compose more complex data transformation and movement. In data mesh, a data pipeline is simply an internal implementation of the data domain and is handled internally within the domain. It's an implementation detail that must be abstracted from outside of the domain. As a result, when transitioning to data mesh, you will be redistributing different pipelines and their jobs to different domains.

For example, the source-aligned domains need to include the cleansing, deduplicating, and enriching of their domain events so that they can be consumed by other domains, without replication of cleansing downstream.

Consider Daff, where the **media player** domain provides audio **play events**. This domain includes a cleansing and standardization data pipeline that provides a stream of deduped near-real-time **play events** that conform to the organization's standards of encoding events.

Equally, we will see that the aggregation stages of a centralized pipeline move into the implementation details of aggregate or fit-for-purpose domain data.

One might argue that this model leads to duplicated effort in each domain to create their own data processing pipeline implementation, technology stack, and tooling. Data mesh addresses this concern with the self-serve data platform, described in Chapter 4.

With data mesh, domains are taking on additional data responsibilities. The responsibilities and efforts shift from a centralized data team to domains, to gain agility and authenticity.

Recap

Arranging data and its ownership around technology has been an impediment to scale; it simply has been orthogonal to how change happens and features develop. Centrally organized data teams have been the source of friction. There is an alternative. The alternative is a tried and tested method to scale modeling at the enterprise level: domain-driven bounded context modeling.

Data mesh adapts the concept of domain bounded contexts to the world of analytical data. It demands domain teams who are closest to the data own the analytical data and serve the domain's analytical data to the rest of the organization. Data mesh supports the creation of new domains' data by composing, aggregating, and projecting existing domains.

There are three fuzzy classifications of domain data:

- Source-aligned (native) analytical data, created and shared by the teams who own the source operational systems.
- Aggregates, analytical data in the middle, between consumers and producers, compositions of multiple upstream data products. Aggregates are owned by the producer or consumer teams, or a newly formed team.
- Consumer-aligned (fit-for-purpose) analytical data, designed for a particular data consumption scenario.

The shift toward domain-oriented data ownership leads to accepting and working with real-world messiness of data, particularly in high-speed and scaled environments:

- Work with multiple models of shared entities, which are linked (mapped) to each other.
- No more pipelines, well not at a high level. There will be pipelines hidden as internal implementations supporting particular domain data.

If you take one thought from this chapter, it would be this:

> All models are wrong, but some are useful.
>
> —George Box

Don't try to design the *domains* of a business up front and allocate and model analytical data according to that. Instead, start working with the seams of your business as they are. If your business is already organized based on domains, start there. If not, perhaps data mesh is not the right solution just yet. Let the evolution of data influence the shape of the organization, and vice versa.

CHAPTER 3

Principle of Data as a Product

One long-standing challenge of existing analytical data architectures is the high friction and cost of using data: *discovering, understanding, trusting, exploring, and ultimately consuming quality data.* There have been numerous surveys surfacing this friction. A recent report from Anaconda, a data science platform company, "The State of Data Science 2020" (*https://oreil.ly/S8XMz*), finds that nearly half of a data scientist's time is spent on data preparation—data loading and cleansing. If not addressed, this problem only exacerbates with data mesh, as the number of places and teams who provide data, i.e., domains, increases. Distribution of the organization's data ownership into the hands of the business domains raises important concerns around accessibility, usability, and harmonization. Further data siloing and regression of data usability are potential undesirable consequences of data mesh's first principle, *domain-oriented ownership.* The principle of *data as a product* addresses these concerns.

The second principle of data mesh, *data as a product*, applies *product thinking* to domain-oriented data to remove such usability frictions and truly delight the experience of the data users—data scientists, data analysts, data explorers, and anyone in between. *Data as a product* expects that the analytical data provided by the domains is treated as a product, and the consumers of that data should be treated as customers—happy and pleased. Furthermore, data as a product underpins the case for data mesh, unlocking the value of an organization's data by dramatically increasing the potential for serendipitous and intentional use.

In his book *INSPIRED* (*https://oreil.ly/mzv7u*), Marty Cagan, a prominent thought leader in product development and management, provides convincing evidence on how successful products have three common characteristics: they are *feasible, valuable,* and *usable.* Data as a product principle defines a new concept, called *data product*, that embodies standardized characteristics to make data *valuable* and *usable.*

Figure 3-1 demonstrates this point visually. This chapter introduces these characteristics. Chapter 4 describes how to make building data products *feasible*.

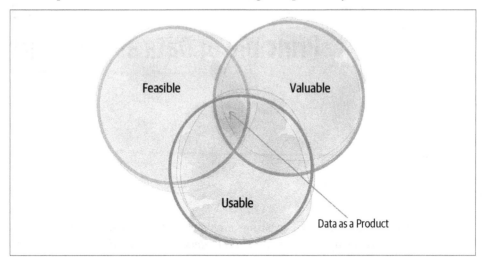

Figure 3-1. Data products live at the intersection of Marty Cagan's characteristics of successful products

For data to be a product it adheres to a set of rules and exhibits a set of traits that make it fit right in the intersection of Cargan's *usability*, *feasibility*, and *valuable* Venn diagram. For data to be a product, it must be valuable to its users—on its own and in cooperation with other data products. It must demonstrate *empathy* for its users and be accountable for its usability and integrity.

I admit that treating data as a product doesn't simply happen out of good intentions. For that, this principle introduces new roles to domains such as the *domain data product owner* and *data product developer* who have responsibility for creating, serving, and evangelizing data products, while maintaining the specific objective measures of data accessibility, quality, usability, and availability over the lifetime of the data products. Chapter 16 will cover further details about these new roles.

Compared to past paradigms, data as a product inverts the model of responsibility. In data lake or data warehousing architectures the accountability of creating data with quality and integrity resides downstream from the source and remains with the centralized data team. Data mesh shifts this responsibility close to the source of the data. This transition is not unique to data mesh; in fact, over the last decade we have seen the trend of *shift left* with testing and operations, on the basis that addressing problems is cheaper and more effective when done close to the source.

I go as far as saying that what gets shared on a mesh is not merely *data*; it is a *data product*.

Data as a product is about applying product thinking to how data is modeled and shared. This is not to be confused with product selling.

Let's unpack how we can apply product thinking to data.

Applying Product Thinking to Data

Over the last decade, high-performing organizations have embraced the idea of treating their internal operational technology like a product, similarly to their external technology. They treat their internal developers as customers and their satisfaction a sign of success. Particularly in two areas, this trend has been strongly adopted: applying product management techniques to internal platforms, which accelerates the ability of internal developers to build and host solutions on top of internal platforms (e.g., Spotify Backstage (*https://oreil.ly/B1fwB*)), and treating APIs as a product to build APIs that are discoverable, understandable, and easily testable to assure an optimal developer experience (e.g., Square APIs (*https://oreil.ly/gG9eL*)).

Applying the magic ingredient of product thinking to internal technology begins with establishing empathy with internal consumers (i.e., fellow developers), collaborating with them on designing the experience, gathering usage metrics, and continuously improving the internal technical solutions over time to maintain ease of use. Strong digital organizations allocate substantial resources and attention to building internal tools that are valuable to the developers and ultimately the business.

Curiously, the magical ingredient of empathy, treating data as a product and its users as customers, has been missing in big data solutions. Operational teams still perceive their data as a byproduct of running the business, leaving it to someone else, e.g., the data team, to pick it up and recycle it into *products*. In contrast, data mesh domain teams apply product thinking with similar rigor to their data, striving for the best data user experience.

Consider Daff. One of its critical domains is the **media player**. The **media player** domain provides essential data such as what songs have been played by whom, when, and where. There are a few different key data users for this information. For example, the **media player support** team is interested in near-real-time events to quickly catch errors causing a degrading customer experience and recover the service, or respond to incoming customer support calls informedly. On the other hand, the **media player design** team is interested in aggregated play events that tell a data story about the listener's journey over a longer period of time, to improve media players with more engaging features toward an overall better listener experience.

With an informed understanding of these use cases and what information the other teams need, the **media player** domain provides two different types of data as its products to the rest of the organization: *near-real-time play events* exposed as infinite event logs, and aggregated *play sessions* exposed as serialized files on an object store. This is product ownership applied to data.

Figure 3-2 shows the **media player** domain data products.

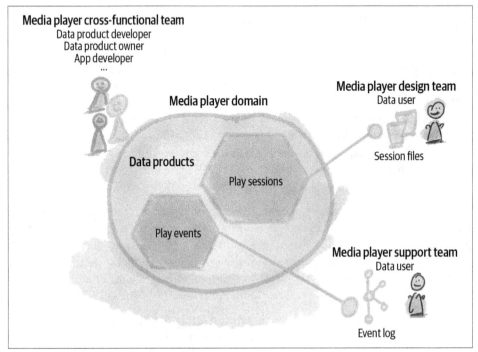

Figure 3-2. Data products example

As you can imagine, you can adopt the majority of the product ownership techniques to data. However, there is something unique about data. The difference between data product ownership and other types of products lies in the *unbounded nature of data use cases*, the ways in which particular data can be combined with other data and ultimately turned into insights and actions. At any point in time, data product owners are aware or can plan for what is known today as viable use cases of their data, while there remains a large portion of unknown future use cases for the data produced today, perhaps beyond their imagination.

This is more true for source-aligned domains and less for consumer-aligned ones. This source-aligned data captures the reality of the business interactions and events as they have happened. They can continue to be used, transformed, and reinterpreted by data users of the future. Source-aligned data products need to balance the immediate known use cases and the unknown ones. They have no choice but to strive to model the reality of the business, as closely as possible, in their data, without too much assumption in how it will be used. For example, capturing all the **play events** as an infinite high-resolution log is a safe choice. It opens the spectrum of future users who can build other transformations and infer new insights from the data that is captured today.

This is the main difference between data product design and software product design.

Baseline Usability Attributes of a Data Product

In my opinion, there is a set of non-negotiable baseline characteristics that a data product incorporates to be considered *useful*. These characteristics apply to all data products, regardless of their domain or archetype. I call these *baseline data product usability attributes*. Every data product incorporates these characteristics to be part of the mesh. Figure 3-3 lists data products' usability attributes.

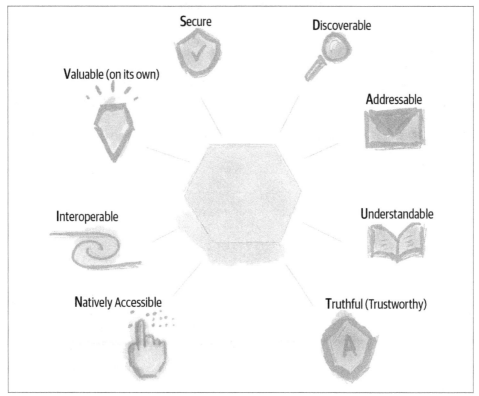

Figure 3-3. The baseline usability attributes of data products (DAUTNIVS)

Note that these *usability characteristics* are oriented around the experience of the data users. These are not intended to express the technical capabilities. Part IV, "Design of Data Quantum Architecture," covers the technical characteristics of data products.

The baseline characteristics listed in this section are an addition to what has been known as FAIR (*https://oreil.ly/2BB7V*) data in the past—data that meets the principles of *findability, accessibility, interoperability,* and *reusability*.[1] In addition to these principles I have introduced characteristics that are necessary to make distributed data ownership work.

Let's put ourselves in the shoes of data users and walk through these attributes.

Discoverable

> Two of the most important characteristics of good design are discoverability and understanding. Discoverability: Is it possible to even figure out what actions are possible and where and how to perform them? Understanding: What does it all mean? How is it supposed to be used? What do all the different controls and settings mean?[2]
>
> —Don Norman

The very first step that data users take in their journey is to discover the world of data available to them and explore and search to find "the one." Hence, one of the first usability attributes of data is to be easily discoverable. Data users need to be able to explore the available data products, search and find the desirable sets, and explore them and gain confidence in using them. A traditional implementation of discoverability is a centralized registry or catalog listing available datasets with some additional information about each dataset, the owners, the location, sample data, etc. Often this information is curated after the fact by the centralized data team or the governance team.

Data product discoverability on data mesh embraces a shift-left solution where the data product itself *intentionally* provides discoverability information. Data mesh embraces the dynamic topology of the mesh, continuously evolving data products and the sheer scale of available data products. Hence, it relies on individual data products to provide their discoverability information at different points of their life cycle—build, deploy, and run—in a standard way. Each data product continuously shares its source of origin, owners, runtime information such as timeliness, quality metrics, sample datasets, and most importantly information contributed by their consumers such as the top use cases and applications enabled by their data.

Part IV, "How to Design the Data Product Architecture", will discuss the technical design of data product discoverability.

---

1 The FAIR principles were published in 2016 in *Scientific Data*, a peer-reviewed scientific journal.

2 Don Norman, *The Design of Everyday Things: Revised and Expanded Edition.* (New York: Basic Books, 2013).

Addressable

A data product offers a permanent and unique address to the data user to programmatically or manually access it. This addressing system embraces the dynamic nature of the data and the mesh topology. It must recognize that many aspects of data products will continue to change, while it assures *continuity of usage.*

The addressing system accommodates the following ever-changing aspects of a data product, among others, while retaining access to the data product through its long-lasting unique address:

Semantic and syntax changes in data products
   Schema evolution

Continuous release of new data over time (window)
   Partitioning strategy and grouping of data tuples associated with a particular time (or time window)

Newly supported modes of access to data
   New ways of serializing, presenting, and querying the data

Changing runtime behavioral information
   For example, service-level objectives, access logs, debug logs

The unique address must follow a global convention that helps users to programmatically and consistently access all data products. The data product must have an addressable aggregate root (*https://oreil.ly/D4M9x*) that serves as an entry to all information about a data product, including its documentation, service-level objectives, and the data it serves.

Understandable

Once a data product is discovered, the next step of the data user's journey is to understand it, which involves getting to know the semantics of its underlying data, as well as various syntax in which the data is encoded.

Each data product provides semantically coherent data: data with a specific *meaning*. A data user needs to understand this *meaning*: what kind of entities the data product encapsulates, what the relationships among the entities are, and their adjacent data products.

Getting back to the **media player** event example, a data user should easily understand what constitutes a player event: the **user**, the **play actions** they have taken, the **time** and **location** of their action, and the **feedback** the action has resulted in. The data user should easily understand the kinds of actions available and that there is a relationship between a listener triggering a player event and a **subscriber** from the adjacent **listener** domain. Data products provide a formal representation of such *semantics*.

In addition to understanding the semantics, data users need to understand how exactly the data is presented to them. How is it serialized, and how can they access and query the data syntactically? What kind of queries can they execute or how can they read the data objects? They need to understand the *schema* of the underlying *syntax* of data. Sample datasets and example consumer codes ideally accompany this information. Examples accompanied with a formalized description of the data improve data users' understanding.

Additionally, dynamic and computational documents like computational notebooks (*https://oreil.ly/k0TmE*) are great companions to tell the story of a data product. Computational notebooks include documentation of the data, as well as code to use it, with immediate feedback that visually demonstrates the code's result.

Lastly, understanding is a social process. We learn from each other. Data products facilitate communication across their users to share their experience and how they take advantage of the data product.

Understanding a usable data product requires no hand-holding. A self-serve method of understanding is a baseline usability characteristic.

Trustworthy and truthful

> [Trust is] a confident relationship with the unknown.[3]
>
> —Rachel Botsman

No one will use a product that they can't trust. So what does it mean to trust a data product, and more importantly what does it take to trust? To unpack this, I like to use the concept of trust offered by Rachel Botsman: *the bridge between the known and the unknown*. A data product needs to close the gap between what data users know confidently about the data, and what they don't know but need to know to trust it. While the prior characteristics like understandability and discoverability close this gap to a degree, it takes a lot more to trust the data for use.

The data users need to confidently know that the data product is truthful, that it represents the fact of the business correctly. They need to confidently know how closely data reflects the reality of the events that have occurred, the probability of truthfulness of the aggregations and projections that have been created from business facts.

---

3 Rachel Botsman, "Trust-Thinkers" (*https://oreil.ly/Q2s3i*), July 26, 2018.

A piece of closing the trust gap is to guarantee and communicate data products' service-level objectives (*https://oreil.ly/41TpM*) (SLOs)—objective measures that remove uncertainty surrounding the data.

Data product SLOs include, among others:

Interval of change
How often changes in the data are reflected

Timeliness
The skew between the time that a business fact occurs and becomes available to the data users

Completeness
Degree of availability of all the necessary information

Statistical shape of data
Its distribution, range, volume, etc.

Lineage
The data transformation journey from source to here

Precision and accuracy over time
Degree of business truthfulness as time passes

Operational qualities
Freshness, general availability, performance

In the traditional approaches to data management, it's common to extract and onboard data that has errors, does not reflect the truth of the business, and simply can't be trusted. This is where the majority of the efforts of centralized data pipelines are concentrated, cleansing data after ingestion.

In contrast, data mesh introduces a fundamental shift that the owners of the data products must communicate and guarantee an acceptable level of quality and trustworthiness—specific to their domain—as an intrinsic characteristic of their data product. This means cleansing and running automated data integrity tests at the point of the creation of a data product.

Providing data provenance and data lineage—the data journey, where it has come from and how it got here—as the metadata associated with each data product helps consumers gain further confidence in the data product. The users can evaluate this information to determine the data's suitability for their particular needs. I'm of the opinion that once the discipline of building trustworthiness in each data product is established, there is less need for establishing trust through investigative processes and applying detective techniques navigating a lineage tree. Having said that, data lineage will remain an important element in a few scenarios, such as postmortem root-cause analysis, debugging, data compliance audits, and evaluation of data's fitness for ML training.

Natively accessible

Depending on the data maturity of the organization there is a wide spectrum of data user personas in need of access to data products. The spectrum spans a large profile of users, as displayed in Figure 3-4: data analysts who are comfortable with exploring data in spreadsheets, data analysts who are comfortable with query languages to create statistical models of data as visualizations or reports, data scientists who curate and structure data and consume data frames to train their ML models, and data-intensive application developers who expect a real-time stream of events or pull-based APIs. This is a fairly wide spectrum of users with equally diverse expectations of how to access and read data.

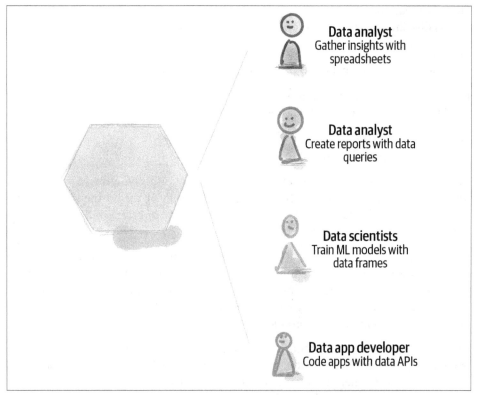

Figure 3-4. Example of a wide spectrum of data product users with different data access patterns

There is a direct link between the *usability* of a data product and how easily a particular data user can access it with their native tools. Hence, a data product needs to make it possible for various data users to access and read its data in their native mode of access. This can be implemented as a polyglot storage of data or by building multiple read adapters on the same data.

For example, the **play events** data product needs to natively support reading data through SQL query to satisfy a data analyst's native mode of access, publishing a stream of events for data-intensive applications, and columnar files for data scientists.

Interoperable

One of the main concerns in a distributed data architecture is the ability to correlate data across domains and stitch them together in wonderful and insightful ways: join, filter, aggregate. The key for an effective composability of data across domains is following standards and harmonization rules that allow *linking data* across domains easily.

Here are a few things data products need to standardize to facilitate interoperability and composability:

Field type
    A common explicitly defined type system

Polysemes identifiers
    Universally identifying entities that cross boundaries of data products

Data product global addresses
    A unique global address allocated to each data product, ideally with a uniform scheme for ease of establishing connections to different data products

Common metadata fields
    Such as representation of time when data occurs and when data is recorded

Schema linking
    Ability to link and reuse schemas—types—defined by other data products

Data linking
    Ability to link or map to data in other data products

Schema stability
    Approach to evolving schemas that respects backward compatibility

For example, let's look at managing polysemes identifiers. At Daff, *artist* is a core business concept that appears in different domains. An artist, while remaining the same global entity, has different attributes and likely different identifiers in each domain. The **play events** data product recognizes the artist differently from the **payment** domain—taking care of invoices and payments for artists' royalties. In order to correlate data about an artist across different domain data products Daff needs to agree on how they identify an artist, globally, across all data products.

Chapter 5 covers the topic of global standards and protocols applied to each data product. Interoperability is the foundation of any distributed system design, and data mesh is no exception.

Valuable on its own

I think it's fairly obvious that a data product must be valuable—it should have some inherent value for the data users in service of the business and customers. After all, if the data product owner can't envisage any value out of the data product, perhaps it's best not to create one. Having said that, it's worth calling out that a data product should carry a dataset that is *valuable* and *meaningful* on its own—without being joined and correlated with other data products.

Of course, there is always higher-order meaning, insight, and value that can be derived by correlating multiple data products. However, if a data product on its own serves no value on its own, it should not exist.

While this may sound obvious, there is a common antipattern when migrating from a warehouse architecture to data mesh: directly mapping warehouse tables to data products can create data products with no value. In the data warehouse, there are glue (aka facts) tables that optimize correlation between entities. These are identity tables that map identifiers of one kind of entity to another. Such identity tables are not meaningful or valuable on their own—without being joined to other tables. They are simply mechanical implementations to facilitate joins.

On the contrary, there are no mechanical data products that solely exist to enable the machines to correlate information across the mesh. Machine optimizations such as indices or fact tables must be automatically created by the platform and hidden from the product products.

Secure

Data users access a data product securely and in a confidentiality-respecting manner. Data security is a must, whether the architecture is centralized or distributed. However, in a distributed architecture like data mesh, the access control is validated by the data product, right in the flow of data, *access*, *read*, or *write*. The access control policies can change dynamically. They continuously get evaluated at every point of access to data products.

Additionally, access to a data product is not quite binary—whether the user can see or can't see the data. In many cases while the user may not be able to see the actual records, it might have sufficient permissions to see the shape of the data and evaluate it using its statistical characteristics.

Access control policies can be defined centrally but enforced at runtime by each individual data product. Data products follow the practice of security policy as code (*https://oreil.ly/zH1k2*). This means to write security policies in a way that they can be versioned, automatically tested, deployed and observed, and computationally evaluated and enforced.

A policy described, tested, and maintained as code can articulate various security-related concerns such as the following, among others:

Access control
> Who, what, and how data users—systems and people—can access the data product

Encryption
> What kinds of encryption—on disk, in memory, or in transit—using which encryption algorithm, and how to manage keys and minimize the radius of impact in case of breaches

Confidentiality levels
> What kinds of confidential information, e.g., personally identifiable information, personal health information, etc., the data product carries

Data retention
> How long the information must be kept

Regulations and agreements
> GDPR, CCPA, domain-specific regulations, contractual agreements

Transition to Data as a Product

In working with my clients, I have found that they are overwhelmingly receptive to data mesh principles, often questioning "Why didn't I think of it myself?" or occasionally saying, "We have been doing something similar but not quite the same." The principles appear to be intuitive and rather natural next steps in their organization's tech modernization journey, an extension to modernization of the operational aspect of organizations, e.g., moving toward domain-oriented ownership of capabilities with microservices and treating internal products like operational APIs as products.

However, a sense of discomfort arises when they go deeper into what it actually takes to implement the transformation toward data mesh. I found in my conversations with data mesh early implementers that while they verbalize the principles and their intention to implement them, the implementations remain heavily influenced by the familiar techniques of the past.

For this reason, I have decided to include a number of thought-provoking transition statements as well as a few pragmatic steps to crystalize the differences between the existing paradigm and truly owning *data as a product*.

I invite you to think of new transition statements that I likely have missed here.

Include Data Product Ownership in Domains

In the past decade, teams have continued to move from being functionally divided to becoming cross-functional. The DevOps movement has led to closing the gap between building and operating business services and forming dev and ops cross-functional teams. Customer-obsessed product development has brought the design and product ownership closer to the developers.

The introduction of analytical data as a product adds to the list of existing responsibilities of cross-functional domain teams and expands their roles to:

Data product developer
> The role responsible for developing, serving, and maintaining the domain's data products as long as the data products live and are being used

Data product owner
> The role accountable for the success of a domain's data products in delivering value, satisfying and growing the data users, and maintaining the life cycle of the data products

Define these roles for each domain and allocate one or multiple people to the roles depending on the complexity of the domain and the number of its data products.

Reframe the Nomenclature to Create Change

One commonly used term in data analytics is *ingestion*, receiving data from an upstream source—often an untrustworthy source that has *egested* data as a *byproduct* of its operation. It's now the job of the downstream pipeline to ingest, clean, and process the data before it can be *consumed* to generate value.

Data mesh suggests reframing receiving upstream data from *ingestion* to *consumption*. The subtle difference is that the upstream data is already cleansed, processed, and *served* ready for consumption. The change of language creates a new cognitive framing that is more aligned with the principle of serving data as a product.

Relatedly, the word *extraction* used in ETL (extract, transform, load) and its other variations needs to be critically evaluated. Extraction evokes a passive role for the provider and an intrusive role for the consumer. As we know, extracting data from an operational database that is not optimized for external use other than its own application creates all kinds of pathological coupling and a fragile design. Instead, we can shift the language to *publish*, *serve*, or *share*. This implies shifting the implementation of data sharing from accessing raw databases to intentionally sharing domain events or aggregates.

By now you probably have picked up on my emphasis on language and the metaphors we use. George Lakoff (*https://oreil.ly/3YZ26*)—professor of cognitive science and linguistics at UC Berkeley—in his book, *Metaphors We Live By*, elegantly demonstrates the consequence of shifting our language around the concept of *argument*, from *war* to *dance*. Imagine the world we would live in and the relationships we would nurture, if instead of *winning* an argument, losing and gaining argument ground, and attacking the weak points of an argument, we would, as dancers, perform a balanced and aesthetically pleasing argument, expressing our ideas and emotions through the beautiful and collaborative ritual of dancing. This unexpected reframing of language has a profound behavioral impact.

Think of Data as a Product, Not a Mere Asset

"Data is an asset." "Data must be managed like an asset." These are the phrases that have dominated our vernacular in big data management.

The metaphor of *asset* used for *data* is nothing new. After all, for decades, TOGAF (*https://oreil.ly/oekyG*), a standard of the Open Group for Enterprise Architecture methodologies and frameworks, explicitly has penciled in "Data Is an Asset" (*https://oreil.ly/Z6Y0y*) as the first principle of its data principles. While this is a rather harmless metaphor on the surface, it has shaped our perceptions and actions toward negative consequences, for example, our actions toward how we measure success. Based on my observations, data as an asset has led to measuring success by *vanity metrics*—metrics that make us look or feel good but don't impact performance—such as the number of datasets and tables captured in the lake or warehouse, or the volume of data. These are the metrics I repeatedly come across in organizations. Data as an asset promotes keeping and storing data rather than sharing it. Interestingly, TOGAF's "Data Is an Asset" principle is immediately followed by "Data Is Shared."

I suggest the change of metaphor to *data as a product*, and a change of perspective that comes with that, for example, measuring success through *adoption of data*, its *number of users*, and their *satisfaction* using the data. This underscores *sharing the data* versus keeping and locking it up. It puts emphasis on the continuous care that a quality product deserves.

I invite you to spot other metaphors and vocabulary that we need to change to construct a new system of concepts for data mesh.

Establish a Trust-But-Verify Data Culture

Data as a product principle implements a number of practices that lead to a culture where data users, by default, can trust the validity of the data and put their focus on verifying its fitness for their use cases.

These practices include introducing a role for long-term ownership of a data product, accountable for the integrity, quality, availability, and other usability characteristics of the data product; introducing the concept of a data product that not only shares data but also explicitly shares a set of objective measures such as timeliness, retention, and accuracy; and creating a data product development process that automates testing of the data product.

Today, in the absence of these data-as-a-product practices, *data lineage* remains a vital ingredient for establishing trust. Data users have been left with no choice but to assume data is untrustworthy and requires a detective investigation through its lineage before it can be trusted. This lack of trust is the result of the wide gap between data providers and data users due to the data providers' lack of visibility to the users and their needs, lack of long-term accountability for data, and the absence of computational guarantees.

Data-as-a-product practices aim to build a new culture, from *presumption of guilt* to the Russian proverb of *trust but verify*.

Join Data and Compute as One Logical Unit

Let's do a test.

When you hear the word *data product*, what comes to your mind? What shape? What does it contain? How does it feel? I can guarantee that a large portion of readers imagine static files or tables, columns and rows, some form of storage medium. It feels static. It's accumulated. Its content is made of bits and bytes that are representative of the facts, perhaps beautifully modeled. That is intuitive. After all, by definition *datum*—singular form—is a "piece of information."[4]

This perspective results in the separation of *code (compute)* from *data*, in this case, separation of the code that maintains the data, creates it, and serves it. This separation creates orphaned datasets that decay over time. At scale, we experience this separation as data swamps (*https://oreil.ly/6ixTI*)—a deteriorated data lake.

Data mesh shifts from this dual mode of data versus code to data and code as one architectural unit, a single deployable unit that is structurally complete to do its job, providing the high-quality data of a particular domain. One doesn't exist without the other.

Data and code coexisting as one unit is not a new concept for people who have managed microservices architecture (*https://oreil.ly/cKogS*). The evolution of operational systems has moved to a model in which each service manages its code and data, schema definition, and upgrades. The difference between an operational system is the relationship between the *code* and its *data*. In the case of microservices architecture, *data* serves the *code*. It maintains state so that code can complete its job, serving business capabilities. In the case of a data product and data mesh this relationship

---

4 Couldn't help but notice that the 18th century Latin meaning of datum is "something given." This early meaning is a lot closer to the spirit of "data product"' valuable facts to give and share.

is inverse: *code* serves *data*. The code transforms the data, maintains its integrity, governs its policies, and ultimately serves it.

Note that the underlying physical infrastructures that host code and data are kept separate.

Recap

The principle of *data as a product* is a response to the data siloing challenge that may arise from the distribution of data ownership to domains. It is also a shift in the data culture toward *data accountability* and *data trust* at the point of origin. The ultimate goal is to make data simply *usable*.

The chapter explained eight nonnegotiable baseline *usability* characteristics of data products including *discoverability, addressability, understandability, trustworthiness, native accessibility, interoperability, independently valuable,* and *security*.

I introduced the role of *data product owner*—someone with an intimate understanding of the domain's data and its consumers—to assure continuity of ownership of data and accountability of success metrics such as *data quality, decreased lead time* of data consumption, and in general *data user satisfaction* through net promoter score (*https://oreil.ly/iFCtM*).

Each domain includes a *data product developer role*, responsible for building, maintaining, and serving the domain's data products. Data product developers will be working alongside their fellow application developers in the domain.

Each domain team may serve one or multiple data products. It's also possible to form new teams to serve data products that don't naturally fit into an existing operational domain.

Data as a product creates a new system of the world, where data is and can be trusted, built, and served with deep empathy for its users, and its success is measured through the value delivered to the users and not its size.

This ambitious shift must be treated as an organizational transformation. I will cover the organizational transformation in Part V of this book. It also requires an underlying supporting platform. The next chapter looks into the platform shift to make data as a product feasible.

CHAPTER 4

Principle of the Self-Serve Data Platform

Simplicity is about subtracting the obvious and adding the meaningful.
—John Maeda

So far I have offered two fundamental shifts toward data mesh: a distributed data architecture and ownership model oriented around business domains, and data shared as a usable and valuable product. Over time, these two seemingly simple and rather intuitive shifts can have undesired consequences: duplication of efforts in each domain, increased cost of operation, and likely large-scale inconsistencies and incompatibilities across domains.

Expecting domain engineering teams to own and share analytical data as a product, in addition to building applications and maintaining digital products, raises legitimate concerns for both the practitioners and their leaders. The concerns that I often hear from leaders, at this point in the conversation, include: "How am I going to manage the cost of operating the domain data products, if every domain needs to build and own its own data?" "How do I hire the data engineers, who are already hard to find, to staff in every domain?" "This seems like a lot of overengineering and duplicate effort in each team." "What technology do I buy to provide all the data product usability characteristics?" "How do I enforce governance in a distributed fashion to avoid chaos?" "What about copied data—how do I manage that?" And so on. Similarly, domain engineering teams and practitioners voice concerns such as, "How can we extend the responsibility of our team to not only build applications to run the business, but also share data?"

Addressing these questions is the reason that data mesh's third principle, *self-serve data infrastructure as a platform*, exists. It's not that there is any shortage of data and analytics platforms, but we need to make changes to them so they can *scale out* sharing, accessing, and using analytical data, in a *decentralized manner*, for a new population of *generalist technologists*. This is the key differentiation of a data mesh platform.

Figure 4-1 depicts the extraction of domain-agnostic capabilities out of each domain and moving to a self-serve infrastructure as a platform. The platform is built and maintained by a dedicated platform team.

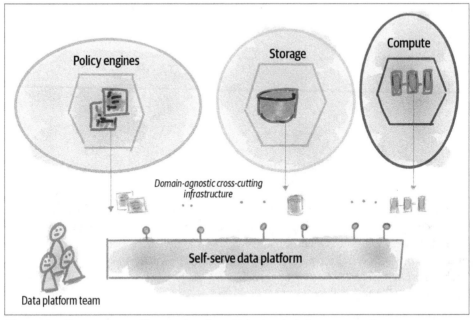

Figure 4-1. Extracting and harvesting domain agnostic infrastructure into a separate data platform

In this chapter, I apply platform thinking to the underlying infrastructure capabilities to clarify what we mean by the term *platform* in the context of data mesh. Then, I share the unique characteristics of data mesh's underlying platform. Later chapters, such as Chapters 9 and 10, will go into further detail about the platform's capabilities and how to approach its design. For now, let's discuss how data mesh's underlying platform is different from many solutions we have today.

In this chapter, I use the phrase *data mesh platform* as shorthand for a set of underlying data infrastructure capabilities. A singular form of the term *platform* does not mean a single solution or a single vendor with tightly integrated features. It's merely a placeholder for a set of technologies that one can use to achieve the objectives mentioned in "Data Mesh Platform Thinking" on page 54, a set of technologies that are independent and yet play nicely together.

Data Mesh Platform: Compare and Contrast

There is a large body of technology solutions that fall into the category of data infrastructure and are often posed as a platform. Here is a small sample of the existing platform capabilities:

- *Analytical data storage* in the form of a lake, warehouse, or lakehouse
- *Data processing frameworks* and computation engines to process data in batch and streaming modes
- *Data querying languages,* based on two modes of computational data flow programming or algebraic SQL-like statements
- *Data catalog* solutions to enable data governance as well as discovery of all data across an organization
- *Pipeline workflow management,* orchestrating complex data pipeline tasks or ML model deployment workflows

Many of these capabilities are still needed to enable a data mesh implementation. However, there is a shift in approach and the objectives of a data mesh platform. Let's do a quick compare and contrast.

Figure 4-2 shows a set of unique characteristics of a data mesh platform in comparison to the existing ones. Note that the data mesh platform can utilize existing technologies yet offer these unique characteristics.

The following section clarifies how data mesh works toward building self-serve platforms further.

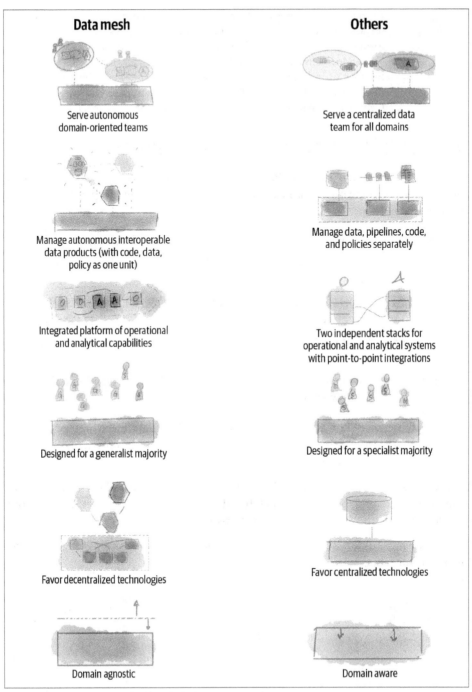

Data mesh	Others
Serve autonomous domain-oriented teams	Serve a centralized data team for all domains
Manage autonomous interoperable data products (with code, data, policy as one unit)	Manage data, pipelines, code, and policies separately
Integrated platform of operational and analytical capabilities	Two independent stacks for operational and analytical systems with point-to-point integrations
Designed for a generalist majority	Designed for a specialist majority
Favor decentralized technologies	Favor centralized technologies
Domain agnostic	Domain aware

Figure 4-2. Data mesh platform's differentiating characteristics

Serving Autonomous Domain-Oriented Teams

The main responsibility of the data mesh platform is to enable existing or new domain engineering teams with the new and embedded responsibilities of building, sharing, and using data products end to end; capturing data from operational systems and other sources; and transforming and sharing the data as a product with the end data users.

The platform must allow teams to do this in an autonomous way without any dependence on centralized data teams or intermediaries.

Many existing vendor technologies are built with an assumption of a centralized data team, capturing and sharing data for all domains. The assumptions around this centralized control have deep technical consequences such as:

- Cost is *estimated and managed monolithically* and not per isolated domain resources.

- *Security and privacy management* assumes physical resources are shared under the same account and don't scale to an isolated security context per data product.

- *A central pipeline (DAG) orchestration* assumes management of all data pipelines centrally—with a central pipeline configuration repository and a central monitoring portal. This is in conflict with independent pipelines, each small and allocated to a data product implementation.

These are a few examples to demonstrate how existing technologies get in the way of domain teams acting *autonomously*.

Managing Autonomous and Interoperable Data Products

Data mesh puts a new construct, a domain-oriented data product, at the center of its approach. This is a new architectural construct that *autonomously* delivers value. It encodes all the behavior and data needed to provide discoverable, usable, trustworthy, and secure data to its end data users. Data products share data with each other and are interconnected in a mesh. Data mesh platforms must work with this new construct and must support managing its autonomous life cycle and all its constituents.

This platform characteristic is different from the existing platforms today that manage behavior, e.g., data processing pipelines, data and its metadata, and policy that governs the data as independent pieces. However, it is possible to create the new data product management abstraction on top of existing technologies, but it is not very elegant.

A Continuous Platform of Operational and Analytical Capabilities

The principle of domain ownership demands a platform that enables autonomous domain teams to manage data end to end. This closes the gap organizationally between the operational plane and the analytical plane. Hence, a data mesh platform must be able to provide a more connected experience. Whether the team is building and running an application or sharing and using data products for analytical use cases, the team's experience should be connected and seamless. For the platform to be successfully adopted with existing domain technology teams, it must remove the barriers to adoption, the schism between the operational and analytical stacks.

The data mesh platform must close the gap between analytical and operational technologies. It must find ways to get them to work seamlessly together, in a way that is natural to a cross-functional domain-oriented data and application team.

For example, today the computation fabric running data processing pipelines such as Spark are managed on a different clustering architecture, away and often disconnected from the computation fabric that runs operational services, such as Kubernetes. In order to create data products that collaborate closely with their corresponding microservice, i.e., source-aligned data products, we need a closer integration of the computation fabrics. I have worked with very few organizations that have been running both computation engines on the same computation fabric.

Due to inherent differences between the two planes, there are many areas of the platform where the technology for operational and analytical systems must remain different. For example, consider the case of tracing for debugging and audit purposes. The operational systems use the OpenTelemetry (*https://opentelemetry.io*) standards for tracing of (API) calls across distributed applications, in a tree-like structure. On the other hand, data processing workloads use OpenLineage (*https://openlineage.io*) to trace the lineage of data across distributed data pipelines. There are enough differences between the two planes to mind their gap. However, it is important that these two standards integrate nicely. After all, in many cases, the journey of a piece of data starts from an application call in response to a user action.

Designed for a Generalist Majority

Another barrier to the adoption of data platforms today is the level of proprietary specialization that each technology vendor assumes—the jargon and the vendor-specific knowledge. This has led to the creation of scarce specialized roles such as data engineers.

In my opinion there are a few reasons for this unscalable specialization: *lack of (de facto) standards and conventions, lack of incentives for technology interoperability,* and *lack of incentive to make products super simple to use.* I believe this is the residue of the big monolithic platform mentality that a single vendor can provide soup to nuts functionality to store your data on their platform and attach their additional services to keep the data there and its processing under their control.

A data mesh platform must break this pattern and start with the definition of a set of open conventions that promote interoperability between different technologies and reduce the number of proprietary languages and experiences one specialist must learn to generate value from data. Incentivizing and enabling generalist developers with experiences, languages, and APIs that are easy to learn is a starting point to lower the cognitive load of generalist developers. To scale out data-driven development to the larger population of practitioners, data mesh platforms must stay relevant to generalist technologists. They must move to the background, fit naturally into the native tools and programming languages generalists use, and get out of their way.

Needless to say, this should be achieved without compromising on the software engineering practices that result in sustainable solutions. For example, many low-code or no-code platforms promise to work with data, but compromise on testing, versioning, modularity, and other techniques. Over time they become unmaintainable.

The phrase *generalist technologist (experts)* refers to the population of technologists who are often referred to as T-shaped (*https://oreil.ly/jHehn*) or Paint Drip (*https://oreil.ly/Durvx*) people. These are developers experienced in a broad spectrum of software engineering who, at different points in time, focus and gain deep knowledge in one or two areas.

The point is that it is possible to go deep in one or two areas while exploring many others.

They contrast with specialists, who only have expertise in one specific area; their focus on specialization doesn't allow them to explore a diverse spectrum.

In my mind, future generalists will be able to work with data and create and share data through data products, or use them for feature engineering and ML training when the model has already been developed by specialist data scientists. Essentially, they use AI as a service.

As of now, the majority of data work requires specialization and requires a large amount of effort to gain expertise over a long period of time. This inhibits the entry of generalist technologists and has led to a scarcity of data specialists.

Favoring Decentralized Technologies

Another common characteristic of existing platforms is the centralization of control. Examples include centralized pipeline orchestration tools, centralized catalogs, centralized warehouse schema, centralized allocation of compute/storage resources, and so on. The reason for data mesh's focus on decentralization through domain ownership is to avoid organizational synchronization and bottlenecks that ultimately slow down the speed of change. Though on the surface this is an organizational concern, the underlying technology and architecture directly influence organizational communication and design. A monolithic or centralized technology solution leads to centralized points of control and teams.

Data mesh platforms need to consider the decentralization of organizations in data sharing, control, and governance at the heart of their design. They inspect every centralized aspect of the design that can result in lockstep team synchronization, centralization of control, and tight coupling between autonomous teams.

Having said that, there are many aspects of infrastructure that need to be centrally managed to reduce the unnecessary tasks that each domain team performs in sharing and using data, e.g., setting up data processing compute clusters. This is where an effective self-serve platform shines, centrally managing underlying resources while allowing independent teams to achieve their outcomes end to end, without tight dependencies to other teams.

Domain Agnostic

Data mesh creates a clear delineation of responsibility between domain teams—who focus on creating business-oriented products, services that are ideally data-driven, and data products—and the platform teams who focus on technical enablers for the domains. This is different from the existing delineation of responsibility where the data team is often responsible for amalgamation of domain-specific data for analytical usage, as well as the underlying technical infrastructure.

This delineation of responsibility needs to be reflected in the platform capabilities. The platform must strike a balance between providing domain-agnostic capabilities, while enabling domain-specific data modeling, processing, and sharing across the organization. This demands a deep understanding of the data developers and the application of product thinking to the platform.

Data Mesh Platform Thinking

> Platform: raised level surface on which people or things can stand.
>
> —Oxford Languages

The word *platform* is one of the most commonly used phrases in our everyday technical jargon and is sprinkled all over organizations' technical strategies. It's commonly used, yet hard to define and subject to interpretation.

To ground our understanding of the *platform* in the context of data mesh I draw from the work of a few of my trustworthy sources:

A digital platform is a foundation of self-service APIs, tools, services, knowledge and support which are arranged as a compelling internal product. Autonomous delivery teams can make use of the platform to deliver product features at a higher pace, with reduced coordination.

—Evan Bottcher, "What I Talk About When I Talk About Platforms" (*https://oreil.ly/EoWNP*)

The purpose of a platform team is to enable stream-aligned teams to deliver work with substantial autonomy. The stream-aligned team maintains full ownership of building, running, and fixing their application in production. The platform team provides internal services to reduce the cognitive load that would be required from stream-aligned teams to develop these underlying services.

The platform simplifies otherwise complex technology and reduces cognitive load for teams that use it.

—Matthew Skelton and Manuel Pais, *Team Topologies*

Platforms are designed one interaction at a time. Thus, the design of every platform should start with the design of the core interaction that it enables between producers and consumers. The core interaction is the single most important form of activity that takes place on a platform—the exchange of value that attracts most users to the platform in the first place.[1]

—Geoffrey G. Parker et al., *Platform Revolution*)

A platform has a few key objectives that I like to take away and apply to data mesh:

Enable autonomous teams to get value from data
A common characteristic that we see is the ability to enable teams who use the platform to complete their work and achieve their outcomes with a sense of autonomy and without requiring another team to get engaged directly in their workflow, e.g., through backlog dependencies. In the context of data mesh, enabling domain teams with new responsibilities of sharing analytical data, or using analytical data for building ML-based products, in an autonomous way, is a key objective of a data mesh platform. The ability to use the platform capabilities through self-serve APIs is critical to enable autonomy.

Exchange value with autonomous and interoperable data products
Another key aspect of a platform is to intentionally design *what value* is being exchanged and *how*. In the case of data mesh, data products are the unit of value exchange, between data users and data providers. A data mesh platform must build in the frictionless exchange of data products as a unit of value in its design.

---

1 Geoffrey G. Parker, Marshall W. Van Alstyne, and Sangeet Paul Choudary, *Platform Revolution*, (New York: W.W. Norton & Company, 2016).

Accelerate exchange of value by lowering the cognitive load

In order to simplify and accelerate the work of domain teams in delivering value, platforms must hide technical and foundational complexity. This lowers the cognitive load of the domain teams to focus on what matters; in the case of data mesh, this is creating and sharing data products.

Scale out data sharing

Data mesh is a solution offered to solve the problem of organizational scale in getting value from their data. Hence, the design of the platform must cater for scale: sharing data across main domains within the organization, as well as across boundaries of trust outside of the organization in the wider network of partners. One of the blockers to this scale is the lack of interoperability of data sharing, securely, across multiple platforms. A data mesh platform must design for interoperability with other platforms to share data products.

Support a culture of embedded innovation

A data mesh platform supports a culture of innovation by removing activities that are not directly contributing to the innovation, by making it really easy to find data, capture insights, and use data for ML model development.

Figure 4-3 depicts these objectives applied to an ecosystem of domain teams sharing and using data products.

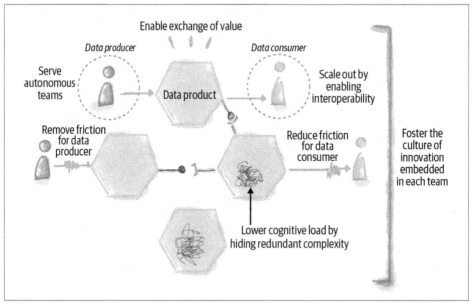

Figure 4-3. Objectives of the data mesh platform

Now, let's talk about how a data mesh platform achieves these objectives.

Enable Autonomous Teams to Get Value from Data

In designing the platform, it is helpful to consider the roles of platform users and their journey in sharing and using data products. The platform can then focus on how to create a frictionless experience for each journey. For example, let's consider two of the main personas of the data mesh ecosystem: *data product developers* and *data product users*. Of course, each of those personas includes a spectrum of people with different skill sets, but for this conversation we can focus on the aspects of their journeys that are common across this spectrum. There are other roles such as data product owner whose journey is as important in achieving the outcome of creating successful data products; favoring brevity, I leave them out of this example.

Enable data product developers

The delivery journey of a data product developer involves developing a data product; testing, deploying, monitoring, and updating it; and maintaining its integrity and security—with continuous delivery (*https://oreil.ly/cmkps*) in mind. In short, the developer is *managing the life cycle* of a data product, working with its code, data, and policies as one unit. As you can imagine, there is a fair bit of infrastructure that needs to be provisioned to manage this life cycle.

Provisioning and managing the underlying infrastructure for life cycle management of a data product requires specialized knowledge of today's tooling and is difficult to replicate in each domain. Hence, the data mesh platform must implement all necessary capabilities allowing a data product developer to build, test, deploy, secure, and maintain a data product without worrying about the underlying infrastructure resource provisioning. It must enable all domain-agnostic and cross-functional capabilities.

Ultimately, the platform must enable the data product developer to just focus on the domain-specific aspects of data product development:

- *Transformation code*, the domain-specific logic that generates and maintains the data
- *Build-time tests* to verify and maintain the domain's data integrity
- *Runtime tests* to continuously monitor that the data product meets its quality guarantees
- Developing a data product's *metadata* such as its schema, documentation, etc.
- Declaration of the required *infrastructure resources*

The rest must be taken care of by the data mesh platform, for example, infrastructure provisioning—storage, accounts, compute, etc. A self-serve approach exposes a set of platform APIs for the data product developer to declare their infrastructure needs and let the platform take care of the rest. This is discussed in detail in Chapter 14.

Enable data product users

Data users' journey—whether analyzing data to create insights or developing machine learning models—starts with discovering the data. Once the data is discovered, they need to get access to it, and then understand it and deep dive to explore it further. If the data has proven to be suitable, they will continue to use it. Using the data is not limited to one-time access; the consumers continue receiving and processing new data to keep their machine learning models or insights up to date. The data mesh platform builds the underlying mechanisms that facilitate such a journey and provides the capabilities needed for data product consumers to get their job done without friction.

For the platform to enable this journey, autonomously, it must reduce the need for manual intervention. For example, it must remove the need to chase the team that created the data or the governance team to justify and get access to the data. The platform automates the process that facilitates requests for access and grants access based on automated evaluation of the consumer.

Exchange Value with Autonomous and Interoperable Data Products

An interesting lens on the data mesh platform is to view it as a multisided platform (*https://oreil.ly/Ugv1S*)—one that creates value primarily by enabling direct interactions between two (or more) distinct parties. In the case of data mesh, those parties are data product developers, data product owners, and data product users.

This particular lens can be a source of unbounded creativity for building a platform whose success is measured directly by exchanging value, i.e., data products. The value can be exchanged *on the mesh*, between data products, or *at the edge* of the mesh, between the end products, such as an ML model, a report, or a dashboard, and the data products. The mesh essentially becomes the *organizational data marketplace*. This particular data mesh platform characteristic can be a catalyst for a culture change within the organization, promoting sharing to the next level.

As discussed in the previous section, an important aspect of exchanging value is to be able to do that *autonomously*, without the platform getting in the way. For data product developers, this means being able to create and serve their data products without the constant need for hand-holding or dependency on the platform team.

Create higher-order value by composing data products

The exchange of value goes beyond using a single data product and often extends to the composition of multiple data products. For example, the interesting insights about Daff's **listeners** are generated by cross-correlating their **behavior** while listening to music, the **artists** they follow, their **demographic**, their interactions with **social media**, the influence of their **friends** network, and the cultural **events** that surround them. These are multiple data products and need to be correlated and composed into a matrix of features.

The platform makes data product compatibility possible. For example, platforms enable data product linking—when one data product uses data and data types (schema) from another data product. For this to be seamlessly possible, the platform provides a standardized and simple way of *identifying* data products, *addressing* data products, *connecting* to data products, *reading* data from data products, etc. Such simple platform functions create a *mesh of heterogeneous domains with homogeneous interfaces*. I will cover this in Chapter 13.

Accelerate Exchange of Value by Lowering the Cognitive Load

Cognitive load was first introduced in the field of cognitive science as the amount of working memory needed to hold temporary information to solve a problem or learn.[2] There are multiple factors influencing the cognitive load, such as the intrinsic complexity of the topic at hand or how the task or information is presented.

Platforms are increasingly considered a way of reducing the cognitive load of developers to get their job done. They do this by hiding the amount of detail and information presented to the developer: *abstracting complexity*.

As a data product developer, I should be able to express *what* my domain-agnostic wishes are without describing exactly *how* to implement them. For example, as a developer I should be able to *declare* the structure of my data, its retention period, its potential size, and its confidentiality class and leave it to the platform to create the data structures, provision the storage, perform automatic encryption, manage encryption keys, automatically rotate keys, etc. This is domain-agnostic complexity that as a data developer or user I should not be exposed to.

There are many techniques for abstracting complexity without sacrificing configurability. The following two methods are commonly applied.

---

2 John Sweller, "Cognitive Load During Problem Solving: Effects on Learning," *Cognitive Science*, 12(2) (April 1988): 257–85.

Abstract complexity through declarative modeling

Over the last few years, operational platforms such as container orchestrators, e.g., Kubernetes (*https://kubernetes.io*), or infrastructure provisioning tools, e.g., Terraform (*https://www.terraform.io*), have established a new model for *abstracting complexity* through *declarative modeling of the target state*. This is in contrast with other methods such as using *imperative* instructions to command how to build the target state. Essentially, the former focuses on the *what*, and the latter focuses on the *how*. This approach has been widely successful in making the life of a developer much simpler.

In many scenarios declarative modeling hits limitations very quickly. For example, defining the data transformation logic through declarations reaches a diminishing return as soon as the logic gets complex.

However, systems that can be described through their state, such as provisioned infrastructure, lend themselves well to a declarative style. This is also true about the data mesh infrastructure as a platform. The target state of infrastructure to manage the life cycle of a data product can be defined declaratively.

Abstract complexity through automation

Removing the human intervention and manual steps from the data product developer journey through automation is another way to reduce complexity, particularly complexity arising from manual errors through the process. Opportunities to automate aspects of a data mesh implementation are ubiquitous. The provisioning of the underlying data infrastructure itself can be automated using infrastructure as code[3] techniques. Additionally, many actions in the data value stream, from production to consumption, can be automated.

For example, today the data certification or verification approval process is often done manually. This is an area of immense opportunity for automation. The platform can automate verifying the integrity of data, apply statistical methods in testing the nature of the data, and even use machine learning to discover unexpected outliers. Such automation removes complexity from the data verification process.

Scale Out Data Sharing

One issue I've noticed in the existing big data technology landscape is the lack of standards for interoperable solutions that lead to data sharing at scale, for example, lack of a unified model for authentication and authorization when accessing data, absence of standards for expressing and transmitting privacy rights with data, and lack of standards in presenting temporality aspects of data. These missing standards

---

3 Kief Morris, *Infrastructure as Code*, (Sebastopol, CA: O'Reilly, 2021).

inhibit scaling the network of usable data beyond the boundaries of organizational trust.

Most importantly, the data technology landscape is missing the *Unix philosophy (https://oreil.ly/pGtte)*:

> This is the Unix philosophy: Write programs that do one thing and do it well. Write programs to work together...
>
> —Doug McIlroy

I think we got incredibly lucky with very special people (McIlroy, Ritchie, Thompson, and others) seeding the culture, the philosophy, and the way of building software in the operational world. That's why we have managed to build powerfully scaled and complex systems through loose integration of simple and small services.

For some reason, we have abandoned this philosophy when it comes to big data systems, perhaps because of those early assumptions (see "Characteristics of Analytical Data Architecture" on page 126) that seeded the culture. Perhaps, because at some point we decided to separate data (the *body*) from its code (the *soul*), which led to establishing a different philosophy around it.

If a data mesh platform wants to realistically scale out sharing data, within and beyond the bounds of an organization, it must wholeheartedly embrace the Unix philosophy and yet adapt it to the unique needs of data management and data sharing. It must design the platform as a set of interoperable services that can be implemented by different vendors with different implementations yet play nicely with the rest of the platform services.

Take observability as an example of a capability that the platform provides—the ability to monitor the behavior of all data products on the mesh and detect any disruptions, errors, and undesirable access, and notify the relevant teams to recover their data products. For observability to work, there are multiple platform services that need to cooperate: the data products emitting and logging information about their operation; the service that captures the emitted logs and metrics and provides a holistic mesh view; the services that search, analyze, and detect anomalies and errors within those logs; and the services that notify the developers when things go wrong. To build this under the Unix philosophy we need to be able to pick and choose these services and connect them together. The key in simple integration of these services is *interoperability*,[4] a common language and APIs by which the logs and metrics are expressed and shared. Without such a standard, we fall back to a single monolithic (but well-integrated) solution that constrains access to data to a single hosting environment. We fail to share and observe data across environments.

---

4 OpenLineage (*https://oreil.ly/8zSHP*) is an attempt to standardize tracing logs.

Support a Culture of Embedded Innovation

To date, continuous innovation must arguably be one of the core competencies of any business. Eric Ries introduced the Lean Startup[5] to demonstrate how to scientifically innovate through short and rapid cycles of *build-measure-learn*. The concept has since been applied to the larger enterprise through Lean Enterprise[6]—a scaled innovation methodology.

The point is that to grow a culture of innovation—a culture of rapidly building, testing, and refining ideas—we need an environment that frees its people from unnecessary work and accidental complexity and friction and allow them to experiment. The data mesh platform removes unnecessary manual work, hides complexity, and streamlines the workflows of data product developers and users, to free them to innovate using data. A simple litmus test to assess how effective a data mesh platform is in doing that is to measure how long it takes for a team to dream up a data-driven experiment and get to use the required data to run the experiment. The shorter the time, the more mature the data mesh platform has become.

Another key point is: *who* is empowered to do the experiments? The data mesh platform supports a *domain team* to innovate and perform data-driven experiments. The data-driven innovations are no longer exclusive to the central data team. They must be *embedded* into each domain team in developing their services, products, or processes.

Transition to a Self-Serve Data Mesh Platform

So far, I have talked about the key differences between existing data platforms and data mesh and covered the main objectives of the data mesh platform. Here, I'd like to leave you with a few actions you can take in transitioning to your data mesh platform.

Design the APIs and Protocols First

When you begin your platform journey, whether you are buying, building, or very likely both, start with selecting and designing the interfaces that the platform exposes to its users. The interfaces might be programmatic APIs. There might be command-line or graphic interfaces. Either way, decide on interfaces first and then the implementation of those through various technologies.

This approach is well-adopted by many cloud offerings. For example, cloud blob storage providers expose REST APIs[7] to post, get, or delete objects. You can apply this to all capabilities of your platform.

---

5 Eric Ries, "The Lean Startup" (*https://oreil.ly/VMQXS*), September 8, 2008.

6 Jez Humble, Joanne Molesky, and Barry O'Reilly, *Lean Enterprise*, (Sebastopol, CA: O'Reilly, 2015).

In addition to the APIs, decide on the communication protocols and standards that enable interoperability. Taking inspirations from internet—the one example of a massively distributed architecture—decide on the *narrow waist*[8] protocols. For example, decide on the protocols governing how data products express their semantic, in what format they encode their time-variant data, what query languages each support, what SLOs each guarantee, and so on.

Prepare for Generalist Adoption

I discussed earlier that a data mesh platform must be designed for the generalist majority ("Designed for a Generalist Majority" on page 52). Many organizations today are struggling to find data specialists such as data engineers, while there is a large population of generalist developers who are eager to work with data. The fragmented, walled, and highly specialized world of big data technologies have created an equally siloed fragment of hyper-specialized data technologists.

In your evaluation of platform technologies, favor the ones that fit better with a natural style of programming known to many developers. For example, if you are choosing a pipeline orchestration tool, pick the ones that lend themselves to simple programming of Python functions—something familiar to a generalist developer— rather than the ones that try to create yet another domain-specific language (DSL) in YAML or XML with esoteric notations.

In reality, there will be a spectrum of data products in terms of their complexity, and a spectrum of data product developers in terms of their level of specializations. The platform must satisfy this spectrum to mobilize data product delivery at scale. In either case, the need for applying evergreen engineering practices to build resilient and maintainable data products remains necessary.

Do an Inventory and Simplify

The separation of the analytical data plane and the operational plane has left us with two disjointed technology stacks, one dealing with analytical data and the other for building and running applications and services. As data products become integrated and embedded within the operational world, there is an opportunity to converge the two platforms and remove duplicates.

In the last few years the industry has experienced an overinvestment in technologies that are marketed as *data* solutions. In many cases their operational counterparts are perfectly suitable to do the job. For example, I have seen a new class of continuous

---

7 See the Amazon S3 API Reference (*https://oreil.ly/Wf2PU*) as an example.

8 Saamer Akhshabi and Constantine Dovrolis, "The Evolution of Layered Protocol Stacks Leads to an Hourglass-Shaped Architecture" (*https://oreil.ly/C3Cuk*), SIGCOMM conference paper (2011).

integration and continuous delivery (CI/CD) tooling marketed under DataOps. Evaluating these tools more closely, they hardly offer any differentiating capability that the existing CI/CD engines can't offer.

When you get started, take an inventory of platform services that your organization has adopted and look for opportunities to simplify.

I do hope that the data mesh platform is a catalyst in simplification of the technology landscape and closer collaboration between operational and analytical platforms.

Create Higher-Level APIs to Manage Data Products

The data mesh platform must introduce a new set of APIs to manage data products as a new abstraction ("Managing Autonomous and Interoperable Data Products" on page 51). While many data platforms, such as the services you get from your cloud providers, include lower-level utility APIs—storage, catalog, compute—the data mesh platform must introduce a higher level of APIs that deal with a data product as an object.

For example, consider APIs to create a data product, discover a data product, connect to a data product, read from a data product, secure a data product, and so on. See Chapter 9 for the logical blueprint of a data product.

When establishing your data mesh platform, start with high-level APIs that work with the abstraction of a data product.

Build Experiences, Not Mechanisms

I have come across numerous platform building/buying situations, where the articulation of the platform is anchored in *mechanisms* it includes, as opposed to *experiences* it enables. This approach in defining the platform often leads to bloated platform development and adoption of overambitious and overpriced technologies.

Take *data cataloging* as an example. Almost every platform I've come across has a *data catalog* on its list of mechanisms, which leads to the purchase of a data catalog product with the longest list of features, and then overfitting the team's workflows to fit the catalog's inner workings. This process often takes months.

In contrast, your platform can start with the articulation of the single experience of *discovering data products*. Then, build or buy the simplest tools and mechanisms that enable this experience. Then rinse, repeat, and refactor for the next experience.

Begin with the Simplest Foundation, Then Harvest to Evolve

Given the length of this chapter discussing the objectives and unique characteristics of a data mesh platform, you might be wondering, "Can I even begin to adopt data mesh today, or should I wait some time to build the platform first?" The answer is to begin adopting a data mesh strategy today, even if you don't have a data mesh platform.

You can begin with the simplest possible foundation. Your smallest possible foundation framework (*https://oreil.ly/hutwF*) is very likely composed of the data technologies that you have already adopted, especially if you are already operating analytics on the cloud. The bottom-layer utilities that you can use as the foundation include the typical storage technologies, data processing frameworks, federated query engines, and so on.

As the number of data products grows, standards are developed, and common ways of approaching similar problems across data products are discovered. Then you will continue to evolve the platform as a harvested framework (*https://martinfowler.com/bliki/HarvestedFramework.html*) by collecting common capabilities across data products and domain teams.

Remember that the data mesh platform itself is a product. It's an internal product—though built from many different tools and services from multiple vendors. The product users are the internal teams. It requires *technical product ownership*, long-term planning, and long-term maintenance. Though it continues to evolve and goes through evolutionary growth, its life begins today as a *minimum viable product* (MVP).[9]

Recap

Data mesh's principle of a *self-serve platform* comes to the rescue to lower the cognitive load that the other two principles impose on the existing domain engineering teams: own your analytical data and share it as a product.

It shares common capabilities with the existing data platforms: providing access to polyglot storage, data processing engines, query engines, streaming, etc. However, it differentiates from the existing platforms in its users: *autonomous domain teams made up primarily of generalist technologists*. It manages a higher-level construct of a *data product* encapsulating data, metadata, code, and policy as one unit.

---

9 Ries, "The Lean Startup."

Its purpose is to give domain teams superpowers, by hiding low-level complexity behind simpler abstractions and removing friction from their journeys in achieving their outcome of exchanging data products as a *unit of value*. And ultimately it frees up the teams to innovate with data. To scale out data sharing, beyond a single deployment environment or organizational unit or company, it favors decentralized solutions that are interoperable.

I will continue our deep dive into the platform in Chapter 10 and talk about specific services a data mesh platform could offer.

CHAPTER 5

Principle of Federated Computational Governance

For peace to reign on Earth, humans must evolve into new beings who have learned to see the whole first.

—Immanuel Kant

A refreshed look at *data governance* is the missing and final piece to make data mesh work. So far, data mesh expects independent teams to own and serve their analytical data. It expects this data to be served as a product, accompanied by behavior that enriches the experience of the data consumer, to discover, trust, and use it for multiple purposes. And it heavily relies on a new set of self-serve data infrastructure capabilities to make it all feasible. Governance is the mechanism that assures that the mesh of independent data products, as a whole, is secure, trusted, and most importantly delivers value through the interconnection of its nodes.

I must admit, *governance* is one of those words that makes me, and perhaps many, feel uneasy. It evokes memories of central, rigid, authoritative decision-making systems and control processes. In the case of *data governance*, it evokes memories of central teams and processes that become bottlenecks in serving data, using data, and ultimately getting value from data.

Data governance teams and processes have noble objectives: ensuring the *availability of safe, high quality, consistent, compliant, privacy-respecting,* and *usable data* across an organization with *managed risk*. These objectives are well intended and necessary. However, traditionally, our approach in achieving them has been a point of friction. In the past, governance has relied heavily on *manual interventions,* complex central *processes of data validation and certification,* and *establishing global canonical modeling* of data with minimal support for *change,* often engaged *too late* after the fact. This approach to governance simply won't work for the decentralized data mesh.

Data mesh governance in contrast embraces constant change to the data landscape. It delegates the responsibility of modeling and quality of the data to individual domains, and heavily automates the computational instructions that assure data is secure, compliant, of quality, and usable. Risk is managed early in the life cycle of data, and throughout, in an automated fashion. It embeds the computational policies in each and every domain and data product. Data mesh calls this model of governance a *federated computational governance.*

Federated and computational governance is a decision-making model led by the federation of domain data product owners and data platform product owners, with autonomy and domain-local decision-making power, while creating and adhering to a set of global rules—rules applied to all data products and their interfaces. The global rules are informed and enabled by global specializations such as legal and security to ensure a trustworthy, secure, and interoperable ecosystem. It addresses what is considered one of the most common mistakes[1] of today's data governance: being an IT initiative with an organizational model that parallels business and is not embedded within the business.

Looking at the word *governance*, its definition softens from "to rule with authority" to its original meaning of "to steer and guide—a vessel." I chose to keep the word *governance* in the data mesh vocabulary, but I intend for it to carry its original meaning and not its later definitions.

In addition to the existing objectives of data governance, data mesh must address a new set of concerns. Distribution of data ownership to individual domains raises concerns around the *interoperability* of the data and *standardization of data communication*, e.g., standardization of data presentation and querying across all domains. Interoperability is an essential characteristic of the mesh to satisfy the majority of data use cases where insights and intelligence are derived from the correlation of independent data products on the mesh, where we create unions, find intersections, or perform other graphs or set operations on data products at scale.

Returning to the Daff example, for Daff to provide a new set of services around **emerging artists** they need to first discover who the emerging artists are. They need to be able to correlate data across **social media** platforms mentioning the emerging artists, looking at the trends of **subscribers listening to artists** and **artist profiles**. Without some level of data product interoperability this task would be impossible.

Not only do we need global standardizations to allow correlating independent data products, but we need to be able to do it easily—with a consistent experience—and securely, without compromising confidential information. Data governance concerns extend to make such a seamless and consistent experience possible.

---

1 Nicola Askham, "The 9 Biggest Mistakes Companies Make When Implementing Data Governance," (2012).

In this chapter, I introduce *how to implement* data governance in the context of data mesh. The focus of this chapter is the high-level modeling of the data governance team and function, and not the individual concerns that governance must assure, like privacy, security, GDPR, or other policies. In short, in this chapter I aim to address the uneasy feeling of loss of control and indeterminism that a decentralized data ownership model like data mesh can arise in many of my tenured data steward and governance colleagues.

To guide tailoring data governance to your organization according to the *federated computational* model, in this chapter, I introduce three complementary and related components: applying *systems thinking to* a complex system of data products and teams, *federation* of the operating model, and *computational execution* of controls and standards by the underlying platform. Figure 5-1 shows the interaction between these three components of data mesh governance.

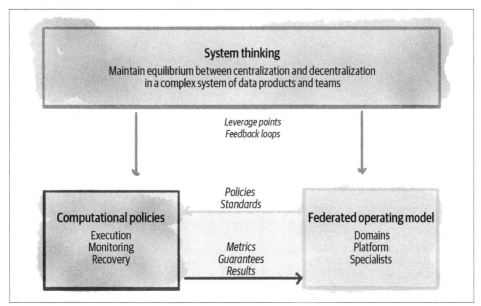

Figure 5-1. Components of data mesh federated computational governance

Let's unpack each.

Apply Systems Thinking to Data Mesh Governance

> Placing a system in a straitjacket of constancy can cause fragility to evolve.
>
> —C. S. Holling

Data mesh architecture creates a complex network of interconnected systems: domain-oriented data products and data owners, interacting with each other, operational applications, and the underlying platform. It follows a distributed system architecture, a collection of independent data products, with independent life cycles, built and deployed by independent teams. For these independent systems to act as cooperative and collaborative members of an ecosystem, data mesh requires a governance model that embraces *systems thinking*. Systems thinking, as described by Peter Senge,[2] is the discipline of "seeing the whole," shifting our focus "from parts to the organization of parts, recognizing interaction of the parts are not static and constant, but dynamic processes." Similarly, data mesh governance must see the mesh more than the sum of its parts and as a collection of interconnected systems—data products, data product providers, data product consumers, and platform teams and services.

Systems thinking applied to data mesh must pay attention to and take advantage of the following characteristics, as demonstrated by Figure 5-2.

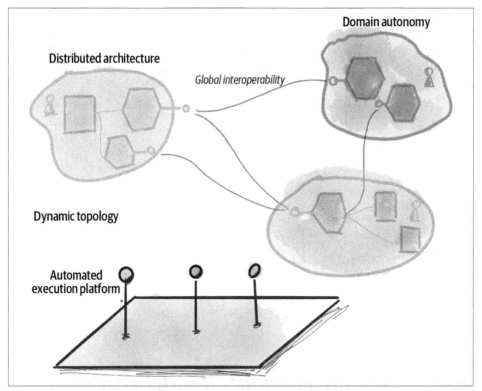

Figure 5-2. Leveraging data mesh characteristics when applying systems thinking

---

2 Peter Senge, *The Fifth Discipline: The Art & Practice of The Learning Organization*, (New York: Currency, 2006).

Maintain Dynamic Equilibrium Between Domain Autonomy and Global Interoperability

One of the main objectives of data mesh governance, through applying system thinking, is to balance the state of the mesh between *decentralization of domains and their autonomy* with *global interoperability and just-enough mesh-level harmony.* While the governance model respects the local control and autonomy of each domain —accountable for the quality and integrity of their data and responsible to share their data with the rest of the ecosystem—it must balance that with a global-level security, legal conformance, interoperability standards, and other mesh-level policies applied to all data products. The art of governing a data mesh ecosystem is in maintaining an *equilibrium between local (domain) optimization and global (the mesh) optimization.*

For example, the governance model needs to balance the equilibrium between allowing each domain to define the model and schema of their own data product with autonomy—a case of local optimization—while making sure the data product model is standardized enough to be joined and stitched with other domains' data products—a case of global optimization. The governance model needs to strike a balance between allowing each domain data product owner to be accountable for the security of their data product—a case of decentralization—while making sure all data products are consistently and reliably secure—a case of centralization.

To continuously influence the delicate balance, we can apply systems thinking. We can look into the work of system thinkers such as Donella Meadows (*https://oreil.ly/wbsbw*). As Donella describes in her classic book, *Thinking in Systems*, using elements of systems thinking, a system can reach the state of *dynamic equilibrium*—while information is continuously flowing, the desired observed state remains the same, like a tub of water with equal inflows and outflows. Maintaining a dynamic equilibrium demands continuously adjusting the behavior in systems using *leverage points* and *feedback loops.* Leverage points are places in the system where a small change could lead to a large shift in behavior. Feedback loops are system structures that either balance or reinforce a change in the state of the system. Let's look at a few examples where data mesh governance can use leverage points and feedback loops to balance the autonomy of the domains with the global harmony and function of the mesh.

Introduce feedback loops

Feedback loops in a system are greatly helpful in adjusting the behavior and the state of the system.

For example, one of the common concerns I hear from the existing governance teams is around "preventing data product duplication and redundant work," basically controlling the chaos that may arise from each domain team making independent decisions and creating duplicate data products. This of course stems from scars they have incurred over the years, seeing teams copying data into many isolated and abandoned databases, each for a single use. Traditionally, this problem has been solved by injecting governance *control* structures that qualify and certify that the data is not a duplicate before it can be used. Despite best intentions, this creates a bottleneck that simply doesn't scale out in a complex system like data mesh.

Instead, we can introduce two feedback loops to get the same outcome without creating bottlenecks. As you will see in Part IV, every data product on the mesh, with the help of the platform, is equipped with self-registration, observability, and discoverability capabilities. Hence, all data products are known to the users of the mesh from the moment of creation throughout their lifetime until they retire. Now imagine the kind of observability and discovery information that each data product supplies— their semantic, syntax, how many users are using them, the users' satisfaction rating, quality metrics, timeliness, completeness, and retention measures. The mesh can use this information to identify duplicate data products and provide additional insights such as identifying groups of data products that serve similar information, and comparison of these data products based on their satisfaction rating, number of users, completeness, etc. This information and the insights made available to the users create two new feedback loops.

The platform "search and discovery" feature can give lower visibility to the duplicate data products that don't have high ratings; as a result, they get gradually degraded on the mesh and hence less used. The platform can inform the data product owners of the state of their data products and nudge them to prune out unused and duplicate data products in favor of others. This mechanism is called a *negative or balancing feedback loop*. The intention of this feedback loop is self-correction, in this case reducing the number of duplicate, low-quality, and less usable data products.

The second feedback loop uses the same information to promote high-quality and highly usable data products with happy users. The mesh discovery function gives higher search ranking to these data products, which then results in higher visibility to the users and increased opportunity for selection and use. This is a *positive feedback loop* that reinforces the success of useful data products, known as "success to the successful."

Figure 5-3 shows the information flow and the feedback loops to keep the system in a state of equilibrium, keep the useful and helpful data products in, and degrade and remove duplicate and redundant data products. The net result of these feedback loops is the outcome of "fewer duplicate data products." This is a kind of automated *garbage collection*.

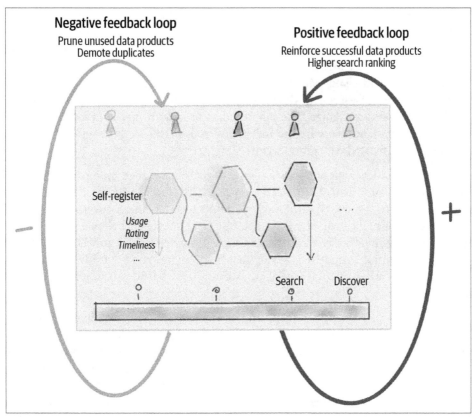

Figure 5-3. Example of feedback loops to maintain a state of dynamic equilibrium

Now, let's look at the leverage points to make sure system balance is maintained.

Introduce leverage points

In her article, Donella introduces 12 aspects of the system that can be used as leverage points, such as controlling the parameters and metrics, controlling the strength of the feedback loops, changing the goals of the system, and so on. These are a great starting point in experimenting with the leverage points that create a high-performing, complex data mesh system.

Let's follow the previous example. Earlier, I introduced the self-reinforcing feedback loop for successful data products. Data products, based on the users' satisfaction and growth, get higher visibility and ranking in the search. Hence, the more successful a data product is, the more opportunity for usage it gets, and as a result it becomes more successful. If this feedback loop is left unchecked, over time we might see undesired side effects: successful data products become bloated, slow, and fragile to change; become a god-like dependency for many other downstream data products;

and ultimately slow down progress of the mesh as a whole. This is where *parameters* and *measurements* can be used as short-term and quick leverage points and change behavior fast. In this case, the mesh governance can place upper bounds on the *lead time to change a data product* to detect data products that are hard to change, or detect an uptick in *change fail ratio* of more fragile products, and that combined with the number of users and downstream dependencies can identify bloated data products that need to change. The job of a data product owner is to keep their data products healthy, and these are the metrics of health. This leads to self-adjusting by breaking down bloated data products into simpler ones.

Another type of leverage point is *the goals of the system*. Everything in the system follows a goal that is articulated clearly, repeated, measured, and insisted upon. This perhaps is one of the most critical leverage points that data mesh governance can put in place to balance the state of the system. But there are some challenges with system goals as leverage points. Jay W. Forrester (*https://oreil.ly/PM0CT*) at MIT, the founder of system dynamics, is quoted as saying that "people (we) know intuitively where the leverage points are" but often "everyone is trying very hard to push it in the wrong direction!"

Let me give you an example of a goal in the wrong direction. Many organizations see the value of the mesh in the number of data products. The larger the mesh and interconnectivity between the data products, potentially the higher value we can leverage by exploiting the available data. However, if the goal of the system becomes "the number of data products," early in the development of the mesh, this leverage point results in a focus on generating data, and not necessarily generating value from the data. This is consequential particularly early in the exploration phase of data mesh evolution ("Evolutionary Execution" on page 286), where organizations are still establishing the practices and creating the foundation or the blueprint of their data products. Overproduction of data products early on leads to a higher cost of exploration, and in fact it becomes an inhibitor to an exploration of what works best. This is a goal pushed in the wrong direction at the wrong time. Conversely, once the platform capabilities are established and the organization has worked out what good looks like during the expansion and growth of data mesh, the goal can shift to the increased population of data products. The governance can use the "rate of new data products" as a leverage point to focus on the growth and diversity of data.

Embrace Dynamic Topology as a Default State

Data mesh is a dynamic system with a continuously changing topology. The shape of the mesh continuously changes. New data products get created, old data products retire, and existing data products continue to morph their logic, data, and structure. The governance model must work with continuous change across the mesh, without interrupting the experience of the mesh consumers. Governance designed with this assumption as the default state of the system, with a pinch of complexity theory applied, looks for simple rules that can underlie a complex adaptive mesh.

For example, in Part IV I introduce the rule of applying bitemporality to all aspects of a data product. All elements of a data product can be a function of time—data, metadata, schema, semantic, etc.—and they change with time. Change of the data product as a function of the passage of time is a basic simple rule that embraces the dynamic nature of the system. Change becomes a default parameter, not an exception.

Utilize Automation and the Distributed Architecture

Distributed architecture is the foundation for building digital ecosystems, in this case data mesh. The governance of an ecosystem such as data mesh needs to rely on a distributed architecture that enables independent life cycle management of each data product while allowing loose interconnectivity and integration between them. The intention behind this architecture is to limit central components and reduce the opportunity of creating fragile bottlenecks as the ecosystem grows. The execution of governance must fit in a distributed architecture, operating in a peer-to-peer mode, instead of relying on single points of control.

A core component of the data mesh ecosystem is the environment within which data products execute, the underlying platform that manages the data products life cycle, from build to deployment to runtime. Most governance system elements such as the leverage points and feedback loop ("Maintain Dynamic Equilibrium Between Domain Autonomy and Global Interoperability" on page 71) described earlier rely on automated mechanisms built by the platform and embedded into the distributed architecture connecting data products. The section "Apply Computation to the Governance Model" on page 83 unpacks the opportunities for automation.

Apply Federation to the Governance Model

Organizationally, by design, data mesh is a federation. It has an organizational structure with smaller divisions, the domains, where each has a fair amount of internal autonomy. The domains control and own their data products. They control how their data products are modeled and served. The domains select what SLOs their data products guarantee, and ultimately they are responsible for the satisfaction of their data products' consumers.

Despite the autonomy of the domains, there are a set of standards and global policies that all domains must adhere to as a prerequisite to be a member of the mesh—a functioning ecosystem.

Data mesh proposes a governance operating model that benefits from federated decision making. It suggests that the governance team organizes itself as a federated group of domain and platform stakeholders. For the group to manage its operation, it defines the following operating elements (illustrated in Figure 5-4):

Federated team ("Federated Team" on page 77)
Composed of domain product owners, subject matter experts such as legal and security

Guiding values ("Guiding Values" on page 78)
Managing the scope and guiding what good looks like

Policies ("Policies" on page 81)
Security, conformance, legal, and interoperability guidelines and standards governing the mesh

Incentives ("Incentives" on page 82)
Leverage points that balance local and global optimization

Platform automations ("Apply Computation to the Governance Model" on page 83)
Protocols, standards, policies as code, automated testing, monitoring and recovery of the mesh governance

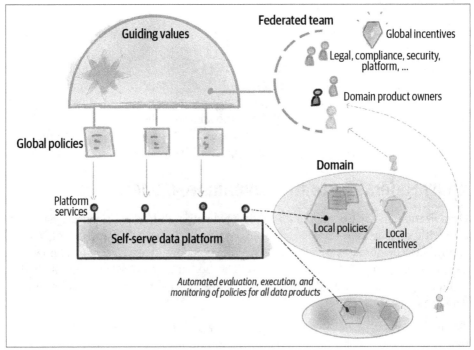

Figure 5-4. Federated computational governance operating model

This operating model is a draft and starting point for you to refine within your organization. Let's look a bit more closely at each of these operating model elements.

Federated Team

Data mesh governance is a collective responsibility, yet with clear accountability of domains; unlike many existing governance functions, it is not outsourced to a third party. The governance is composed of a cross-functional team of representatives from domains, as well as platform experts and subject matter experts from security, compliance, legal, etc.

The following section lists some of the basic and essential roles that make up a multidisciplinary federated team. The team collectively takes the responsibility of:

- Deciding what policies must be implemented by all data products
- How the platform must support these policies computationally
- How data products adopt the policies

Domain representatives

Data product owners are the long-term owners of the domains' data products. They intrinsically care about the longevity and success of their data product as a *member of the mesh*. They have accountability for the security, quality, and integrity of their data. Given the guiding principle of *executing decisions locally*, the data product owners are ultimately accountable for making sure the global governance decisions are executed at the level of every single data product. Early buy-in and contribution of domains to define the global policies is crucial in adoption of them.

Their role is different from what is traditionally known as data stewards as the main accountability and responsibility lives within a business-aligned-tech domain. They are a member of a cross-functional team that is accountable for the success of the business domain, and one of those success criteria is to manage and share their analytical data as a product, as well as use other data products in embedding ML/analytics in their business processes and applications.

Their role as a member of the governance team is contributing to the definition of policies that govern the data products on the mesh.

Data platform representatives

Nearly all governance decisions rely on platform automation. This demands close collaboration between the platform team and the governance function. The automations may be in the form of enablement, monitoring, or recovery. For example, the platform can automate de-identification of personally identifiable information (PII) during write/read of data, or implement standardized APIs for accessing each data product's discoverability information. Given the importance of the platform in policy automation, platform representatives must be part of the governance team, with roles such as data platform product owner and platform architect. The *platform product owner* ("The platform product owner" on page 326) designs the experience and prioritizes the platform features—the what—and the *platform architect* designs the implementation of computational policy configuration and execution—the how.

Subject matter experts

Domains are responsible for ensuring their data products are in compliance and secure. They either have the subject matter expertise internally or the governance team offers experts who know the expected, security, compliance and legal concerns.

Legal teams often are the source of the latest data privacy regulations. These regulations need to be translated into platform capabilities and applied to all data products. Global governance creates the structure for continuous and close collaboration between other subject matter experts to inform and influence the prioritization and design of platform features and their adoption by all data products.

Facilitators and managers

Bringing a group of people from different disciplines and scope of influence with somewhat competing priorities is no easy task. It requires allocated management and administrative roles to facilitate and support the process of governance under the federated and computational model.

Guiding Values

The cornerstone of any governance system is the clarity of the *value system* that *guides* how decisions are made and what their scope of influence is. These guides influence how to decide whether the global governance function should bother with a particular concern, or if there is a conflict in decision making, how to resolve it.

The following is a demonstrative list of guides and representative of the spirit of the data mesh value system.

Localize decisions and responsibility close to the source

Data mesh gives the ownership of the decision and accountability for execution to the people who have the most relevant knowledge and scope of influence. For example, data mesh pushes the responsibility of assuring data quality to the domains. Contrary to prior models, data quality is neither a centralized governance team concern nor a downstream data team. Domains decide, define, and then guarantee the quality of their data products. The same applies to domain data modeling. The modeling of data products is left to the domains since they are best positioned to represent their data as close to the reality of their business as possible.

Identify cross-cutting concerns that need a global standard

While data mesh governance, by default, assumes that decisions should be made at the most local level, there are often cross-cutting aspects of data products that require global standards. Cross-cutting concerns include ensuring confidentiality compliance with regulations, access control, and security. How these cross-cutting concerns are implemented—how they are defined, configured, and applied—in a common way is ideally something that individual data products influence but leave to the platform to automate. If there is enough commonality between the individual data products or if a concern affects all the data products based on regulations, the governance function defines the hows globally, the platform automates it, and data products execute it.

For example, the execution of the "right to be forgotten" according to GDPR regulation is a cross-cutting concern applied to all data products. How and when such an administrative function is triggered, and how each data product assures the execution of this function, is a global concern as it applies equally to all data products.

Globalize decisions that facilitate interoperability

There is a subset of cross-cutting concerns that enable interoperability between data products as well as interoperability between data products and the platform components.

Imagine Daff is experimenting to find if there is a correlation between **weather conditions** and **listenership behavior**, at a point in time. Exploiting a pattern between the two can enhance its recommendation engine, perhaps recommending melancholic music on rainy days. This requires querying and correlating two data products, the **near-real-time play events** and **hourly weather report files**, on the dimension of time.

In order to perform the query, the data products must standardize on a few things:

- Inclusion of the temporal dimensions in the data: this includes the timestamp of the real event or state (event time), e.g., the date of the weather, and the timestamp when the data product has become aware of the event (processing time). I will be discussing further details on this topic later in Part IV, "Design the Data Quantum Architecture."
- Standardization on the date and time representation, e.g., using the ISO 8601 (*https://oreil.ly/KWdDg*) date and time format.
- Standardization of how the time dimension is represented in the query, e.g., SQL:2011 (*https://oreil.ly/2ixZe*) standardizing SQL for temporal databases.

Defining a consistent way for encoding and querying temporal data allows users to run time-sensitive queries and data processing across disparate data products.

Identify consistent experiences that need a global standard

An imbalance between domain autonomy and global harmony can result in a fragmented and disconnected experience for data users. Imagine you are a data scientist and running an experiment that requires data about **listeners** across all domains: **subscribers**, **podcasts**, **play events**, **streams**, **concerts**, etc. To run this experiment, the data scientist first uses the platform's search and discovery features to locate the data products that know something about **listeners**. Then, the data scientist deep dives into each of the data products to learn about them further, reading documentation, schemas, and other metadata. Naturally, each data product provides its own documentation, schema, SLOs, etc. However, imagine if each data product chooses a different format or technology to present documentation, schema, and metadata to the data scientist. This experiment will be fragmented, and it will not be inviting to run mesh-wide experiments. To provide a consistent experience of understanding data products across the mesh, the decision of how data products encode and share their semantic and syntax schema becomes a global concern. This decision will be automated by the platform to provide a set of tools to create, verify, and share data product schemas. Each data product utilizes the platform tooling to comply with this global standard.

While this is an ideal state, given the dynamic nature ("Embrace Dynamic Topology as a Default State" on page 74) of the mesh, it is not possible to guarantee that all data products will be using the same schema language, or the same version of the language, at a point in time. This is where systems thinking ("Apply Systems Thinking to Data Mesh Governance" on page 69) nudges the system toward global consistency over time.

Execute decisions locally

The global governance function makes decisions that have a radius of impact beyond the internals of a single domain. While these decisions are made globally, they are executed locally as close as possible to each domain's data product.

For example, consider the global decision about how access to data products is granted, revoked, and verified. While the decision on how we configure and apply access control is made globally, the configuration of the access control policies is encoded for each data product and evaluated and executed at the time of access to a data product. A similar approach is taken in operational systems with the implementation of a service mesh (*https://oreil.ly/v47zp*) and zero trust architecture (*https://oreil.ly/nTQQl*), where access control policies are defined for each single service endpoint and enforced live at the time of access to the endpoint.

Policies

The output of a system of governance can be distilled to the definition of a set of guides or rules, *policies*, that specify what good looks like and how to ensure it's maintained. In the case of data, for example, it can be distilled to what *secure data* looks like and how security is maintained; the same goes for *data accessibility*, *data quality*, *modeling data*, and many other cross-functional characteristics of data shared on the mesh.

Local policies

Data mesh governance pushes the *power of decision making and execution* around these policies as close as possible to the people who are affected by those decisions. For example, execution of many traditional aspects of governance such as assuring data quality, data modeling, and data integrity is shifted to people who are producing the data in the first place, as close to the source as possible. These decisions are made locally as *local policies* and executed locally.

For example, the decision around the *timeliness* of a **play event** is best made and maintained by the **player** team. They know best how soon after an event has occurred it can be reliably shared. The domain has the most-informed understanding of the behavior of the **player** and its capabilities. That, combined with an understanding of its data users, results in the **player** domain defining a local policy around the data product's guaranteed *timeliness*.

Global policies

Global policies apply consistently to all data products. They cover the seams, the interconnectivity, and the gap between the data products. They impact the scope of the mesh as a whole and not the internal implementation of a data product. Earlier, our look at guiding values ("Guiding Values" on page 78) demonstrated how global policies are identified.

Another decision that falls in the gap between data products is the decision of *data ownership*: which team shall own a new data product. This also can be treated as a *global policy*. In the case where the data product is closely representing the analytical data produced from an operational system—it is *source-aligned*—the operational team must own it. The **player** team building and hosting the player devices own the **player events** data product. In the case of a *fit-for-purpose* data product, the team whose use case is the primary consumer of the data can maintain and own the data product. For example, the **emerging artist** business unit that has many use cases for the data products around **artist classification** naturally owns it. However, the ownership of the *aggregate* data products is not as clear. As an example, **longitudinal listener behavior** as an *aggregate* of all listener touchpoints doesn't naturally fit into existing domains. In this case, the federated governance team can create a set of heuristics to help make such a decision: either an existing source domain like **listener** is incentivized, or the marketing team is empowered to own it as the primary consumers of it, or a new domain must be formed.

Ideally, we would want to minimize global policies to reduce friction. Implementing and updating global policies that affect the mesh is hard. Limiting their number and scope and relentlessly implementing them through automated platform capabilities are our only options to make them effective.

Incentives

Bringing data mesh to life not only requires a shift in technology and architecture, but also depends on an organizational transformation. Change in the data governance operating model is one aspect of such transformation. In fighting through the pain of change, motivation has a big role.

Incentives, as motivators, are leverage points ("Introduce leverage points" on page 73) that impact the behavior of the governance function, particularly in balancing the priorities of the domain representatives between their local and global priorities. A careful design of the incentives has an important role in getting the domain representatives to not only contribute to the definition of global policies but also execute them within their scope of influence—domains. The incentive structure creates two leverage points: *global incentives* that encourage building a richly interconnected mesh of data products and not silos, and *local incentives* that encourage speed and autonomy of individual domains.

The governance operating model must create, monitor, and continuously tune the local and global incentives of their members. Keep in mind that getting leverage points right requires experimentation and continuous tuning and is often counterintuitive. The examples given in the following are experimental and extrinsic. In Chapter 16, "Organization and Culture", I will discuss the intrinsic motivators.

Introduce local incentives

Locally within domains, data product owners measure their success based on the satisfaction and growth of their data product users. This encourages them to prioritize work that leads to the creation of new data products for their consumers or the addition of content to the existing ones. For example, the **player** team is incentivized to provide various aggregations of **play events** that capture a larger audience of data users. They are incentivized to not only provide **play events** to real-time data users, but also **play sessions** that aggregate the listeners' interactions over a longer period of time for other data users.

Local incentives are driven by product thinking, with the objective of creating successful data products. Introduce these local incentives to strengthen and increase domain autonomy.

Introduce global incentives

Now let's assume that the federated governance team has decided to standardize how domain data products measure and share their data quality metrics. The governance is introducing a new set of quality metrics that each data product must report through a consistent set of APIs. This is a global policy that must apply to all data products to achieve a mesh-level observability. However, from the perspective of the domains' product owners conforming to this policy and implementing the data quality reporting APIs, it is somewhat in competition with their domain priorities, building richer and featureful data products.

To resolve this conflict and encourage the domains to participate in global policies, the incentives of data product owners must be augmented. In addition to their local incentives, they need to be rewarded and motivated by the degree of adoption of global policies. In this case, the measure of success for their data product must include reporting its quality metrics based on the latest global policy.

Apply Computation to the Governance Model

In an optimal state of the mesh, the governance function is invisible. It's out of the way of data providers and consumers. It's automated and abstracted by the platform, embedded into each data product, and applied at the right moment. Let's look at a few ways of achieving this—what I call the *computational governance*.

The data mesh platform programmatically manages the life cycle of each data product. It executes each stage of a data product life cycle, such as build, test, deploy, run, access, read, etc. It's best positioned to enable data product developers and data governance team members to define policies and execute them computationally, at the right point in a data product life cycle. The platform is able to embed the execution of these policies into each and every data product without friction. It's essential for the self-serve platform to abstract the complexity of executing various policies and make it easy to do the right thing. Additionally, it's necessary for the platform to automatically and continuously verify that the policies are in place across the mesh and notify if they are not.

In the operational plane, a similar computational governance has recently been demonstrated by service mesh platforms. For example, Istio (*https://istio.io*), an open source implementation of a service mesh, embeds the configuration of traffic routing policies in each endpoint of every single service and executes them locally right at the time of making a request. A domain's service developer simply defines the routing policies around how many times they wish for their service to retry a failed request or when to time out an outstanding request. Beyond this declarative configuration of the routing policy, the service developer does not need to do anything else. The platform automatically executes the routing policies at the right time. Simplicity and effectiveness of computational routing policy incentivizes all service developers to build more resilient services without incurring extra overhead.

Let's look at the different ways that the platform can support governance policies, computationally: *standards as code, policies as code, automated tests,* and *automated monitoring.*

Standards as Code

Many policies fall into the *standards* category—behavior, interfaces, and data structure that is expected to be implemented in a consistent way across all data products. Here are a few examples of standards that can be coded and supported by the platform:

Data product discovery and observability interfaces
APIs that expose discoverability information, documentation, schema, and SLOs

Data product data interfaces
APIs that expose the data

Data and query modeling language
Modeling of semantics and syntax of data and the query language operating on the data

Lineage modeling
Modeling of the traces of data flows and operations across connected data products

Polysemes identification modeling
Modeling of identity systems that globally identify and address common business concepts across different data products

Take the SLO APIs as an example. The platform can inject a *sidecar* ("Data Product Sidecar" on page 165)—an execution context deployed with every single data product that implements cross-cutting capabilities—to implement the SLO APIs consistently for all data products.

Policies as Code

All data products must implement *global policies* such as compliance, access control, access audit, and privacy. The platform is the key enabler in embedding these policies in all data products. Data products can define the *policy configurations as code and test and execute them* during their life cycle. The platform offers the underlying engine that implements the management of policies as code.

Take *compliance* as an example; all data products must *protect PII* yet enable ML or analytical workloads that inherently require access to such information across a population. For example, **listeners** data products must protect access to PII data types such as name, age, address, etc., while enabling population analysis to detect cohorts of listeners' demographics across age or geographical locations. To enable such a policy, data products can implement techniques such as differential privacy (*https://oreil.ly/qkSqU*), providing access to anonymized data that sustains the statistical characteristics of the population while refraining access to an individual's PII. The platform provides the means for the **listeners** data product to codify the policy definition by simply declaring what attributes are PII and who can run population analysis on them. It's the platform's job to apply differential privacy techniques such as Randomized Aggregatable Privacy-Preserving Ordinal Response (RAPPOR) (*https://oreil.ly/fDlom*) to the underlying data during data access.

Here are a few other examples of policies that the platform can help computationally configure and execute as code:

Data privacy and protection
Strategies to prevent data from being stolen, lost, or accidentally deleted. Ensure that sensitive data is accessible only to approved parties.

Data localization
Requirements around geolocation of data storage and its processing.

Data access control and audit
Control who can access what elements of the data and keep track of all accesses.

Data consent
Track and control what information the data owners allow to be preserved and shared.

Data sovereignty
Preserving the ownership of data and its control.

Data retention
Managing the availability and storage of data according to the defined retention duration and policy.

Automated Tests

Another way that the platform supports data governance computationally is to run automated tests. Automated testing makes sure that the data product complies with its guarantees in terms of data quality and integrity. The platform sets up and runs CI/CD pipelines that data product developers utilize to add testing to their data products code. Automated tests intend to provide rapid feedback loops to the developers to detect and address errors as early and cheaply as possible.

Automated Monitoring

Maintaining policies demands a continuous monitoring system that observes the state of the mesh and its data products at runtime. The mesh monitoring system can detect whether data products are complying with global policies or drifting. Runtime monitoring verifies whether data products are moving toward or away from the intended objectives. They get configured with a tolerance threshold and armed with alarms and notification systems.

For example, the governance team can configure the monitoring system with an SLO compliance function. These functions automatically scan the mesh and poll data from the products' SLO metrics APIs. Failure to respond to the required version of the SLO APIs is the first signal in detecting lack of compliance, leading to a range of actions from notification of the teams to degrading the data products' trustworthiness.

Transition to Federated Computational Governance

So far, I have introduced a framework for operating and implementing federated computational governance. This section summarizes the key shifts that transform your organization to this model, particularly if you are operating a centralized governance model.

Delegate Accountability to Domains

If your organization has adopted data governance, likely influenced by the work of original thinkers such as Seiner,[3] it is centralized. Governance of data mesh calls for a federated team ("Federated Team" on page 77) of domain product owners, subject matter experts, and central facilitators. Moving from a central custodianship of the data to a federated model of data product ownership requires establishing a new accountability structure led by the domains. This can be achieved by moving some of the existing data stewards into the business-tech-aligned teams with the new role of a data product owner.

---

3 Robert S. Seiner (2014). *Non-Invasive Data Governance*. Basking Ridge, NJ: Technics Publications.

Embed Policy Execution in Each Data Product

A data governance team today is not only responsible for defining the policies and introduction of regulatory requirements but also heavily involved in their execution and assurance. Their supervision and control are injected into the value stream of delivering quality and trustworthy data.

In contrast, data mesh's global governance is accountable for defining and designing the policies and standards. The execution of these policies is left to the platform. The responsibility of application of the policies is given to the domains and built into and embedded in each data product.

The global data governance function is no longer required to be injected into the data creation or access value stream with the manual steps of checking and qualifying data.

For example, the governance function is accountable to define *what constitutes data quality* and how each data product communicates that in a standard way. It's no longer accountable for the quality of each data product. The *platform* team is accountable to build capabilities to validate the quality of the data and communicate its quality metrics, and each domain (data product owner) is accountable to adhere to the quality standards and provide quality data products.

Similarly, the global governance function is not accountable for *securing the data*. However, it is responsible to define what data security entails, such as the data sensitivity levels that each data product must support. The platform builds in capabilities that describe and enforce sensitivity levels, and each *domain data product owner* is accountable for making their data products securely utilize the platform, according to the governance definition.

Automate Enablement and Monitoring over Interventions

The data technology landscape today is filled with incredibly sophisticated data governance tools. These tools are developed to facilitate the workflow of data governance teams and apply the governance policies after the fact—after the data is generated and collected into a lake or a landing zone. Such tools allow the data governance function to intervene in the data sharing value stream after the data has been provided and try to retrospectively qualify and fix problems.

Data mesh governance shifts these controls left to the source domain of the data. It favors enabling *doing the right thing* early, through seamless automation, over methods of intervening. This changes the nature of the tools from policing to enabling, from fixing problems late to detecting and recovering the issues as early as possible.

This naturally leads to a different approach to the management of errors and risk. The role of the platform and the accountability structure leads to the detection of errors as close as possible to the source. Global governance turns its focus to defining the recovery mechanisms for the platform to put in place in case of an error.

Model the Gaps

Data governance teams today spend a large amount of their time creating the one true canonical model of the centralized body of enterprise data. While the model is composed of smaller models, nevertheless they have a key role in defining the centralized model—whether placed in a warehouse or lake. In contrast, data mesh leaves the modeling of data to the domains, the people closest to the data. However, in order to get interoperability and linkage between data across domains, there are data entities in each domain that need to be modeled in a consistent fashion across all domains. Such entities are called polysemes. Standardizing how polysemes are *modeled*, *identified*, and *mapped* across domains is a global governance function.

Measure the Network Effect

Data governance today has a tremendous responsibility to centrally support enterprise-level data. This responsibility has led to measuring the success of the governance function by the *volume* of data that has gone through the qualification process. I have been in too many conversations where the number of petabytes or thousands of data tables have been mentioned as a sign of pride and success. While it's understandable what has led to such metrics, there is no direct and reliable link from the volume to the value.

Data mesh introduces a new way for the governance team to demonstrate success, based on the usage of data. The stronger the interoperability of the mesh and the trust in the data, the larger the number of *interconnections* between the nodes—consumer and providers—on the mesh. Governance success is measured based on the network effect of the mesh and the number of these interconnections.

Embrace Change over Constancy

Today's governance practices such as defining the enterprise-wise canonical data model or access control policies stem from the need to reduce change and disruption to downstream data users. While practices to reduce change and impose constancy might be feasible at a smaller scale, as the scope of enterprise data grows to many domains and many use cases, it very quickly becomes an impossible mission.

Data mesh governance practices must embrace constant change: change from the continuous arrival of fresh data, change of data models, rapid change in use cases and users of the data, new data products being created, and old data products being retired.

Recap

Some of the common questions about the feasibility of data mesh revolve around governance concerns, now in a decentralized manner. How can we make sure individual data products comply with a set of common policies that make them secure, compliant, interoperable, and trustworthy? Particularly, how can we have any guarantees when each domain owns and controls its own data products and there is no longer a central team getting its arms around the data? What happens to the centralized governance team?

The answer to these questions lies within the data mesh governance model, called federated computational governance. Data mesh, like its predecessors the lake and warehouse, meets a similar set of governance objectives. But it differs in its operating model and how these objectives are met.

The data mesh governance model consists of three complementary pillars. First and foremost, it requires *systems thinking*, looking at the mesh as an ecosystem of interconnected data product and platform systems, and their independent and yet connected teams. Then try to find the leverage points and feedback loops to control the behavior of the mesh as a whole toward its objective, creating value through sharing data products at scale.

Second, apply a federated operating model. From the social and organizational perspective, create a *federated* team of individual domains and platform representatives. Create incentives that are aligned with both domains' data product success as well as the success of the wider ecosystem. Let domains have autonomy and responsibility for the majority of policies that are in the sphere of their influence and control, while leaving cross-functional and a small set of policies to be defined globally.

Finally, from a practical and implementation perspective, data mesh governance heavily relies on embedding the governance policies into each data product in an automated and computational fashion. This of course heavily relies on the elements of the underlying data platform, to make it really easy to do the right thing.

To bring these three pillars together, Figure 5-5 shows an example of this model.

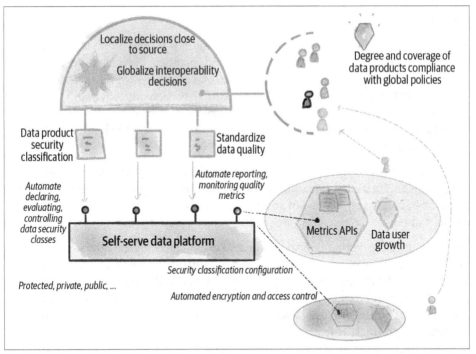

Figure 5-5. Example of data mesh governance operating model

Data mesh governance seeks to improve the existing approach to data governance at the intersection of a decentralized value system meeting automation and computation.

Data mesh governance is the method by which we define and apply what is right and how to do the right thing in an ecosystem of data product teams. The definition of what is right and how to do the right thing has occupied the great minds for centuries (*https://oreil.ly/eOqi6*), from Aristotle in Ancient Greece to the German Idealism era to modern political systems. As human beings we have wrestled with the definition and regulation of what is *right* somewhere in between *common good* (*https://oreil.ly/TlAyl*) and *utilitarianism* (*https://oreil.ly/nMQpg*)—approaches that achieve maximum benefit and happiness of the community—and *individualism* (*https://oreil.ly/7KJjw*), which is prioritizing an individual's happiness and liberty and doing what is right for them.

While data mesh is not a field of philosophy, it wrestles with a similar dilemma: how to do the right thing while maintaining the autonomy, freedom, and individualism of different domains and also achieving the greater good through consistency and standardization across all data products. It defines an approach to data governance that attempts to continuously find the *dynamic equilibrium* between localization of decisions so that the domains can go *fast* versus globalization and centralizations of decisions for everyone to go *far*.

I do think catalysts such as computational governance and dual-system incentive structures can lead to domain behaviors that ultimately result in the greater good of the mesh ecosystem. However, the mesh will not reach an optimal state unless the majority of domains become intelligently augmented—with embedded ML-based systems in each of their products and systems. The continuous need for trustworthy and useful data across multiple domains to train ML-based solutions will be the ultimate motivator for the adoption of data mesh governance and doing the right thing.

PART II

Why Data Mesh?

By doubting we are led to question, by questioning we arrive at the truth.
—Pierre Abélard

Organizational transformation is difficult, costly, and takes time. Data mesh transformation is no exception. The story of Daff, Inc. (Prologue: Imagine Data Mesh), and the description of data mesh principles in Part I demonstrate the substantial impact of data mesh on data culture, architecture, and technology and how this affects how an organization values, shares, and uses analytical data at scale.

So why should any organization make this shift, and why now? I will answer these questions in Part II of the book.

In Chapter 6, "The Inflection Point", I will look at the macro drivers, the current realities that have pushed us to a tipping point, where our past evolutionary approaches no longer serve us. In Chapter 7, "After the Inflection Point", I introduce the core outcomes of data mesh and how it achieves them. And in the last chapter of Part II, Chapter 8, "Before the Inflection Point", I briefly review the history of analytical data management architecture and why what got us here will no longer take us to the future.

CHAPTER 6

The Inflection Point

A strategic inflection point is a time in the life of a business when its fundamentals are about to change. That change can mean an opportunity to rise to new heights. But it may just as likely signal the beginning of the end.[1]
—Andrew S. Grove

Data mesh is what comes after an inflection point, shifting our approach, attitude, and technology toward data. Mathematically, an inflection point is a magic moment at which a curve stops bending one way and starts curving in the other direction. It's a point that the old picture dissolves, giving way to a new one.

This won't be the first or the last inflection point in the evolution of data management. However, it is the one that is most relevant now. There are drivers and empirical signals that point us in a new direction. I personally found myself at this turning point in 2018, when many companies were seeking a new data architecture that could respond to the scale, complexity, and data aspirations of their business. After reading this chapter, I hope you also arrive at this critical point, where you feel the urge for change, to wash away some of the fundamental assumptions made about data and imagine something new.

Figure 6-1 is a simplistic demonstration of the inflection point in question. The x-axis represents the trend of macro drivers that have pushed us to this inflection point. The drivers include ever-increasing business complexity combined with uncertainty, diversity of data expectations and use cases, and the proliferation of data available from ubiquitous sources. On the y-axis we see the impact of these drivers. The impacts affect business agility, the ability to get value from data, and resilience to change. In the center is the inflection point, where we have a choice to make: to

---

1 Andrew S. Grove, *Only the Paranoid Survive*, (New York: Currency, 1999).

continue with our existing approach and, at best, reach a plateau of impact or take the data mesh approach with the promise of reaching new heights.

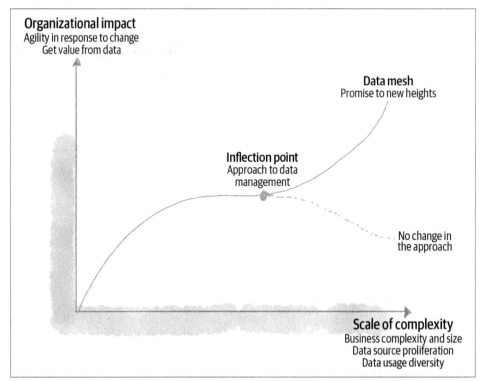

Figure 6-1. The inflection point in the approach to analytical data management

In this chapter, I share today's data landscape realities that act as the main drivers for data mesh.

Great Expectations of Data

One of the perks of being a technology consultant is traveling through many industries and companies and getting to know their deepest hopes and challenges. Through this journey, one thing is evident: building a data-oriented business remains one of the top strategic goals of executives. Data is front and center in creating intelligent services and products, and it backs real-time business decisions.

Here are a few examples, all truly inspiring:

> Our mission at Intuit (*https://oreil.ly/QEoLj*) is to power prosperity around the world as an AI-driven expert platform company, by addressing the most pressing financial challenges facing our consumer, small business and self-employed customers.
>
> —Financial SaaS company

Our mission is to improve every single member's experience at every single touchpoint with our organization through data and AI.

—Healthcare provider and payer company

By People, For People: We incorporate human oversight into AI. With people at the core, AI can enhance the workforce, expand capability and benefit society as a whole.

—Telco (*https://oreil.ly/UOkCj*)

No matter the industry or the company, it's loud and clear that we want to become intelligently empowered[2] to:

- Provide the best customer experience based on data and personalization.
- Reduce operational costs and time through data-driven optimizations.
- Empower employees to make better decisions with trend analysis and business intelligence.

All of these scenarios require data—a high volume of diverse, up-to-date, and truthful data that can, in turn, fuel the underlying analytics and machine learning models.

A decade ago, many companies' data aspirations were mainly limited to business intelligence (BI). They wanted the ability to generate reports and dashboards to manage operational risk, respond to compliance, and ultimately make business decisions based on the facts, on a slower cadence. In addition to BI, classical statistical learning has been used in pockets of business operations in industries such as insurance, healthcare, and finance. These early use cases, delivered by highly specialized teams, have been the most influential drivers for many past data management approaches.

Today, data aspirations have evolved beyond BI to every aspect of an organization, for example using machine learning in the design of products, such as automated assistants; in the design of services and the customer experience, such as personalized healthcare; and streamlining operations such as optimized real-time logistics. Not only that, but the expectation is to democratize data so that the majority of the workforce can put data into action.

Meeting these expectations requires a new approach to data management—an approach that can seamlessly fulfill the diversity of uses for data. Diversity of data usage demands diversity of modes of access to data, ranging from simple structured views of data for reporting to continuously reshaping semi-structured data for machine learning training, or from real-time and fine-grained access to events to batch aggregations. We need to meet these expectations with an approach and

---

2 Christoph Windheuser, "What Is Intelligent Empowerment?" (*https://oreil.ly/jQ9OO*). Thoughtworks, March 23, 2018.

architecture that natively supports diverse use cases without requiring copying data from one technology stack to another across the organization.

More importantly, the widespread use of machine learning requires a new attitude toward application development and data. The approach shifts from deterministic and rule-based application development—where given a specific input data, the output can be determined—to nondeterministic and probabilistic data-driven applications, where given specific input data, the output could be a range of possibilities that can change over time. This approach to application development requires continuous refining of machine learning models over time and continuous, frictionless access to the latest data.

The great and diverse expectations of data require us to step back and wonder if there is a simpler approach to data management that can universally address the diversity of needs today and beyond.

The Great Divide of Data

Many of the technical complexities organizations face today stem from how we have divided data—*operational* and *analytical data*:[3] how we have siloed the teams that manage them, how we have proliferated the technology stacks that support them, and how we have integrated them.

Today, operational data is collected and then transformed into analytical data. Analytical data trains the machine learning models that then make their way into the operational systems as intelligent services (Figure 6-2).

 Over time, the analytical data plane itself has diverged into two generations of architecture and technology stacks. Initially there was a *data warehouse*, and this was followed by a *data lake* (*https://oreil.ly/qew01*), with data lakes supporting data science access patterns and preserving data in its original form, and data warehouses supporting analytical and BI reporting access patterns with data conforming to a centrally unified ontology. In recent years, the two technology stacks have begun to converge, with data warehouses attempting to onboard data science workflows and data lakes attempting to serve data analysts and BI, in an architecture called *lakehouse* (*https://oreil.ly/PltYF*).

---

3 Chapter 1 introduces the two types of data.

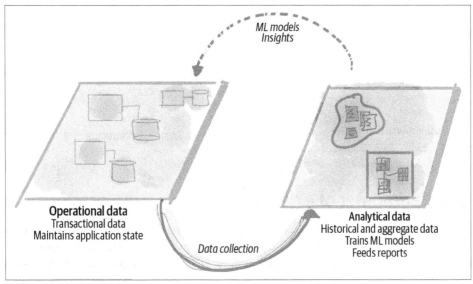

Figure 6-2. The two planes of data

The current state of data technology, architecture, and organization design is reflective of the divergence of the analytical and operational data planes—two levels of existence, integrated yet separate. Each plane operates under a different organizational vertical. BI, data analytics, and data science teams, under the leadership of a chief data and analytics officer (CDAO), manage the analytical data plane, while business units and their collaborating technology team manage the operational data. From a technology perspective, two fragmented technology stacks have grown to each serve a plane. There is limited overlap between the two stacks.

This divergence has led to the two-plane data topology and a fragile integration architecture between the two. The operational data plane feeds the analytical data plane through a set of scripts or automated processes often referred to as ETL jobs—extract, transform, and load. Often operational databases have no explicitly defined contracts with the ETL pipelines for sharing their data. This leads to fragile ETL jobs where unanticipated upstream changes lead to downstream pipeline failures. Over time the ETL pipelines grow in complexity, trying to provide various transformations over the operational data, flowing data from the operational data plane to the analytical plane and back to the operational plane (Figure 6-3).

The challenges of two-plane data management, including the brittle integration architecture of the pipelines and a centralized data warehouse or lake to access data, are one of the major drivers to imagine a future solution.

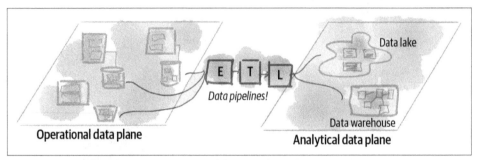

Figure 6-3. Pipeline-based integration of the two data planes

Scale: Encounter of a New Kind

Since the mid-2000s, the data industry has evolved its technology solutions to deal with the scale of data in terms of *volume, velocity,* and *variety.* The early generations of large-scale parallel data processing[4] addressed the large volume of data that web applications and touchpoints generated. Stream processing backbones[5] have been created to handle the high speed of data that started flowing from mobile devices. Since then, general and purpose-built storage systems have been created to manage a variety of data formats[6]—text, imaging, voice, graphs, files, time series, etc.

Today, we are encountering a new kind of scale, the *origins* and *location of the data.* Data-driven solutions often require access to data beyond a business domain, organizational, or technical boundary. The data can be originated from every system that runs the business, from every touchpoint with customers, and from other organizations. The next approach to data management needs to recognize the proliferation of the origins of data and their ubiquitous nature.

The most interesting and unexpected insights emerge when we connect data from a variety of sources. For example, the future of intelligent healthcare requires a longitudinal human record of a patient's diagnostics, pharmaceutical records, personal habits, and lab results in conjunction with all other patient longitudinal records. These sources are beyond a single organization's control. Another example involves the future of intelligent banking, which requires data beyond the financial transactions that customers perform with their banks. They'll need to know customers' housing

---

4 Google pioneered MapReduce (*https://oreil.ly/ObWvl*) in the early 2000s.

5 While David Luckham (*https://oreil.ly/WDCvC*) at Stanford was one of the early pioneers of event processing, the open source technologies for high volume and velocity event and stream processing only became available in early 2010s with the likes of Apache Kafka (*https://oreil.ly/1sSUc*).

6 Perhaps the most impactful work on storage for storing a variety of data types has been object storage and its first cloud-based implementation by AWS S3 (*https://oreil.ly/L57Ob*) in the mid-2000s.

needs, the housing market, their shopping habits, and their dreams and needs to offer them the services they need when they need them.

This unprecedented scale of the diversity of sources requires a shift in data management—a shift away from collecting data from sources in one big, centralized place to *connecting data*, wherever it is.

Beyond Order

I'm writing this book during the pandemic of 2020–2021. If there was any doubt that organizations need to navigate *complexity, uncertainty,* and *volatility,* the pandemic has made that abundantly clear. Even on a good day, in the absence of the pandemic, organizations must see *volatility and change* as a default state of existence.

The complexity that rises from the ever-changing landscape of business is reflected in data. Rapid delivery of new features to products, new and changed offerings, new touchpoints, new partnerships, new acquisitions, etc., all result in a continuous reshaping of data.

More than ever now, organizations need to have the pulse of their data and the ability to act quickly and respond to change with *agility.*

What does this mean for data management? It requires access to high quality and trustworthy facts of the business at the time they happen. Data platforms must *close the distance*—time and space—between when an event happens and when it gets analyzed. Analytics solutions must guide *real-time decision making.* Rapid response to change is no longer a premature optimization[7] of business: it's a baseline feature.

Data management of the future must build in embracing change, by default. Rigid data modeling and querying languages that expect to put the system in a straitjacket of a never-changing schema can only result in a fragile and unusable analytics system.

Data management of the future must embrace the complex nature of today's organizations and allow for *autonomy* of teams with *peer-to-peer* data collaborations.

Today, the complexity has stretched beyond the surface of the business to its physical platforms. In many organizations, data platforms span multiple clouds and on-prem providers. The data management of the future must support managing and accessing data across multiple hosting platforms, by default.

---

7 Donald Knuth made the statement "(code) premature optimization is the root of all evil."

Approaching the Plateau of Return

In addition to the seismic shifts listed earlier, there are other telling signs: the discord between data and AI investments and their returns. To get a glimpse of this, I suggest you browse the NewVantage Partners annual reports (*https://oreil.ly/Qhclv*),[8] an annual survey of senior corporate C-level executives on the topics of data and AI adoption. What you find is the recurring theme of an increasing effort and investment in building the enabling data and analytics platforms. While the majority of companies report successful outcomes from their investments, they are finding the transformational results middling.

For example, in their 2021 report, only 24.4% of firms reported *having forged a data culture*. Only 24.0% of firms reported that they have *become data-driven*, and only *41.2%* of firms reported that they are *competing using data and analytics*. It's too small of result for the pace and amount of investment; 99% of surveyed companies are investing in big data and AI, with 62% reporting investments exceeding $50M.

I recognize that organizations face a multifaceted challenge in transforming to become data-driven, migrating from decades of legacy systems, resistance of a legacy culture to using data, and competing business priorities.

The future approach to data management must look carefully at this phenomena, at why the solutions of the past are not producing a comparable result to the human and financial investment we are putting in today. Some of the root causes include lack of skill sets needed to build and run data and AI solutions, organizational, technology, and governance bottlenecks, and friction in discovering, trusting, accessing, and using data.

Recap

Data mesh embraces the data realities of organizations today and their trajectory. It is created as an acknowledgment of the limitations of today's data solutions.

Figure 6-4 summarizes the realities of the inflection point moving toward data mesh.

---

8 NewVantage Partners LLC, *Big Data and AI Executive Survey 2021: Executive Summary of Findings*, (2021).

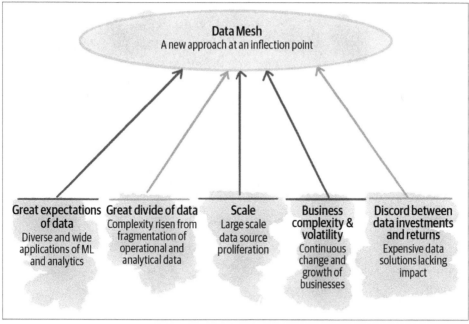

Figure 6-4. Macro drivers for the creation of data mesh

Data mesh assumes a new default starting state: proliferation of data origins within and beyond organizations' boundaries, on one or across multiple cloud platforms. It assumes a diverse range of use cases for analytical data. It works with the grain of a highly complex and volatile organizational environment, and not against it.

Next, we look at our expectations from data mesh as a post-inflection-point solution, namely, what organizational impacts we expect to see and how data mesh achieves them.

CHAPTER 7

After the Inflection Point

The only way to make sense out of change is to plunge into it, move with it, and join the dance.

—Alan Watts

Standing at an inflection point is a magical experience. It's where we look at what has come before, learn from it, and choose a new path. It's a point where we have a choice to turn to a new direction, with an eye on a different destination. This chapter introduces the destination and the outcomes to expect when choosing data mesh at your organization's inflection point.

Data mesh assumes the environmental conditions I introduced in the previous chapter as a default state. By default, data mesh assumes the *ubiquitous nature of data*. Data can be of any origin; it can come from any system within an organization, or outside, and across boundaries of organizational trust. Any underlying platform can serve it on one cloud hosting service or another. Data mesh assumes the *diversity of data use cases* and their unique modes of access to data. The data use cases range from historical data analysis and reporting to training machine learning models and data-intensive applications. And lastly, data mesh assumes *complexity of the business landscape*—continuous growth, change, and diversity—as a natural state of being.

Data mesh learns from the past solutions and addresses their shortcomings. It reduces *points of centralization* that act as coordination bottlenecks. It finds a new way of decomposing the data architecture without slowing the organization down with synchronizations. It removes the gap between where the data originates and where it gets used and *removes the accidental complexities*—aka pipelines—that happen in between the two planes of data. Data mesh departs from data myths such as a single source of truth, or one tightly controlled canonical data model.

Ultimately, data mesh's goal is to enable organizations to *get value from data at scale*, using data to not only improve and optimize their business but also reshape it. Data mesh outcomes can be summarized as (Figure 7-1):

- Respond gracefully to change: a business's essential complexity, volatility, and uncertainty
- Sustain agility in the face of growth
- Increase the ratio of value from data to the investment

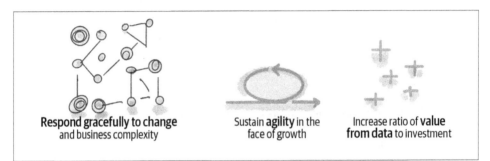

Figure 7-1. Data mesh outcomes for organizations

In this chapter, I describe each of these outcomes and how data mesh principles accomplish them.

Respond Gracefully to Change in a Complex Business

Businesses are complex systems, composed of many domains that each have their own accountability structure and goals; they each change at a different pace. The behavior of the business as a whole is the result of an intricate network of relationships between its domains and functions and their interactions and dependencies. The volatility and rapid change of the markets and regulations within which the businesses operate compound their complexity.

How can businesses manage the impact of such complexity on their data? How can organizations keep going through change while continuing to get value from their data? How can businesses avoid the increased cost of managing the change of their data landscape? How can they provide truthful and trustworthy data without disruption, in the face of continuous change? This comes down to *embracing change in a complex organization*.

Let's look at a few ways data mesh achieves embracing change despite the increased complexity of the business.

Align Business, Tech, and Now Analytical Data

One way to manage complexity is to break it down into independently managed parts. Businesses do so by creating domains. For example, Daff breaks down its business domains according to relatively independent outcomes and functions—managing podcasts, managing artists, player applications, playlists, payments, marketing, etc.

This allows each domain to move fast without tight synchronization dependencies on other parts of the business.

Just as a business divides its work through business domains, technology can, and should, align itself to these business divisions. Modern digital businesses orient their technology staff around their business units, allowing each business unit to be supported, enabled, and shaped by dedicated digital products and services, built and maintained by a long-standing dedicated technology team. The recent movement toward microservices is largely about performing this kind of decomposition. Business units control and manage their operational applications and data, supported by their partnering technology team.

The first principle of data mesh carries out the same decomposition for analytical data, resulting in the *domain ownership of data*.[1] Each business unit takes on the responsibility for analytic data ownership and management. This is because the people closest to the data are best able to understand what analytical data exists and how it should best be interpreted.

Domain ownership results in a distributed data architecture, where the data artifacts—datasets, code, metadata, and data policies—are maintained by their corresponding domains.

Figure 7-2 shows the concept of business, technology, and data alignment applied to Daff. Each domain has a business function and goal, enabled and shaped by a set of technology solutions—applications and services—and empowered by data and analytics. Domains have dependencies through explicitly defined data and service contracts.

---

1 Chapter 2 elaborates on this. The information provided here is sufficient for understanding why this principle is needed to manage complexity of data.

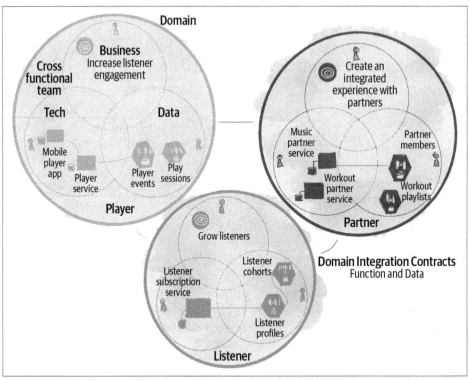

Figure 7-2. Aligning business, tech, and data to manage complexity

Close the Gap Between Analytical and Operational Data

To make good decisions in the moment, analytical data must reflect *business truthfulness*. It must be as close as possible to the facts and reality of the business at the moment the decision is made. This is hard to achieve with two separate data planes—analytical and operational—that are far from each other and connected through fragile data pipelines and intermediary data teams. Data pipelines must dissolve and give way to a new way of providing the analytical data and capabilities as close to the source as possible.

How can changes in the business, such as adding new features to a product, introducing new services, or modifying a business process be reflected in near real time in the analytical data?

Data mesh suggests closing the gap and feedback loop between the two planes, through data shared as a product and oriented around the domains. Data mesh connects the two planes under a new structure—a network of peer-to-peer connected data products and applications, a mesh that exchanges analytical data.

The *data mesh principle* of *data as a product* introduces a new accountability for each domain to share their analytical data as a product, with the goal of delighting the experience of data users by streamlining their experience in discovering, understanding, trusting, and ultimately using quality data. The data as a product principle is designed to address data quality and the age-old siloed data problem and unhappy data users.[2]

Figure 7-3 shows data mesh's approach to integrating operational and analytical planes with tighter and faster feedback loops. The concept of centralized pipelines across the two planes is eliminated. Here, the planes are divided by business domains. The integration between data products, the analytical data plane, and their corresponding domain's operational plane services are rather simple and unintelligent and a matter of simple movement of data. Data products will embed and abstract the intelligence and code required to transform the operational data into its analytical form.

By embedding machine intelligent decisions and actions into modern systems through embedding analytics in digital experiences, the boundaries between the analytical and operational planes are dissolving. Data mesh continues to respect the fundamental technical differences between operational data and analytical data, while it closes the gap and tightly integrates the two as demonstrated in this section.

---

2 Chapter 3 elaborates upon this concept. For now, the introduction here is sufficient to understand the role of data products in responding to the organizational complexity.

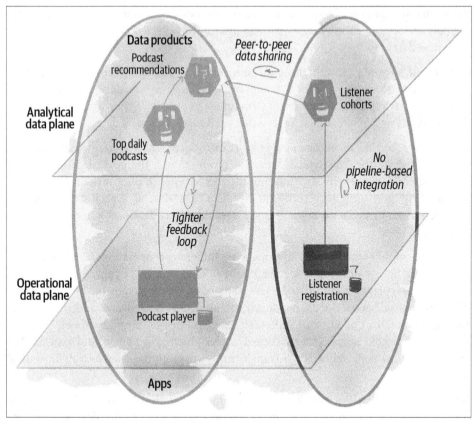

Figure 7-3. Closing the gap between operational and analytical data

Localize Data Changes to Business Domains

Data mesh allows for data models to change continuously without fatal impact to downstream data users or slowing down access to data. It does so by removing the shared global canonical data model and hence removing the need for synchronizing changes. Data mesh localizes change to domains and gives them autonomy to model their data based on their most intimate understanding of the business without the need for central coordination of a single shared canonical model.

Data mesh imposes well-defined and guaranteed data contracts to share domain data. Domain data contracts support older revisions until they gracefully migrate their data users to the new revision. This liberates domains to change their data models continuously.

Reduce Accidental Complexity of Pipelines and Copying Data

As Fred Brooks laid out in his widely popular paper, "No Silver Bullet—Essence and Accident in Software Engineering" (*https://oreil.ly/HV9yG*), there are two types of complexity when building software systems. First, we have the essential complexity that is essential and inherent to the problem space. This is business and domain complexity. Second, there is accidental complexity: the complexity that we—engineers, architects, and designers—create in our solutions. Accidental complexity can and should be reduced.

The world of analytical solutions is full of opportunities to remove accidental complexities. Let's talk about a few of the accidental complexities that data mesh reduces.

Today, we keep copying data around because we need the data for yet another mode of access, or yet another model of computation. We copy data from operational systems to a landing zone and then to the data lake and after that to feature stores for data scientists. We copy the data again from the lake into lakeshore marts for data analyst access and then into the downstream dashboard or reporting databases for the last mile. We build complex and brittle pipelines to do the copying. The copying journey continues from one technology stack to another and from one cloud vendor to another. Today, to run analytical workloads you need to decide up front which cloud provider copies all of your data in its lake or warehouse before you can get value from it.

Data mesh addresses this problem by creating a new architectural unit that encapsulates a domain-oriented data semantic while also providing multiple modes of access to the data suitable for different use cases and users. This architectural unit is called the *data product quantum* (*data quantum* for short). A data quantum has an explicit set of contracts and guarantees for each of its native access modes—SQL, files, events, etc. It can be accessed anywhere across the internet, in case it chooses to provide data to external data users. It provides access control and policy enforcement on each of its interfaces at the time of access. A data quantum encapsulates the code that transforms and maintains its data. Data pipelines break down and become internal implementations of data quantum logic. A data quantum shares data without the need for intermediary pipelines. Removing complex, brittle, and labyrinth pipelines reduces the opportunity for failure in case of an upstream data change.

Sustain Agility in the Face of Growth

Today, the success of businesses is predicated on their multifaceted growth—new acquisitions, new service lines, new products, geolocation expansions, and so on. All this leads to new sources of data to manage and new data-driven use cases to build. Many organizations slow down or plateau in the speed of delivering value from their data, onboarding new data, or serving the use cases as they grow.

Data mesh's approach to *sustaining agility in the face of growth* can be summarized in a few techniques that aim to reduce organization-wide bottlenecks, coordination, and synchronization. Agility relies on business domains' ability to achieve outcomes autonomously with minimal dependencies.

Remove Centralized and Monolithic Bottlenecks

A centralized data team managing a monolithic data lake or warehouse limits agility, particularly as the number of sources to onboard or number of use cases to serve grow. Data mesh looks carefully for centralized bottlenecks, particularly where they are the focal point of a multiparty synchronization, from both the architecture and human communication perspective. Architecturally, these bottlenecks include data lakes and data warehouses.

Data mesh proposes an alternative, a peer-to-peer approach in data collaboration when serving and consuming data. The architecture enables consumers to directly discover and use data from the source data products. For example, an ML training function or a report can directly access independent data products, without the intervention of a centralized architectural component such as a lake or warehouse and without the need for an intermediary data (pipeline) team.

Figure 7-4 demonstrates the conceptual shift. Each data product provides versioned interfaces that allow peer-to-peer consumption of data. The data from multiple data products can be composed and aggregated into new higher-order data products.

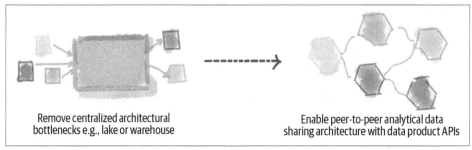

Remove centralized architectural
bottlenecks e.g., lake or warehouse

Enable peer-to-peer analytical data
sharing architecture with data product APIs

Figure 7-4. Data mesh removes centralized architecture bottlenecks

Reduce Coordination of Data Pipelines

In recent decades, technologies that have exceeded their operational scale have one thing in common: they have *minimized coordination and synchronization*. Asynchronous I/O has scaled the throughput of networked applications over blocking I/O. Reactive (*https://oreil.ly/fFk2P*) applications have resulted in faster parallel processing of messages. MapReduce functional programming has distributed large-volume data processing across many servers. Choreographed event-driven microservices (*https://oreil.ly/qpnuH*) have scaled business workflows.

Despite the relentless effort to remove coordination and synchronization in core technologies, we have, for the most part, neglected organizational and architectural coordination. As a result, no matter how fast our computer systems run, achieving outcomes have fallen behind coordinating activities of teams and humans.

Data mesh reduces architectural and human coordination.

Existing architectures build on the technical decomposition of components—i.e., pipeline tasks such as ingestion, processing, serving, etc. This style of architectural decomposition results in heavy coordination between these functions each time a new data source or a new use case is delivered. Data mesh moves away from technical partitioning of data management to domain-oriented partitioning. Domain-oriented data products develop and evolve independently of other data products. This domain-oriented decomposition reduces the need for coordination to achieve an outcome. For the most part, the domain-oriented data product team can take care of the new data sources for their new use cases. In cases where a new use case requires access to a new data product outside of the domain, the consumer can make progress by utilizing the standard contracts of the new data product, mocks, stubs (*https://oreil.ly/XV0zh*), or synthetic data[3] interfaces, until the data product becomes available. This is the beauty of contracts, as they ease the coordination between consumer and provider during development. Figure 7-5 shows the shift in reducing pipeline coordination.

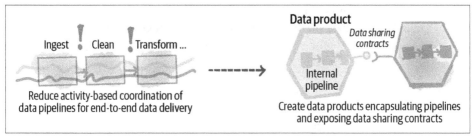

Figure 7-5. Reduce architectural coordination of pipelines

Reduce Coordination of Data Governance

Another major coordination bottleneck is the central function of data governance. Today, data governance coordination is necessary to permit access to data, approve the quality of data, and validate the conformance of data changes with the organization's policies. The central and heavily manual processes of data governance inhibit agility in data sharing.

---

3 Data with similar statistical and structural properties as the real data, without exposing the private information found in real data.

Data mesh reduces governance coordination friction through two functions:

- Automating and embedding *policies as code* in each data product
- Delegating central responsibilities of governance to individual domain data product owners

These changes are implemented by data mesh's *federated and computational data governance model.*[4]

Operationally, the governance team is composed of the individual domain data product owners—the long-term product owners responsible for domain data sharing. Architecturally, the governance function embeds policy execution into every data product in a computational and automated fashion. This vastly improves the function of governance today, which is one of the main synchronization points for discovering data, approving data, and making sure it follows the necessary policies.

As you can imagine, the autonomy of the domains can have undesirable consequences if not checked: isolation of domains, incompatibility and disconnection of one domain's data product from others, and a fragmented experience when consuming multiple domains' data. Data mesh governance heavily relies on the automation of governance concerns for a consistent, connected, and trustworthy experience using the domains' data products.

Figure 7-6 shows the replacement of manual and central governance functions with automated delivery of data products with policies embedded as code.

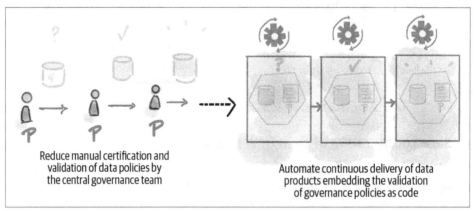

Reduce manual certification and validation of data policies by the central governance team

Automate continuous delivery of data products embedding the validation of governance policies as code

Figure 7-6. Reduce synchronization of data governance

---

4 Chapter 5 discusses this further. For now, it's sufficient to know what impact this principle has on organizational agility.

Enable Autonomy

The correlation between team autonomy and team performance has been the subject of team management studies (*https://oreil.ly/jorX7*). Empirical studies show that teams' freedom in decision making to fulfill their mission can lead to better team performance. On the other hand, too much autonomy can result in inconsistencies, duplicated efforts, and team isolation.

Data mesh attempts to strike a balance between team autonomy and interteam interoperability and collaboration. It gives domain teams autonomy to take control of their local decision making, for example, choosing the best data model for their data products, while it uses computational governance policies to impose a consistent experience across all data products, for example, standardizing the data modeling language that all domains utilize. Data mesh gives domain teams autonomy to build and maintain their data products, while it places a domain-agnostic data platform in place for teams to do so in a consistent and cost-effective way.

The *principle of a self-serve data platform* essentially makes it feasible for domain teams to manage the life cycle of their data products with *autonomy* and utilize the skillsets of their generalist developer to do so.[5] The self-serve data infrastructure allows data product developers to build, deploy, monitor, and maintain their data products. It allows data consumers to discover, learn, access, and use the data products. The self-serve infrastructure makes it possible for the mesh of data products to be joined, correlated, and used as a whole, while maintaining the independence of the domain teams.

Increase the Ratio of Value from Data to Investment

Industry reports, such as the NewVantage Partners report I shared in the previous chapter, and my personal experience, point to the fact that we are getting little value from data compared to our investments in data management. If we compare the value we get from our data teams and data solutions, compared to other technical investments such as app development infrastructure, it's evident that we are facing headwinds when it comes to data.

Data mesh looks at ways to improve the ratio of value over effort in analytical data management: the creation of a new archetype of data platform that abstracts today's technical complexity through open data interfaces that enable sharing data across organizational trust boundaries or physical locations and through applying product thinking to remove friction from the experience of data users.

---

5 Chapter 4 further expands on the function and form of the data mesh infrastructure. For now, it's sufficient to know its impact on organizational agility.

Abstract Technical Complexity with a Data Platform

Today's landscape of data management technology is undoubtedly too complex. The litmus test for technical complexity is the ever-growing need for *data engineers* and *data experts*. We don't seem to ever have enough of them. Another litmus test is the low value to effort ratio of data pipeline projects. Much effort is spent with little value returned—i.e., getting frictionless access to quality datasets.

Data mesh looks critically at the existing technology landscape and reimagines the technology solutions as a *data-product-developer (or user)-centric* platform. It intends to remove the need for data specialists and enable generalist experts to develop data products.

Additionally, data mesh defines a set of open and standard interfaces for different affordances that all data products share—discovering, requesting access, querying, serving data, securing data, etc.—to enable a more collaborative ecosystem of technologies. This is to reduce the cost of integration across vendors.[6]

Embed Product Thinking Everywhere

Data mesh introduces a few shifts to get us laser focused on value, as perceived by the data users. It shifts our thinking from data as an *asset* to data as a *product*. It shifts how we measure success from data volume to data user happiness.

Data is not the only component of a data mesh ecosystem that is treated as a product. The self-serve data platform itself is also a product. In this case, it serves the data product developers and data product users. Data mesh shifts the measure of success of the platform from the number of capabilities to the impact of its capabilities on improving the experience of data product development and reducing the lead time to deliver, or discover and use, a data product.

Product thinking leads to reduced effort and cost, hidden in the everyday experience of data product users and developers.

Go Beyond the Boundaries

Improvement to a business function almost always requires insights beyond the unit's boundary. It needs data from many different business domains. Similarly, the data-driven value that an organization generates in serving its customers, employees, and partners requires data beyond what it generates and controls.

Consider Daff. In order to provide a better experience to the listeners with auto-play music, it not only requires data from listeners' playlists, but also their network of

---

6 Chapter 11 lists the open interfaces shared across data products.

friends and their social and environmental influences and behaviors. It requires data from many corners of Daff and beyond—including news, weather, social platforms, etc.

Multidomain and multiorg access to data is an assumption built into data mesh. Data mesh's data quantum concept can provide access to data no matter where the data physically resides. A data quantum provides a set of interfaces that essentially allow anyone with the proper access control to discover and use the data product independent of its physical location. The identification schema, access control, and other policy enforcement assumes using open protocols that are enabled over the internet.

Data mesh architecture delivers more value by connecting data beyond organizational boundaries.

Recap

After reading this chapter you might assume that data mesh is a silver bullet. Quite the contrary. Data mesh is an important piece of the solution. It enables us to truly democratize access to data. However, to close the loop of deriving value from data, there is much more to be done beyond sharing data. We need to continuously deliver repeatable and production-quality analytical and ML-based solutions. But, to bootstrap, we need data sharing at scale, and that is what data mesh focuses on.

The data mesh goals listed in this chapter invite us to reimagine data, specifically how to design solutions to manage it, how to govern it, and how to structure our teams. In this chapter, I linked data mesh goals to their enablers. That was a lot to cover, so allow me to summarize it in Table 7-1.

Table 7-1. Summary of after the inflection point with data mesh

Data mesh goal	What to do	How to do it
Manage changes to data gracefully in a complex, volatile, and uncertain business environment	Align business, tech, and data	Create cross-functional business, tech, and data teams each responsible for long-term ownership of their data *Principle of domain data ownership*
	Close the gap between the operational and analytical data planes	Remove organization-wide pipelines and the two-plane data architecture Integrate applications and data products more closely through dumb pipes *Principle of data as a product*
	Localize data changes to business domains	Localize maintenance and ownership of data products in their specific domains Create clear contracts between domain-oriented data products to reduce impact of change *Principle of data as a product*

Data mesh goal	What to do	How to do it
Manage changes to data gracefully in a complex, volatile, and uncertain business environment (*continued*)	Reduce the accidental complexity of pipelines and copying of data	Breakdown pipelines, move the necessary transformation logic into the corresponding data products, and abstract them as an internal implementation *Principle of data as a product* *Data product quantum architectural component*
Sustain agility in the face of growth	Remove centralized architectural bottlenecks	Remove centralized data warehouses and data lakes Enable peer-to-peer data sharing of data products through their data interfaces *Principle of domain ownership* *Principle of data as a product*
	Reduce the coordination of data pipelines	Move from a top-level functional decomposition of pipeline architecture to a domain-oriented decomposition of architecture Introduce explicit data contracts between domain-oriented data products. *Principle of domain ownership* *Principle of data as a product*
	Reduce coordination of data governance	Delegate governance responsibilities to autonomous domains and their data product owners Automate governance policies as code embedded and verified by each data product quantum *Principle of federated computational governance*
	Enable team autonomy	Give domain teams autonomy in moving fast independently. Balance team autonomy with computational standards to create interoperability and a globally consistent experience of the mesh. Provide domain-agnostic infrastructure capabilities in a self-serve manner to give domain teams autonomy. *Principle of federated computational governance* *Principle of the self-serve data platform*
Increase value from data over cost	Abstract complexity with a data platform	Create a data-developer-centric and a data-user-centric infrastructure to remove friction and hidden costs in data development and use journeys Define open and standard interfaces for data products to reduce vendor integration complexity *Principle of data as a product* *Principle of the self-serve data platform*
	Embed product thinking everywhere	Focus and measure success based on data user and developer happiness Treat both data and the data platform as a product *Principle of the self-serve data platform* *Principle of data as a product*
	Go beyond the boundaries of an organization	Share data across physical and logical boundaries of platforms and organizations with standard and internet-based data sharing contracts across data products *Principle of data as a product* *Principle of the self-serve data platform*

In the next chapter, I will give an overview of what has happened before the inflection point: why the data management approach that got us here won't take us to the future.

CHAPTER 8

Before the Inflection Point

Today's problems come from yesterday's "solutions."
—Peter M. Senge, *The Fifth Discipline*

Organizational complexity, proliferation of data sources, growth in data expectations: these are the forces that have put stress on our existing approaches to analytical data management. Our existing methods have made remarkable progress scaling the machines: managing large volumes of a variety of data types with planet-scale distributed data storage, reliably transmitting high-velocity data through streams, and processing data-intensive workloads concurrently and fast. However, our methods have limitations with regard to organizational complexity and scale, the human scale.

In this chapter, I briefly introduce the current landscape of data architectures, their underlying characteristics, and the reasons why, moving into the future, they limit us.

Evolution of Analytical Data Architectures

How we manage analytical data has gone through evolutionary changes, changes driven by new consumption models, ranging from traditional analytics in support of business decisions to intelligent products augmented with ML. While we have seen an accelerated growth in the number of analytical data technologies, the *high-level architecture* has seen very few changes. Let's browse the high-level analytical data architectures, followed by a review of their unchanged characteristics.

The underlying technologies supporting each of the following architectural paradigms have gone through many iterations and improvements. The focus here is the architectural pattern, not the technology and implementation.

First Generation: Data Warehouse Architecture

Data warehousing architecture today is influenced by early concepts such as facts and dimensions formulated in the 1960s. The architecture intends to move data from operational systems to business intelligence (BI) systems. BI systems have traditionally served management with operational planning of an organization. While data warehousing solutions have greatly evolved, many of the original characteristics and assumptions of their architectural model remain the same. Data is:

- Extracted from many operational databases and sources
- Transformed into a universal schema—represented in a multidimensional and time-variant tabular format
- Loaded into the warehouse tables
- Accessed through SQL-like queries
- Mainly serving data analysts for reporting and analytical visualization use cases

The data warehouse approach has been refined to data marts with the common distinction that a data mart serves a single department in an organization, while a data warehouse serves the larger organization integrating across multiple departments. Regardless of their scope, from an architectural modeling perspective, they both have similar characteristics.

The difficulty and cost of creating a single technology capable of organizational-scale data warehousing has led to enterprise data warehouse (*https://oreil.ly/nqSol*) solutions that are often proprietary and expensive and require specialization to use. Over time, they include thousands of ETL jobs, tables, and reports that only a specialized group can understand and maintain. Given their age and origin, they often don't lend themselves to modern engineering practices such as CI/CD and incur technical debt over time and an increased cost of maintenance. Organizations attempting to escape this technical debt find themselves in a perpetual cycle of migrating from one data warehouse solution to another. Figure 8-1 shows the light-level architecture of the data warehouse architecture.

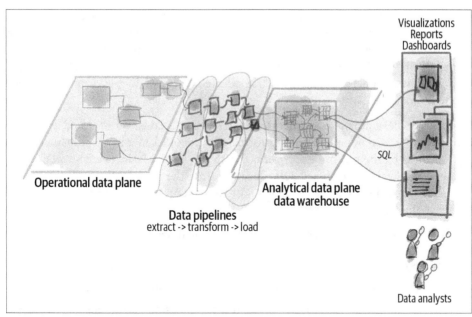

Figure 8-1. Analytical data architecture: warehouse

Second Generation: Data Lake Architecture

Data lake architecture was introduced in 2010 (*https://oreil.ly/Hlq5t*) in response to the challenges of data warehousing architecture in satisfying the new uses of data: access to data by data scientists in the machine learning model training process. Data scientists need data in its original form, as close to the reality of the business as possible. Since data scientists can't predict how exactly the data needs to be modeled, they prefer access to raw data. Additionally, machine learning training demanded massively parallelized data reads.

Data lake architecture, similar to a data warehouse, assumes that data gets extracted from operational systems and loaded into a central repository often in the format of an object store—storage of any type of data. However, unlike data warehousing, a data lake assumes very little or no transformation and modeling of the data up front; it attempts to retain the data close to its original form. Once the data becomes available in the lake, the architecture gets extended with elaborate transformation pipelines to model the higher value data and store it in lakeshore marts or feature stores at the edge of the lake. There are refinements to this approach, with allocated "zones" in the lake, storing data with varying degrees of cleansing and transformation, to organize the lake a bit better.

This evolution to data architecture aims to improve this ineffectiveness and the friction of extensive up-front modeling that data warehousing demands. The up-front transformation is a blocker and leads to slower iterations of model training. Additionally, it alters the nature of the operational system's data and mutates the data in a way that models trained with transformed data fail to perform against real production queries.

In our example, a **music recommender**, when trained against transformed and modeled data in a warehouse, fails to perform when invoked in an operational context, e.g., invoked by the recommender service with the logged-in listener's session information. The heavily transformed data used to train the model either misses some of the listener's attributes or has encoded a different representation of them. Data lake comes to the rescue in this scenario.

Notable characteristics of a data lake architecture include:

- Data is extracted from many operational databases and sources.
- Data represents as much as possible of the original content and structure.
- Data is minimally transformed to fit the popular storage formats, e.g., Parquet, Avro, etc.
- Data—as close as possible to the source schema—is loaded to scalable object storage.
- Data is accessed through the object storage interface—read as files or data frames, a two-dimensional array-like structure.
- Data scientists mainly access the lake storage for analytical and machine learning model training.
- Downstream from the lake, lakeshore marts are created as fit-for-purpose data marts.
- Lakeshore marts are used by applications and analytics use cases.
- Downstream from the lake, feature stores are created as fit-for-purpose columnar data modeled and stored for machine learning training.

Figure 8-2 shows the high-level architecture of the data lake.

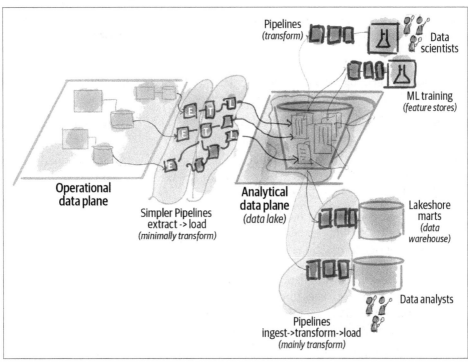

Figure 8-2. Analytical data architecture: data lake

Data lake architecture suffers from complexity and deterioration. It creates complex and unwieldy pipelines of batch or streaming jobs operated by a central team of hyper-specialized data engineers. It deteriorates over time. Its unmanaged datasets, which are often untrusted and inaccessible, provide little value. The data lineage and dependencies are obscured and hard to track.

Third Generation: Multimodal Cloud Architecture

The third and latest generation of data architectures, prior to data mesh, is more or less similar to the previous generations, with a few modern twists, as those data architectures:

- Support streaming for near real-time data availability with architectures such as Kappa (*https://oreil.ly/zpfeK*).

- Attempt to unify batch and stream processing for data transformation with frameworks such as Apache Beam (*https://oreil.ly/bJksG*).

- Fully embrace cloud-based managed services and use modern cloud-native implementations with isolated compute and storage. They leverage the elasticity of the cloud for cost optimization.

- Converge the warehouse and lake into one technology, either extending the data warehouse to include embedded ML training, or alternatively building data warehouse integrity, transactionality, and querying systems into data lake solutions.[1]

These third-generation data platforms are addressing some of the gaps of the previous generations such as real-time data analytics, while also reducing the cost of managing big data infrastructure. However, they suffer from many of the underlying characteristics that have led to the limitations of the previous generations.

Let's look at the limiting characteristics of the existing analytical data architectures.

Characteristics of Analytical Data Architecture

From a quick glance at the history of analytical data architecture, it is apparent that it has gone through evolutionary improvements. In the meantime, technology and the products supporting it have gone through a Cambrian explosion. The dizzying view of FirstMark's[2] annual landscape and "state of the union" in big data and AI (Figure 8-3) is an indication of the sheer number of innovative solutions developed in this space.

---

1 At the time of this writing, Google BigQuery ML or Snowflake Snowpark are examples of traditional data warehouse solutions that embed some ML capabilities, and Databricks Lakehouse is an example of a traditional lake storage solution with warehouse-like transactions and query support.

2 An early-stage venture capital firm in New York City.

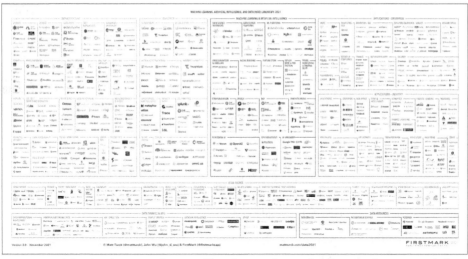

Figure 8-3. The Cambrian explosion of big data and AI technologies: it's not intended to be read—just glance and feel dizzy (courtesy of FirstMark (https://oreil.ly/pCK1o))

So the question is, what hasn't changed? What are the underlying characteristics that all generations of analytical data architecture carry? Despite the undeniable innovation, there are fundamental assumptions that have remained unchallenged for the last few decades and must be closely evaluated:

- Data must be centralized to be useful—managed by a centralized organization, with an intention to have an enterprise-wide taxonomy.

- Data management architecture, technology, and organization are monolithic.

- The enabling technologies drive the paradigm—architecture and organization.

The architectural characteristics discussed in this chapter, including centralization, are applied only to the logical architecture. Physical architecture concerns, such as where data is physically stored, are out of scope for our conversation, and it's independent of the logical architecture concerns. The logical architecture focuses on the experience layer of the data developers and consumers, such as whether data is being managed by a single team or not (data ownership), whether data has a single schema or not (data modeling), and whether a change on one data model has tight coupling and impact on downstream users (dependencies).

Let's look more closely at each of these underlying assumptions and the limitations each imposes.

Monolithic

The core assumption that data mesh challenges is the monolithic nature of data architecture, organization and technology. Let's look at each of these.

Monolithic architecture

> Architecture styles can be classified into two main types: monolithic (single deployment unit of all code) and distributed (multiple deployment units connected through remote access protocols).
>
> —*Fundamentals of Software Architecture*[3]

At 30,000 feet, the data platform architecture looks like Figure 8-4; it is a monolithic architecture whose goal is to:

- *Ingest data* from all corners of the enterprise and beyond, ranging from operational and transactional systems in domains that run the business to external data providers that augment the knowledge of the enterprise.

- For example, in the case of Daff, the data platform is responsible for ingesting a large variety of data: media player performance, how listeners interact with players, songs they play, artists they follow, labels and artists that the business has onboarded, financial transactions with artists, and external market research data such as customer demographic information.

- *Cleanse, enrich, and transform* the source data into trustworthy data that can address the needs of a diverse set of consumers. In Daff's example, one of the transformations turns **listener clicks stream** into **meaningful listener journeys**. This attempts to reconstruct the journey and behavior of the listener into an aggregate longitudinal view.

- *Serve* datasets to a variety of consumers with a diverse set of needs. This ranges from data exploration and machine learning training to business intelligence reports. In the case of Daff, the platform must serve **media player errors** in near real time through a distributed log interface and at the same time serve the batched aggregate view of a particular **artist record** to calculate monthly financial payments.

---

3 Mark Richards and Neal Ford, *Fundamentals of Software Architecture*, (Sebastopol, CA: O'Reilly, 2020).

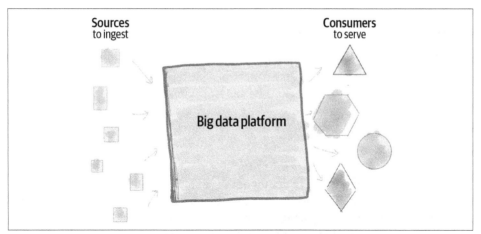

Figure 8-4. The 30,000-foot view of the monolithic data platform

While a monolithic architecture can be a good and a simple starting point for building a solution—e.g., managing one code base, one team—it falls short as the solution scales. The organizational complexity and proliferation of sources and use cases create tension and friction on the architecture and organizational structure:

Ubiquitous data and source proliferation

As more data becomes ubiquitously available, the ability to consume it all and harmonize it in one place, logically, under the control of a centralized platform and team diminishes. Imagine the domain of **customer information**. There are an increasing number of sources inside and outside an organization's boundaries that provide information about existing and potential customers. The assumption that we need to ingest and harmonize the data under a central customer master data management to get value creates a bottleneck and slows down our ability to take advantage of diverse data sources. The organization's response to making data available from new sources slows down as the number of sources increases.

Organizations' innovation agenda and use case proliferation

The need for rapid experimentation by organizations introduces a larger number of use cases that consume data from the platform. This implies an ever-growing number of transformations to create data—aggregates, projections, and slices—that can satisfy the test and learn cycle of innovation (*https://oreil.ly/pKPjB*). The long response time to satisfy data consumer needs has historically been a point of organizational friction and remains so in the modern data platform architecture. The disconnect between people and systems who are in need of data and understand the use case, from the actual sources, teams, and systems who originated the data and are most knowledgeable about the data, impedes a company's data-driven innovations. It lengthens the time needed to access the right data, becomes a blocker for hypothesis-driven development, and lowers data quality and trust in data.

Organizational complexity

When we add the volatility and continuous change of the data landscape to the mix, this monolithic architecture becomes a synchronization and prioritization hell. Aligning the organization's shifting data priorities and activities at large with the centralized data platform is a no-win situation.

Monolithic technology

From a technology perspective, the monolithic architecture has been in harmonious accordance with its enabling technology; technologies supporting data lake or data warehouse architecture, by default, assume a monolithic architecture. For example, data warehousing technologies such as Snowflake (*https://oreil.ly/g1isJ*), Google Big-Query (*https://oreil.ly/LPNUQ*), and Synapse (*https://oreil.ly/xaf4z*) all have a monolithic logical architecture. While at the physical and implementation layer there has been immense progress in resource isolation and decomposition—for example, Snowflake separates compute resource scaling from storage resources, and BigQuery uses the latest generation distributed file system—the user experience of the technology remains monolithic.

Data lake technologies such as object storage and pipeline orchestration tools can be deployed in a distributed fashion. However, by default, they do lead to the creation of monolithic lake architectures. For example, data processing pipeline directed acyclic graph (DAG) definitions and orchestrations lack constructs such as interfaces and contracts that abstract pipeline jobs dependencies and complexity, leading to a big ball of mud monolithic (*https://oreil.ly/5KVDc*) architecture with tightly coupled labyrinthic pipelines, where it is difficult to isolate change or failure to a single step in the process. Some cloud providers have limitations on the number of lake storage accounts, having assumed that there will be only a small number of monolithic lake setups.

Monolithic organization

From an organizational perspective, Conway's law has been at work and in full swing with monolithic organizational structures—business intelligence teams, data analytics groups, or data platform teams—responsible for data across the organization.

> Any organization that designs a system (defined broadly) will produce a design whose structure is a copy of the organization's communication structure.
>
> —Melvin Conway, 1968

When we zoom close enough to observe the lives of the people who build and operate a data platform, we find a group of hyper-specialized data engineers siloed from the operational units of the organization, where the data originates or where it is used. The data engineers are not only siloed organizationally but also separated and grouped into a team based on their technical expertise of data tooling, often absent of business and domain knowledge (Figure 8-5).

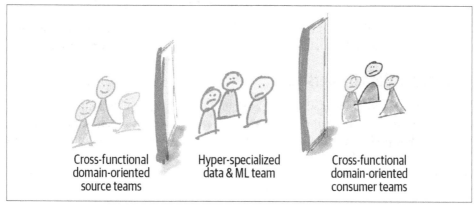

Cross-functional domain-oriented source teams   Hyper-specialized data & ML team   Cross-functional domain-oriented consumer teams

Figure 8-5. Siloed hyper-specialized data team

I personally don't envy the life of a data engineer in a monolithic data organization. They need to consume data from operational teams who are not incentivized to share meaningful, truthful, and correct data, based on an agreed-upon contract. Given the data team's organizational silo, despite best efforts, these data engineers have little understanding of the source domains that generate the data and lack the domain expertise in their teams. They need to provide data for a diverse set of needs, operational or analytical, without a deep understanding of how data is used.

For example, at Daff, on the source side we have a cross-functional **media player** team that provide signals of how users interact with media player features, e.g., **play song events**, **purchase events**, and **play audio quality**; and on the other end sits a cross-functional consumer team such as the **song recommendation** team, the **sales team** reporting sales KPIs, the **artist payment** team that calculates and pays artists based on play events, and so on. Sadly, in the middle sits the data team that through sheer effort provides analytical data on behalf of all sources and to all consumers.

In reality what we find are disconnected source teams, frustrated consumers fighting for a spot on top of the data team's backlog, and an overstretched and underappreciated data team.

The complicated monolith

Monolithic architectures when they meet scale—here, the scale in diversity of sources, consumers, and transformations—all face a similar destiny, becoming complex and difficult to maintain.

The complexity debt (*https://oreil.ly/amHMJ*) of the sprawling data pipelines, the duct-taped scripts implementing the ingestion and transformation logic, the large number of datasets—tables or files—with no clear architectural and organizational modularity, and the thousands of reports built on top of those datasets keep the team busy paying the interest of the debt instead of creating value.

In short, a monolithic architecture, technology, and organizational structure are not suitable for analytical data management of large-scale and complex organizations.

Centralized Data Ownership

It's an accepted convention that the monolithic data platform hosts and owns the data that belongs to different domains, e.g., **play events, sales KPIs, artists, albums, labels, audio, podcasts, music events**, etc., collected from a large number of disparate domains (Figure 8-6).

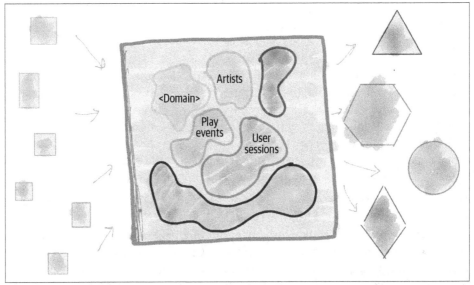

Figure 8-6. Centralized data ownership with no clear domain boundaries

While over the last decade we have successfully applied domain-driven design and bounded context (*https://oreil.ly/2RhbM*) to the design of our operational systems to manage software complexity at scale, we have largely disregarded domain-driven design paradigm for data. DDD's strategic design (*https://oreil.ly/OHz8I*) introduces a set of principles to manage software modeling at scale in a large and complex organization. It encourages moving away from a single canonical model to many bounded context models. It assumes multiple models each owned and managed by a unit of organization. And it explicitly articulates the relationships between these models.

While operational systems have applied DDD's strategic design techniques toward domain-oriented operational data ownership—aligning the services and their data with existing business domains—analytical data systems have retained centralized data ownership outside of the domains.

While this centralized model can work for organizations that have simpler domains with a smaller number of use cases, it fails for enterprises with rich and complex domains.

In addition to limitations of scale, other challenges of data centralization are data quality and resilience to change. This is because business domains and teams that are most familiar with the data are not responsible for data quality. The central data team, far from the source of the data and isolated from the domains of the data, is tasked with building quality back into the data through data cleansing and enriching pipelines. Often, the data that pops out of the other end of the pipelines into the central system loses its original form and meaning.

Centralization of analytical data has been our industry's response to siloed and fragmented application databases, commonly known as *dark data* (*https://oreil.ly/eTY5x*). Coined by Gartner, dark data refers to the information assets organizations collect, process, and store during regular business activities, but generally fail to use for analytical or other purposes.

Technology Oriented

Looking back at different generations of analytical data architectures, from warehouse to lake and all on the cloud, we have heavily leaned on a technology-driven architecture. A typical solution architecture of a data management system merely wires together various technologies, each performing a technical function, a piece of the end-to-end storage and processing flow. This is evident from a glance at any infrastructure provider's modern solution architecture diagram, like the one in Figure 8-7. The core technologies listed in the figure are powerful and helpful in enabling a data platform. However, the proposed solution architecture decomposes and then integrates the components of the architecture based on their technical function and the solution supporting the function. For example, first we encounter the *ingestion* function supported by Cloud Pub/Sub and then *publishing data* to Cloud Storage, which then *serves data* through BigQuery. This approach leads to a *technically partitioned architecture* and consequently an *activity-oriented team decomposition*.

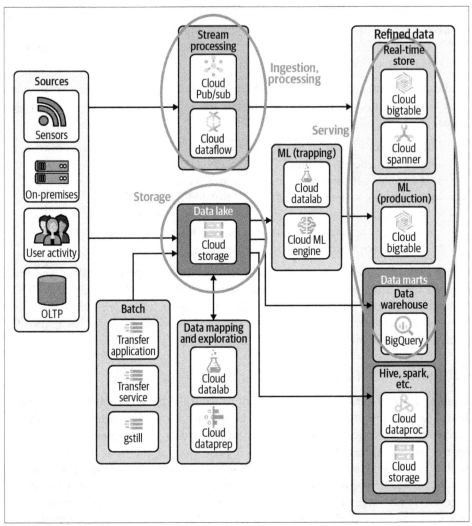

Figure 8-7. Example of a modern analytical architecture influenced by a technology-oriented decomposition

Technically partitioned architecture

One of the limitations of data management solutions today is how we have attempted to manage its unwieldy complexity, how we have decomposed an ever-growing monolithic data platform and team to smaller partitions. We have chosen the path of least resistance, a *technical partitioning*.

Architects and technical leaders in organizations decompose an architecture in response to its growth. The need to onboard numerous new sources or respond to the proliferation of new consumers requires the platform to grow. Architects need to find a way to scale the system by breaking it into its top-level components.

As defined by *Fundamentals of Software Architecture* (*https://oreil.ly/kMene*) (O'Reilly), *top-level technical partitioning* decomposes the system into its components based on their technical capabilities and concerns; it's a decomposition that is closer to the implementation concerns than business domain concerns. Architects and leaders of monolithic data platforms have decomposed monolithic solutions based on a pipeline architecture into its technical functions such as *ingestion, cleansing, aggregation, enrichment*, and *serving* (Figure 8-8). The top-level functional decomposition leads to synchronization overhead and slow response to data changes. An alternative approach is a *top-level domain-oriented partitioning*, where these technical functions are embedded in every domain, where the change to the domain can be managed locally without top-level synchronization.

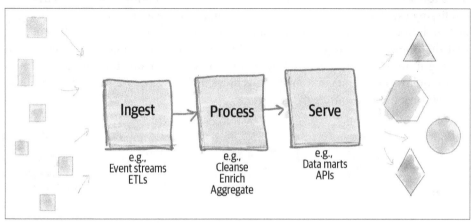

Figure 8-8. Top-level technical partitioning of monolithic data architecture

Activity-oriented team decomposition

One of the motivations behind breaking a system down into its architectural components is to create independent teams that can each build and operate an architectural component. These teams in turn can parallelize work to reach higher operational scalability and velocity. The consequence of top-level technical decomposition is decomposing teams into *activity-oriented groups*, each focused on a particular activity required by a stage of the pipeline, for example, a team focusing on *ingestion* of data from various sources or a team responsible for *serving* the lakeshore marts. Each team attempts to optimize their activity, for example find patterns of *ingestion*.

Though this model provides some level of scale, by assigning teams to different activities of the flow, it has an inherent limitation that does not scale what matters: delivery of outcome—in this case, delivery of new quality and trustworthy data. Delivering an outcome demands synchronization between teams and aligning changes to the activities. Such decomposition is *orthogonal to the axis of change or outcome*, slows down the delivery of value, and introduces organizational friction (Figure 8-9).

Conversely, an outcome-oriented team decomposition (*https://oreil.ly/df5Xo*) optimizes for an end-to-end outcome, delivered rapidly and with low synchronization overhead.

Let's look at an example. Daff started its services with songs and albums and then extended to music events, podcasts, and radio shows. Enabling a single new feature, such as visibility to the podcast play rate, requires a change in all components of the pipeline. Teams must introduce new ingestion services, new cleansing and preparation services, and new data aggregates for viewing podcast play rates. This requires synchronization across implementations of different components and release management across teams. Many data platforms provide generic and configuration-based ingestion services that can cope with extensions such as adding new sources easily or modifying existing ones. However, this does not remove an end-to end-dependency hell of introducing new datasets from the consumer point of view. The smallest unit that must change to cater to a new functionality, unlocking a new dataset and making it available for new or existing consumption, remains the whole pipeline—the monolith. This limits our ability to achieve higher velocity and scale in response to new consumers or sources of the data.

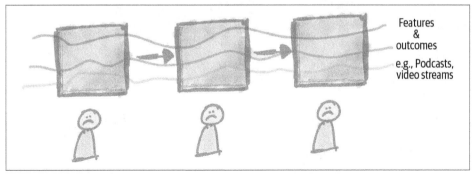

Figure 8-9. Architecture and team decomposition is orthogonal to the axis of change (outcome)

We have created an architecture and organization structure that does not scale and does not deliver the promised value of creating a data-driven organization.

 In recent years, there has been a move toward decomposing the central data team into domain-oriented data teams. While this is an improvement, it does not solve the issue of long-term data ownership and data quality. The data team remains far from the actual domains, out of sync with domain system changes and their needs. This is an antipattern.

Recap

> The definition of insanity is doing the same thing over and over again and expecting different results.
>
> —Albert Einstein

This chapter aimed to give you a perspective on the progression of analytical data architecture and organizational structure. It gave an overview of different styles of two-plane data architectures: warehouse, lake, and multimodal. It pointed out that all of these approaches have a pipeline-based integration model that remains fragile and hard to maintain.

While the evolution of data architecture has been necessary and an improvement, all of the existing analytical data architectures share a common set of characteristics that inhibit them from scaling organizationally. They are all monolithic with centralized ownership and technically partitioned.

These characteristics are the consequence of an age-old assumption that to satisfy analytical use cases, data must be extracted from domains and consolidated and integrated under the central repositories of a warehouse or a lake. This assumption was valid when data use cases were limited to low-frequency reports. It was valid when data was being sourced from a handful of systems. It is no longer valid when data gets sources from hundreds of microservices and millions of devices from within and outside of enterprises. It is no longer valid when tomorrow's use cases for data are beyond our imagination today.

This chapter concludes Part II. With an understanding of what data mesh is and why you should care about it, let's discuss its technical architecture in Part III.

PART III

How to Design the Data Mesh Architecture

The supreme goal of all theory is to make the irreducible basic elements as simple and as few as possible without having to surrender the adequate representation of a simple datum of experience.

—Albert Einstein

Up to this point in the book, I've left the technical design of a data mesh architecture to your imagination. This was necessary. We first needed to share a common understanding of what data mesh is (Part I) and agree on why we need to shift toward it (Part II). Now it's time to model an architecture that enables a technical implementation of the data mesh.

The Scope

At the time of this writing, data mesh is in its early years of development. We still have a long way to go to learn about its optimal design. Hence, the scope of this part is respectful of the fact that data mesh design and implementation will continue to evolve. Nevertheless, we have to start somewhere. So I've decided to dedicate this chapter to *the important stuff*[1] that matters today, aspects of architecture that I think will continue to last and influence the development of future implementations.

---

[1] Martin Fowler's summary definition of architecture (*https://oreil.ly/IdXKQ*) influenced by Ralph Johnson.

What is the *important stuff?*

It's important to have a shared understanding of *logical architecture.* In Chapter 9, "The Logical Architecture", I will define the main logical components of data mesh architecture such as *domains, data product as an architecture quantum,* and *multiple planes of data platform* and how they interact with each other.

Chapter 10, "The Multiplane Data Platform Architecture", defines the capabilities that an infrastructure platform must offer to build, run, and operate an implementation of data mesh. It offers an overall approach to designing the platform, independent of its technologies.

What is not included in this book is the physical layer of the architecture and specific technologies that one can use today to implement the architectural components. For example, whether you should use Apache Airflow, Prefect, or Azure Data Factory to manage data product transformation flow is out of scope here.

The intention of this section is to remove room for misinterpretation and misuse of data mesh, while being open enough to allow creative thinking and creation of a new set of technologies and tools to bring this paradigm to life, elegantly.

Figure III-1 demonstrates a few examples of areas that are in scope and out of scope for this book.

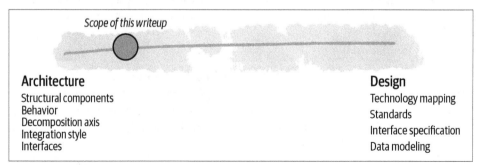

Figure III-1. The scope is more on the architecture and less on design for implementation

Maturity

This part of the book is partly based on my experience implementing data mesh architectures and partly on personal opinion. Some concepts are implemented and tested, and some are more speculative and require further experimentation and testing.

What you find in this part of the book is my suggestion to how a data mesh architecture can be implemented, today, based on available technologies. It's one way of instantiating the principles of data mesh. It is influenced by approaches that have proven successful in similar scaled-out architectures and adapted to the data problem space.

I will make it clear when a topic is experimental and requires further exploration and refinement.

CHAPTER 9

The Logical Architecture

Form ever follows function.
—Louis Sullivan

In this chapter I present the logical architecture of data mesh, including its high-level structural components and their relationships.

To arrive at the architecture, I'll walk you through the data mesh principles and show how each of these principles influences the overall architecture with new components and integrations—*we follow the function and intention to arrive at the form.*

Here is a quick summary of architectural concepts that I will unpack in this chapter, driven by each principle:

Domain ownership extends domains with analytical data sharing interfaces
> Domain ownership of data results in a domain-centric organization of analytical data. This means that a domain's interfaces must extend to sharing its analytical data. Figure 9-1 demonstrates this extension notationally.

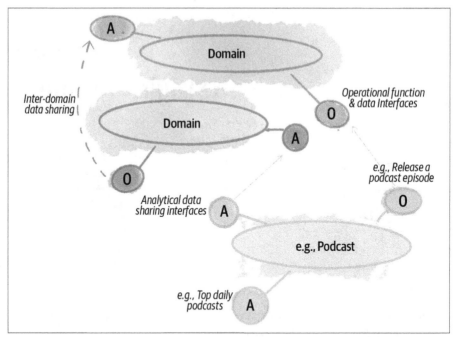

Figure 9-1. Domain interfaces extended with analytical data sharing interfaces

Data as a product introduces a new architecture quantum, aka data quantum

Data mesh represents each data product as an architecture quantum. As an architectural quantum, a data product encapsulates all the necessary components needed to implement its usability characteristics and the behavior of securely sharing analytical data.

A data quantum is the foundational unit of a data mesh architecture. It holds the domain-oriented data and the code that performs the necessary data transformations and shares the data and the policies governing the data. Figure 9-2 shows the main constituents of a data quantum.

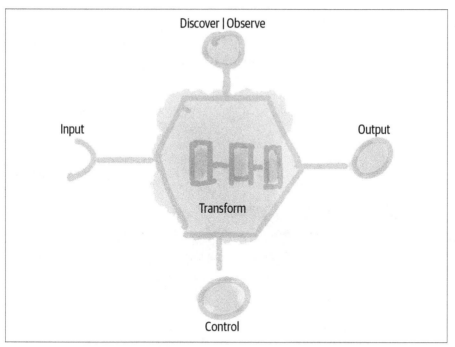

Figure 9-2. A new unit of architecture, the data (product) quantum

The self-serve data platform drives a multiplane platform architecture

The self-serve platform offers a proliferation of services that empower a wide spectrum of the data mesh users to do their job: data producers (data product developers, data product owners), data consumers (data analysts and data scientists), and members of the data governance function. Data mesh designs this platform as three planes—groups of collaborating services arranged based on the experience of data mesh users. Figure 9-3 shows the planes of the platform.

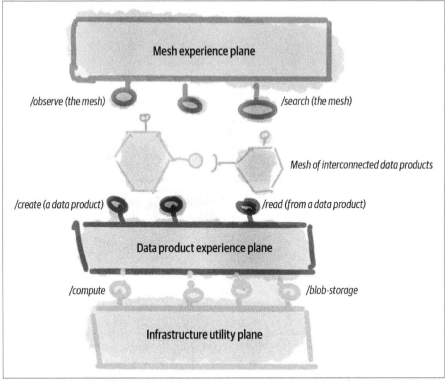

Figure 9-3. A multiplane data platform with declarative interfaces

Federated computational governance embeds computational policies into each data product

The principle of federated computational governance leads to an extension of each data product with a computational container that can host a *sidecar* process that embeds the computational policies in each and every data product and executes them at the right time and in the flow of data—e.g., build, deploy, access, read, or write.

A data product *sidecar* is a process that shares the execution context of a data product and is only responsible for domain-agnostic and cross-cutting concerns such as policy execution. In addition to policy execution, the sidecar process can be extended to implement other standardized features of a data product such as discovery.

The sidecar implementation is common across all data products.

Figure 9-4 introduces the concept of a data product sidecar sharing a computational container (context) with its data product.

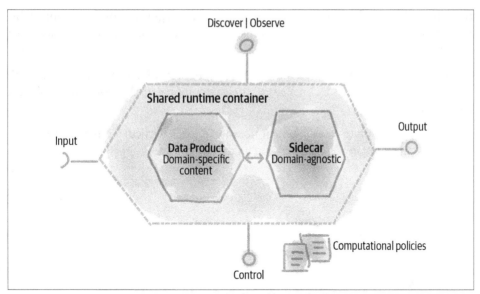

Figure 9-4. A data product extended with a sidecar to embed the configuration and execution of policies

At the time of this writing, there are multiple private implementations of these architectural components that I have been involved with working with clients. Each of these implementations has been different. Hence, there are no de facto standards or reference implementations publicly available yet. I hope that changes in the coming years.

Let's look a bit more closely at each of these architectural components.

Domain-Oriented Analytical Data Sharing Interfaces

To promote a domain-oriented decomposition of data ownership, we need to model an architecture that arranges the analytical data[1] by domains. In this architecture, a domain's interface to the rest of the organization not only includes the operational capabilities but also shares the analytical data that a domain generates and owns.

For example, the **podcast** domain provides operational APIs to, semantically, create a new podcast episode but also provides an analytical data interface for retrieving all podcast episodes data and their usage stats over a long period of time.

Each domain controls its data—operational and analytical. My assumption is that domains already have operational interfaces, the application APIs. This is not

---

1 Chapter 1 defines analytical and operational data.

something that data mesh introduces, but data mesh integrates with operational APIs. In addition to operational APIs, domains control and manage their analytical data sharing APIs.

To scale, the architecture must support the autonomy of the domain teams with regard to the release and deployment of their operational applications and analytical data products.

Figure 9-5 demonstrates the graphical notation I use to articulate that each domain can expose one or many operational and analytical interfaces.

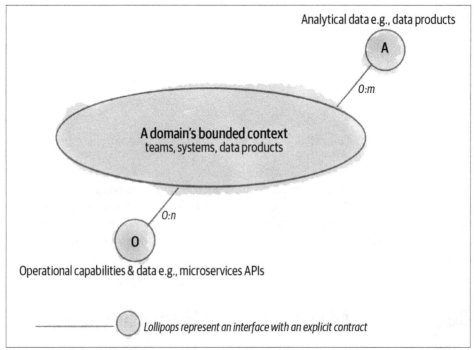

Figure 9-5. Notation: a domain and its analytical and operational interfaces

Let's look a bit more closely at each of these interfaces and their dependencies.

Operational Interface Design

Today, domains implement their operational capabilities with a range of solutions. For example, a domain can have customer-facing GUI applications, head-less applications, legacy systems, SaaS products, microservices, or event-driven functions as a service.

Regardless of the type of solutions, logically, each domain serves its users—systems or people, internal or external to the organization—through a set of interfaces.

For example, in the case of a microservice implementing a domain function, the domain interface includes the APIs—GraphQL, REST, gRPC, etc.—that the microservice exposes. These domain interfaces are depicted by the "O" lollipop in the previous diagram.

Operational interfaces semantically implement a function, e.g., pay an artist or subscribe a listener. Syntactically, these functions can be implemented as operations on declarative resources that get modified with CRUD operations, e.g., HTTP POST/ artists-payments.

The operational interfaces are typically designed to access smaller volume data, and they provide the current near-real-time snapshot of the state known to the system. For example, an operational API of the **listener subscription** service can have the affordance to get the list of subscribed listeners, in North America, now with pagination, e.g., HTTP GET/listeners-subscriptions?region=NA.

Data mesh does not change this preexisting aspect of the enterprise architecture; it simply acknowledges its existence. In some cases, data mesh uses the operational interfaces to create data products.

Analytical Data Interface Design

A new set of interfaces is introduced with the extension of the domain's responsibility to share analytical data. These interfaces are marked as "A" in Figure 9-5.

Analytical interfaces are the APIs that data products expose to get *discovered, understood, and observed* and to *share* their data. At the time of this writing there are no widely accepted conventions on high-level APIs that encapsulate all these functions.

For analytical data sharing, the APIs may choose to redirect the clients to the underlying storage of the data, once the access policies are enforced. Depending on the data product's implementation, the data sharing interface can redirect access to either a blob storage (e.g., Parquet files from AWS S3) or an event stream (e.g., Kafka Topic), or a table (e.g., BigQuery Table) or something completely different.

Interdomain Analytical Data Dependencies

Naturally, each domain can have dependencies to other domains' operational and analytical data interfaces.

In the following example (Figure 9-6), each domain provides a few operational and analytical interfaces. For example, the **podcast** domain provides a few operational APIs to create a podcast episode or release a podcast episode. It also provides analytical data such as **get podcast (listener) demographics** and **get top daily podcasts**.

There are dependencies between each domain. For example, the **podcast** domain consumes information about **listener demographics** from the **listener** domain, to provide a picture of the demographic of podcast listeners.

The mechanics of establishing the dependency—asynchronously using events or pulled synchronously—is an implementation concern. But the important point is that a data product explicitly defines its dependencies to its sources.

In data mesh architecture, the data dependency is defined and controlled by a data product to its upstream source. A data product is in full control of what its sources are and what data it consumes from them and how.

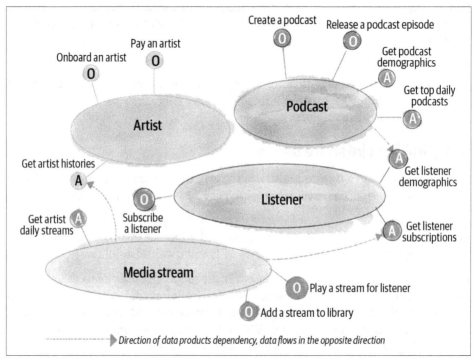

Figure 9-6. Example: domain-oriented data dependencies

> In this example, the labels I have used for the interfaces define the semantic of the interface and not its syntax. For example, syntactically, the semantic of **pay an artist** can be implemented as a declarative resource—RESTful resource or GraphQL query—such as **artist-payments**.

Data Product as an Architecture Quantum

An *architectural quantum* (*https://oreil.ly/Lrd6t*), defined in *Building Evolutionary Architectures* (O'Reilly), is the smallest unit of architecture that can be independently deployed, has high functional cohesion, and includes all the "structural elements required for its function."

In the case of data mesh, a data product is an architectural quantum. It is the smallest unit of architecture that can be independently deployed and managed. It has high functional cohesion, i.e., performing a specific analytical transformation and securely sharing the result as domain-oriented analytical data. It has all the structural components that it requires to do its function: the transformation code, the data, the metadata, the policies that govern the data, and its dependencies to infrastructure.

In a strictly architectural discussion, like this chapter, I may abbreviate *data product (as an architecture quantum)* and use *data product quantum*, or lazily, *data quantum*. All these are interchangeable.

Data quantum is data mesh's opinionated way of designing the architecture of a data product.

You may find it helpful to know why I have chosen the seemingly big and, to many, unfamiliar phrase *data quantum*. Why not a data service, data actor, data agent, data operator, data transformer, etc. They may all seem like OK choices. Most of the names such as operator, transformer, etc., heavily emphasize a single aspect of the data quantum, its task, and transformation execution. Similarly, data service emphasizes another aspect, serving data. Quantum, first introduced in *Building Evolutionary Architectures* and later expanded in the book *Software Architecture: The Hard Parts* (O'Reilly), perfectly embodies the intention of data quantum: all that is required to do its job autonomously—whatever the job is. I hope you accept my reasoning for the neologism in the heavily populated tech vocabulary.

An architecture quantum is the axis over which a system can scale out. Data mesh scales out by adding and connecting more data products. An architecture quantum integrates with other components through static coupling (e.g., build-time libraries) or dynamic coupling (e.g., asynchronous runtime APIs). A data product integrates with other data products through a dynamic coupling of data sharing interfaces.

Part IV is a deep dive into different aspects of a data product as an architecture quantum.

A Data Product's Structural Components

A data product encapsulates more than just the data. It needs to contain all the structural components needed to manifest its baseline usability characteristics—discoverable, understandable, addressable, etc.—in an autonomous fashion, while continuing to share data in a compliant and secure manner.

At a high level, data products have three types of structural components: *code*, *data (and metadata and configuration)*, and the specifications of its *infrastructure dependencies* (Figure 9-7).

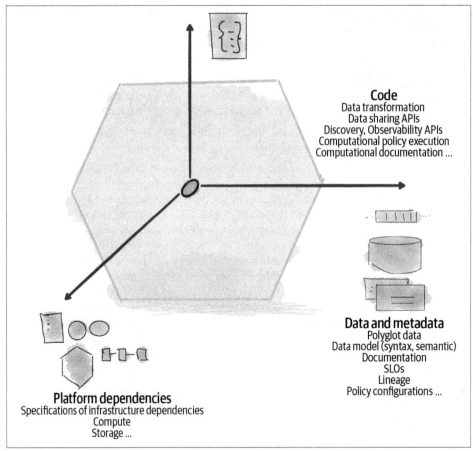

Figure 9-7. Types of structural elements of a data product

The code

For a data product to independently control the life cycle of analytical data—maintain the business logic that generates it, control its revisions, manage access to it, and share its content—it must include code and run it within its computational context. This is a fundamental difference between what data mesh calls a data product and other forms of data artifacts. A data product is active while other data artifacts like files or tables are passive.

Let's look at a few different types of code that a data product controls.

Data transformation as code. Data products either transform data received from an upstream source, e.g., from their adjacent operational system, or originate the data themselves. Either way, there is a need for an analytical computation to generate and share data.

For example, **podcast demographics** consumes **listener demographics** and **played podcasts** by listeners. Its analytical transformation code aggregates the two, derives and adds other information about the demographic of listeners based on their podcast listening behavior such as the category of podcasts they listen to, and then shares the result as **podcast demographics**. It runs this code continuously as new podcasts are played.

In traditional architectures, this code lives outside of a data product, as a *data pipeline*. A pipeline is managed as an independent artifact, perhaps a DAG configuration. Its output data is managed independently, perhaps as a table in a warehouse.

Data mesh removes the concept of an *external* pipeline and introduces the *internal* transformation code. This code may be implemented as a pipeline, or not. The important differentiating point is that the code is encapsulated as an internal implementation of a data product. Its life cycle is controlled by the data product, and it runs in the execution context allocated to the data product.

The transformation code is domain-specific and encapsulates tasks such as a *domain's business logic as well as aggregating and modeling data*. This is the code on which data product developers spend the majority of their time and attention. Figure 9-8 shows the notation I use in this book to demonstrate a data product's transformation code.

The code includes both the implementation and the automated tests that verify it.

Note that I have left out the traditional data pipeline steps such as *data ingestion* or *data cleansing* from the transformation code. This is to further demonstrate the difference between data mesh and traditional pipelines.

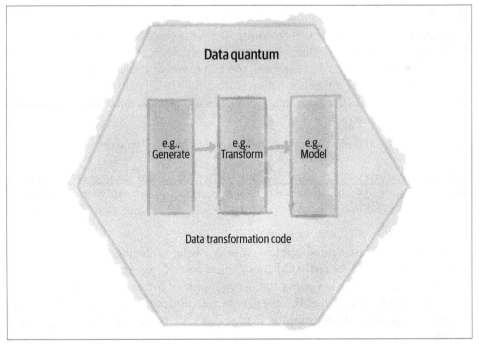

Figure 9-8. A data product's transformation code

Data cleansing is almost always the responsibility of the upstream source—e.g., data products. It provides data with integrity. Hence, the typical cleansing activities are rarely required in a data product code. Traditionally, data cleansing activities in pipelines include handling incomplete, incorrect, inaccurate, or irrelevant data. Expecting data to be dirty is a norm. In the case of data mesh, upstream data products provide cleansed data, according to their guarantees. For example, in the case of **listener demographics**, the data product guarantees a level of quality in terms of completeness of data, integrity of data, and timeliness of data. The data sharing interfaces specify these guarantees and communicate them. Receiving dirty data surprises is an error, an exception, and not a norm. It's likely that these guarantees are good enough for **podcast demographics**, which consumes this data for further aggregation. Hence, it requires no further cleansing.

There could be cases where the level of a guarantee is lower than the need of the downstream data product, in which case their transformation code can include cleansing. For example, the **listener subscriptions** data product generates near-real-time events of subscriptions without the payment information, since Daff handles the subscription asynchronously from the actual payments. In this case, you can imagine a downstream **subscription payments** data product that needs to consolidate the events with payment information to create a complete picture of subscriptions. Even in this case, I don't call **listener subscriptions** dirty data. It's a perfectly reasonable data product, even with missing information, for many other use cases. The missing payment information is part of its contract. If you find yourself building a cleansing task, I suggest that is a sign that something upstream needs to be fixed.

Regarding the ingestion, I consider this part of the *input* function of the data product and not its transformation code. I will discuss that further later in this chapter.

Interfaces as code. A data product provides access to its data, discoverability information, usability documentation, observability metrics, SLOs, etc., through its *interfaces* (APIs). These APIs follow defined *contracts*—agreements on what information the data product communicates and how.

To implement such interfaces there is code involved in providing the necessary information and serving them. The lollipop notation encapsulates the interface and its supporting code. Figure 9-9 demonstrates a list of these interfaces:

Output data APIs
There is a set of collaborating APIs that share the output data of a data product in a way that can be understood and trusted.

Output data APIs can receive and run remote queries on their data, for example an interface to run SQL queries on the underlying tables holding data. Output APIs share the data in multiple formats. For example, APIs read semi-structured files from blob storage or subscribe to an event stream.

Input data APIs
These APIs are used internally by the data product to configure and read data from the upstream sources. They can be implemented as a subscription to upstream output data APIs and asynchronously receive data as it becomes available. They can be implemented as queries executed on an upstream source and read as data frames. The arrival of input data triggers the transformation code.

Discovery and observability APIs
These APIs provide additional information about the data product to help with its discoverability and debugging. For example, a discovery API can provide information about the team maintaining the data products, tags that help to search for it, description of its semantic, etc.

The governance standardizes the definition of these interfaces across all data products, and the platform provides the mechanisms to implement them.

Data mesh uses the phrase *port* interchangeably for its interface APIs. The implementation of these APIs can be synchronous, such as REST, or asynchronous—ideally—e.g., using pub/sub messaging.

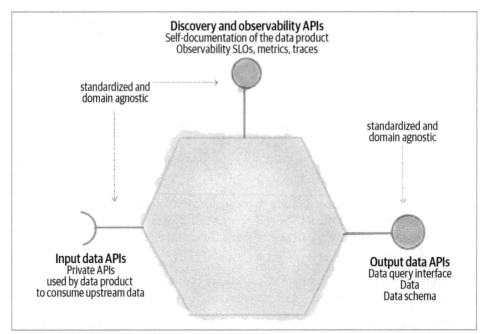

Figure 9-9. Data product APIs as code

Traditionally, a centralized and shared service implements these interfaces. The API life cycles are independent of the domain's data or pipeline. For example, to access the data, a data consumer goes to a central catalog to find the dataset and then directly from the central catalog reaches into the bowels of the platform storage system. In contrast, data mesh introduces intentionally designed interfaces made available by each data product as code, to discover and access the data. These interfaces may ultimately direct access to the underlying storage, but in a manner that data products can control—at runtime—where and how to do that. The interfaces stay versioned and in sync with the rest of the data product code and its data.

Policy as code.   The last category of code encapsulated by a data product implementation is the code responsible for configuring and executing various behavioral and structural policies, such as encryption, access control, quality, and compliance.

For example, if a data product sets a privacy classification, protected, its data will be encrypted on write and on read unencrypted only after verifying that the reader has the necessary privileges. The code involved in interpreting and validating the privacy class, verifying the readers' privileges, encrypting and decrypting data, etc., are executed in the flow of data and within the computational context of a data product.

This code is provided by the platform but invoked in the flow to data product read and write functions.

I further explain this in the section "Embedded Computational Policies" on page 164.

The data and metadata

Access to analytical data is the reason that a data product exists. A data product manages the life cycle of its domain data. It provides access to it in multiple modes—files, tabular, columnar, etc.—depending on the nature of the data and the needs of its data users. Data products' transformation code keeps the data fresh. Data sharing APIs share this data.

Analytical data reflects the facts of the business that have happened, the trends observed, or projections and recommendations for the future.

For data to be usable, data products maintain and serve an associated set of information about the data—often called *metadata*. For example, this includes the data's documentation, semantic and syntax declarations, and SLOs. The life cycle of metadata and how often it changes depends on its type. For example, data models—semantic or syntax—change less often and change at build time. However, most metadata changes as a data product generates new data, including statistical properties of the data, and its current SLO metric values.

I rarely use the term *metadata* in data mesh vocabulary. I often find this generic catchall term confusing and even harmful. It conflates many semantically different concepts that deserve their own intentional design and system support into a bucket of all stuff called *metadata*. This conflation leads to fragile and centralized architectures that become a tangled complexity over time. Data mesh architecture expects metadata and its categories and types to be part of the contract of the data product interfaces.

The big departure from a traditional data architecture is that a data product itself is responsible for generating the metadata, as opposed to traditional systems where metadata is extracted, extrapolated, and projected by an external system—often *after* the data has been generated. In the traditional world an external system such as a central data catalog attempts to extract, collect, and serve metadata from all datasets.

The platform dependencies

The platform enables building, deploying, and running data products. While the platform manages infrastructure resources centrally, it provisions and allocates resources with isolation per data product to support its autonomous operation. It's important that deployment or update of one data product doesn't impact other data products. For example, deploying one data product to its hosting infrastructure should not disrupt the operation of others on a shared infrastructure.

A data product defines and controls its expected target state and its dependencies to the platform. For example, the expectations around how long its data needs to be retained or the types of modes of access to its output data can be expressed as platform dependencies and used by the platform to provision and manage the right type of storage.

Data Product Data Sharing Interactions

The majority of data product interactions are about sharing data—serving and consuming. Figure 9-10 zooms into the domain and analytical interface that I introduced in the previous section. It demonstrates how data products integrate with their collaborating source operational system(s) or other data products.

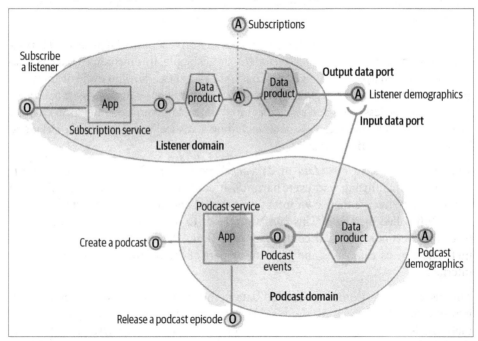

Figure 9-10. Example of data sharing interactions

Each domain can have multiple data products. In this example, the **listener** domain has two data products: **subscriptions** and **listener demographics**. These data products and their data sharing interfaces—aka *output data ports*—become the analytical interfaces that the domain exposes.

A data product can consume data from its collaborating operational system or an upstream data product. In this example, the **podcast demographics** data product consumes **podcast events** from its collaborating operational application **podcast service** and an upstream data product **listener demographics**. Its input interface—

aka *input data port*—implements integration with the sources and receiving data from them.

The underlying technology implementing a data product's input data port and output data port may vary in different implementations of data mesh, but it shares the following common properties.

Input data ports

These are internal integration mechanisms that a data product implements to consume data from one or multiple sources. For example, a data product may consume near-real-time domain events from its collaborating microservice and then convert them into historical long-term-retention analytical data.

Alternatively, the input data port could be a time-triggered query that the data product invokes on an upstream data product to receive the result of the query and transform it to aggregate data.

In Figure 9-10, **podcast demographics** is an aggregate data product that provides a statistical summary of listeners' population characteristics. It uses a classification machine learning model to identify cohorts of the podcasts based on the demographics of their listeners. This is helpful analytical information to both podcast producers as well as Daff to better match podcasts with listeners.

The **podcast demographics** data product uses its input data ports to continuously receive data from its collaborating microservice **podcast service** as well as the **listener** domain's data product **listener demographics**.

Output data ports

These are externally addressable APIs that share the underlying data of a data product. Each data product may have one or multiple output data ports. Data mesh suggests having standardized APIs for the output data port that all consumers invoke before getting access to the data. These APIs enforce policies such as access control before redirecting the consumer to the underlying data.

In Figure 9-10, **podcast demographics** classifies and augments podcasts based on their listeners. It continuously serves the newly classified podcast demographics via its output data port.

Data Discovery and Observability APIs

Data products provide the information necessary to be discovered, understood, debugged, and audited through a set of interfaces—synchronous or asynchronous. For example, the discovery APIs share the data product's identifier, the team owning it, the data semantic, documentation, tags that help searching for it, etc. The observability APIs provide access logs, lineage, and metrics around data sharing.

Part IV expands on the content and function of these APIs.

The Multiplane Data Platform

One can imagine the long list of capabilities and services the data platform must provide to meet the promises of data mesh as discussed in Chapter 4: in short, to empower cross-functional domain teams to manage data products autonomously, and to allow data users to discover, learn, and consume a mesh of data products, all done securely and in compliance with the mesh policies.

There are two general approaches in designing such a platform: adopt a single and tightly integrated platform—often bought from a main vendor—or use a set of loosely integrated services that expose standard and open interfaces, often implemented as a combination of build and buy from different vendors.

Data mesh platform design falls into the second camp. It favors breaking a complex platform into its capabilities, served through APIs, with open interfaces to integrate with other collaborating capabilities.

While the idea of a single platform is appealing—i.e., it is simpler to deal with one vendor—it has limitations to scale. For example, a single platform limits where the services and data can be hosted and creates lock-in to a vendor. Nonetheless, over time, organization complexity leads to the adoption of multiple platforms. But these platforms don't play nicely with each other as each imagines being the sole controller of the data or applications. This leads to ad hoc and costly integrations and expensive copying of data across platforms.

Data mesh, by default, embraces the fact that organization complexity leads to multiplatform, multihosting environments. To support this model, data mesh offers an approach to platform architecture that composes services with standard interfaces. So data can be shared across different services and hosting environments.

For example, managing a data product life cycle requires a collection of capabilities such as *initializing a data product, building the data product, testing the data product, deploying the data product, monitoring the data product*, etc. The data mesh platform emphasizes the design of the (open) interfaces that abstract these capabilities. The API-driven approach allows flexibility in the face of growing complexity. It allows extending the experience of data product management with new capabilities over time or moving data product management to different infrastructure without interruption to the mesh users.

I have intentionally avoided using the term *layer* for the platform *planes*. Layers are often imagined with strict hierarchical access, with the flow of information and control moving from one layer to the next one. For example, the concept of layered application architecture requires hiding database access at the lowest layer and only allowing access to data via the mapped objects of higher layers.

In the case of platform planes, a mesh user can choose to use the higher abstraction plane services or the lower ones, depending on their needs.

A Platform Plane

In the logical design of data mesh platform capabilities I use the notion of a *plane*. A plane is a logical collection of capabilities with complementary objectives and high functional cohesion in satisfying an end-to-end outcome.

Each plane, like a *surface*, abstracts infrastructure complexity and offers a set of interfaces (APIs) for the capabilities it implements. The plane capabilities are accessed through its interfaces.

An end user, such as a data product developer, can interact directly with multiple planes of the platform. While there is a loose dependency between the planes, there is no strong notion of layering or a hierarchical access model. The planes embrace the *separation of concerns* without strong layering constraints.

The logical architecture of the data mesh platform focuses only on the planes' interfaces, accessed programmatically or manually. It focuses on protocol design to access platform capabilities to achieve a particular outcome in developing, deploying, managing, or using data products on the mesh.

In the architecture modeling I only call out logical interfaces. The physical implementation of the interface—whether through a command-line interface (CLI), APIs, or a GUI and the actual number of physical calls for each logical interface—is out of the scope of the architectural design.

Figure 9-11 demonstrates the notation I will be using to describe a specific plane of the infrastructure platform, with a focus on the logical interfaces that one plane provides. The users of a plane—systems or humans, data products, other planes or users—should be able to use the interfaces in a self-serve manner and be able to discover the interfaces and understand, access, and invoke them.

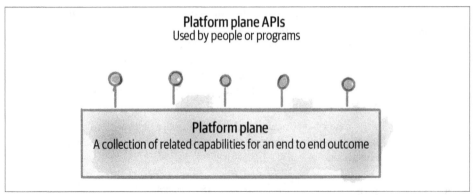

Figure 9-11. Notation: A platform plane surfacing APIs

Given the complexity of the data mesh platform and its wide range of capabilities, its logical architecture is composed of multiple planes. Thus far I have identified three different planes for data mesh infrastructure.

Data Infrastructure (Utility) Plane

This plane is responsible for managing the low-level infrastructure resources to build and run the mesh, e.g., storage, compute, identity system, etc. It integrates and overlaps with the digital application infrastructure that builds and runs operational systems. For example, the data infrastructure could share the same CI/CD engine for data products that the rest of the domain team uses to develop applications. Another example is the management of common storage types such as object stores for both analytical and operational systems.

Data Product Experience Plane

This is a higher-level abstraction to build, maintain, and consume data products, built using the infrastructure plane. Its interfaces work directly with a data product. For example, it supports data product developers in managing the life cycle of a data product—building a data product, deploying a data product, etc. It also supports data product consumers in using a data product, e.g., subscribing to a data product output and reading data.

Mesh Experience Plane

This plane abstracts the mesh-level capabilities operating on multiple data products. For example, it supports operations such as searching for data products on the mesh or traversing the lineage—the link between the input and output data products—across multiple data products on the mesh.

Example

Figure 9-12 shows the bird's-eye view of the platform planes and a sample of logical interfaces they can each provide. While there is no strict layering imposed by the planes, meaning that any authorized user—program or person—can access the interfaces of any of the planes, there is a dependency between the planes.

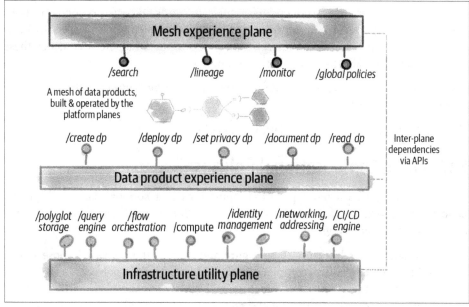

Figure 9-12. Multiple planes of the self-serve data platform

The *mesh experience plane* depends on the interfaces of the *data product plane*—as it aggregates them—and the *data product experience plane* relies on the interfaces of the lower level *infrastructure utility plane*—as it abstracts them.

> The interfaces mentioned in Figure 9-12 are only examples and are not exhaustive. For clarity, I have used an imperative language where in reality they will likely use a declarative resource-oriented design. For example, in order to be clear about the interface's intention I have used */deploy* dp to indicate the capability of "deploying a data product as one unit," while in practice one can design a declarative API, e.g., HTTP POST/data-product-deployments.

In existing platforms such as a service mesh, the concept of two separate collaborating planes, *control* and *data planes,* is borrowed from network routing. While this separation of concerns can be applied to the data mesh platform as well (one can imagine that the data products constitute the data plane, and the platform constitutes the control plane), I have intentionally stayed away from this design.

I have used the concept of *experience* to focus on *affordances* and experiences that the platform provides at different levels, at the level of individual data products and at the level of their collection as a mesh. For example, the platform offers the experience of *service discovery* and *addressability*: the ability for other data products to programmatically find other data products, by name, and address them to consume their data. This can of course then be imagined as the implementation of a control-like plane that implements a dynamic registry, addressing, routing, etc. I consider these implementation details that will follow the experience.

Essentially data mesh architecture designs the platform *by contract* of the experience it provides to its users.

Chapter 10 dives deeper into the platform capabilities.

Embedded Computational Policies

Chapter 5 introduced a few types of computations that support data mesh governance: *computational policies*, *data product standardized protocols*, and *automated tests* and *automated monitoring*.

How we model the architecture to configure and execute the policies, impose standards, and keep data products compliant with quality expectations has a direct impact on how effective the governance function will be. Architecture is the conduit for effective governance, getting the policies and standards applied to every data product on the mesh.

Data quantum is a powerful and extensible construct to embed computational policies in a distributed fashion. It can define and execute *policies as code*.

The policies expressed as code—uniformly across the mesh—are made available to each data product, which then can evaluate and apply them at the right time.

Data mesh architecture introduces a few more logical components to manage data product policies as code:

Data product sidecar
A sidecar is a process that implements the policy execution and other aspects of data products that need to be standardized across the mesh. It is provided by the platform. It deploys and runs with a data product as one unit.

Data product computational container
A way for the platform to encapsulate the execution policies as one deployable unit with the data product. For brevity I sometimes call this a *data container*.

Control port

The *control* port provides a set of standard interfaces to manage and control the data products' policies.

Figure 9-13 shows these logical components. Ideally, the platform supplies and standardizes the domain-agnostic components such as the sidecar, control port implementation, and input and output ports.

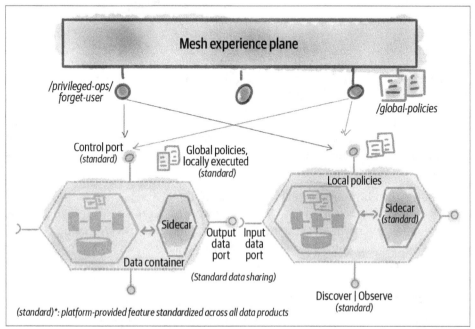

Figure 9-13. The logical architectural components of embedded computational policies

Note that each of these logical components can be implemented as one or many physical components. For example, a sidecar is an extensible and logical placeholder for different kinds of policy enforcement agents.

Data Product Sidecar

A sidecar is a logical component that decorates each data product's runtime context and executes cross-cutting concerns that are expected to be standardized across the mesh.

A sidecar is often implemented as a separate process to create a dynamic and loose coupling with a data product. It is often injected at deployment time into the data product container. Over time we may have more than one sidecar or extend the sidecar with additional cross-functional capabilities. Nevertheless, its design must be extensible to include more policies over time.

Let's look at a few ways that a sidecar can be extended to support consistency across data products.

Policy execution

One of the responsibilities of the data product sidecar is executing policies. While data mesh governance embraces diversity of data products across many dimensions such as data modeling, it does require certain policies to be applied consistently to all data products.

In a distributed architecture like data mesh, the objective is to remove any accidental points of contention and bottlenecks. For this reason, it is best to configure and execute policies within the localized execution context of each data product, independently, as opposed to a centralized gateway.

A common strategy to achieve this is injecting the policy execution into the local context. In this case, the data product sidecar accompanying each data product can evaluate and apply access control policies when an output port is accessed or apply encryption when a data product writes new data.

This strategy has been implemented in the operational systems architecture with a sidecar pattern (*https://oreil.ly/IILMb*). The sidecar is a process that augments the application behavior with cross-cutting concerns. For example, this pattern is used by a service mesh to implement routing, security, resilience, and other policies on a service's inbound and outbound calls.

Standardized protocols and interfaces

An important objective of governance is to create an interoperable ecosystem of data products. Data product interfaces that surface their data and behavior—*input data ports*, *discovery port*, *output data ports*, and *control port*—are fundamental to interoperability across data products.

The sidecar, placed in the flow of all inbound and outbound communications of data products, can offer standardized APIs. For example, the sidecar can provide a standardized API for exposing SLO metrics from each data product. The data product's implementation uses the standard implementation of these APIs to expose their unique content.

Data Product Computational Container

As you can see in Figure 9-13, quite a few structural components are bundled together to create an autonomously usable data product: the sidecar, the policy configurations, the data product transformation code, the data product data, its data sharing interfaces, etc.

Another element to make the federated governance effective is the container that wraps all the structural elements of a data product as an architecture quantum.

The data product experience plane consistently provides the implementation of the container for all data products.

Control Port

Computational governance introduces a new interface on all data products, the control port. The control port exposes a set of APIs to (1) configure policies for each data product, and (2) execute a small set of highly privileged operations to meet governance requirements.

Configure policies

The control port is the interface to configure policies that must be executed within the context of a data product. These policies can be authored and controlled locally, by the data product itself, or centrally by the mesh experience plane.

For example, the policies around data anonymization are best *authored locally* by declaring the data product's PII attributes. The domain data product owners have the most relevant information to know and configure if the data product has PII. In contrast, the definition of roles and their access controls are often authored centrally and enforced locally on each data product.

Both forms of policy authoring—*locally configured* or *centrally configured*—can coexist for a single data product.

The design of a control port must be extensible to support new types of policies as they get introduced to the mesh.

Privileged operations

The governance function needs a way to execute a small set of highly privileged operations on all data products, for example, an operation to execute GDPR's *right to be forgotten*—an individual's right to erase all their data collected by an organization.

Imagine if in the Daff examples one of the listeners decides to erase all their information preserved by Daff; the global governance function needs to have a way to flag this to all data products on the mesh. *Control ports* can expose a specific highly privileged interface that implements the *right to be forgotten* for an individual.

The platform standardizes the control port for all data products.

Recap

This chapter offered a logical architecture that made data mesh principles more concrete and closer to implementation.

At the time of writing various aspects of the logical architecture are in different stages of maturity—some are implemented and tested, and some are more experimental. Table 9-1 clarifies their state of maturity.

The components are deemed to be logical, and their physical implementation may take different forms. For example, the idea of policy execution through a sidecar might physically be implemented as an accompanying process (service) to the data quantum (dynamically coupled) or it can be implemented as a shared library (statically coupled). My hope is that the technology evolves to the point that we can get the logical architecture and its physical implementation as close to each other as possible.

Table 9-1 summarizes the logical architectural components I introduced in this chapter.

Table 9-1. Data mesh logical architectural components and their maturity

Architectural component	Description
Domain	Systems, data products, and a cross-functional team aligned to serve a business domain function and outcomes and share its analytical and operational capabilities with the wider business and customers. *This is a well-established concept.*
Domain analytical data interfaces (see "Analytical Data Interface Design" on page 149)	Standardized interfaces that discover, access, and share domain-oriented data products. *At the time of writing, the implementation of these APIs is custom or platform specific.* The proprietary platforms need to offer open interfaces to make data sharing more convenient and interoperable with other hosting platforms.
Domain operational interfaces (see "Operational Interface Design" on page 148)	APIs and applications through which a business domain shares its transactional capabilities and state with the wider organization. *This concept has mature implementations.* It is supported by de facto standards such as REST, GraphQL, gRPC, etc.
Data (product) quantum (see "Data Product as an Architecture Quantum" on page 151)	Data product implemented as an architecture quantum that encapsulates all the structural components it needs to do its job—code, data, infrastructure specifications, and policies. It is referred to in architectural discussions. It is used interchangeably with data products. *At the time of writing this is an experimental concept with custom implementations.*
Data (product) container (see "Data Product Computational Container" on page 166)	A mechanism to bundle all the structural components of a data product, deployed and run as a single unit with its sidecar. *At the time of writing this is an experimental concept with custom implementations.*
Data product sidecar (see "Data Product Sidecar" on page 165)	The accompanying process to the data product. It runs with the context of a data product container and implements cross-functional and standardized behaviors such as global policy execution. *At the time of writing this is an experimental concept with custom implementations.*

Architectural component	Description
Input data port (see "Input data ports" on page 159)	A data product's mechanisms to continuously receive data from one or multiple upstream sources. *At the time of writing this has custom implementations with existing event streaming and pipeline management technologies.*
Output data port (see "Output data ports" on page 159)	A data product's standardized APIs to continuously share data. *At the time of writing this has vendor-specific custom implementations.* *A mature implementation of the concept requires open data sharing standards with support for multiple modes of access to temporal data.*
Discovery and observability APIs (see "Data Discovery and Observability APIs" on page 159)	A data product's standard APIs to provide discoverability information—to find, address, learn, and explore a data product—and observability information such as lineage, metrics, logs, etc. *At the time of writing custom implementations of these APIs have been built.* *A mature implementation requires open standards for discoverability and observability information modeling and sharing. Some standards[a] are currently under development.*
Control port (see "Control Port" on page 167)	A data product's standard APIs to configure policies or perform highly privileged governance operations. *At the time of writing this concept is experimental.*
Platform plane (see "A Platform Plane" on page 161)	A group of self-serve platform capabilities with high functional cohesion surfaced through APIs. *This is a general concept and well established.*
Data infrastructure utility plane (see "Data Infrastructure (Utility) Plane" on page 162)	Platform plane providing low-level infrastructure resource management—compute, storage, identity, etc. *At the time of writing the services that constitute the infrastructure plane are mature and provided by many vendors with support for automated provisioning.*
Data product experience plane (see "Data Product Experience Plane" on page 162)	Platform plan providing operations on a data product. *At the time of writing, custom implementation of services constituting a data product experience plane has been implemented. No reference implementation publicly exists.*
Mesh experience plane (see "Mesh Experience Plane" on page 162)	Platform plane providing operations on the mesh of connected data products. *At the time of writing, custom implementations of some of the services constituting a mesh experience plane, such as discovery and search services, have been implemented. No reference implementation publicly exists.*

[a] OpenLineage (*https://oreil.ly/366Nj*) is an example of an observability open standard that data products can adopt.

CHAPTER 10

The Multiplane Data Platform Architecture

The real truth of existence is sealed, until after many twists and turns of the road.
—Rumi

The previous chapter introduced the multiplane data platform, a high-level component of data mesh architecture. Many questions are yet to be answered in the gap between this high-level architecture and the actual implementation. What exact technologies to buy or build? How to evaluate these technologies? How to integrate them?

This chapter walks you through a framework that you can apply to answer these questions, in the context of your organization and available technology stack. It provides examples of what constitutes a platform to help you kickstart your creative journey. It shows you the road to follow with all its twists and turns to discover what is truthful for your organization.

By now you have some familiarity with the concept of the data mesh platform and have a language to describe it.

Chapter 4 introduced the platform as:

> A collection of interoperable domain-agnostic services, tools, and APIs that enable cross-functional domain teams to produce and consume data products with lowered cognitive load and with autonomy.

Chapter 9 proposed a multiplane platform to distinguish between different classes of platform services based on their scope of operation without imposing a strict layering.

The three planes of the platform include:

Data infrastructure (utility) plane
> Atomic services to provision and manage physical resources such as storage, pipeline orchestration, compute, etc.

Data product experience plane
> Higher-level abstraction services that operate directly with a data product and enable data product producers and consumers to create, access, and secure a data product, among other operations that run on a data product.

Mesh experience plane
> Services that operate on a mesh of interconnected data products such as searching for data products and observing the data lineage across them.

All of these planes can be directly accessed by the consumers of the platform: data product developers, consumers, owners, the governance function, etc.

Figure 10-1 illustrates the platform planes and their users' personas.

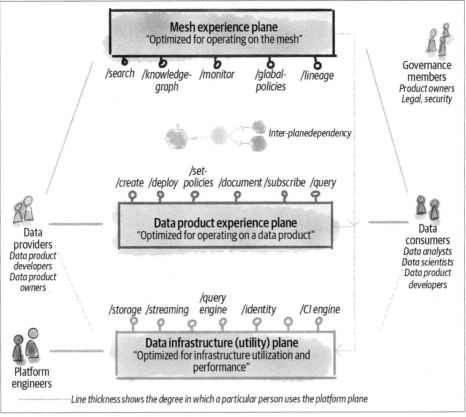

Figure 10-1. Multiplane self-serve platform and platform users

The mesh experience plane optimizes the experience of people who need to operate, govern, and query the mesh as a whole. For example, members of the governance team and data product owners interact with the services in this plane to evaluate the current state of policies, monitor the general operational health of the mesh, and search for existing data products. It is also used by data product consumers and providers in scenarios where they need to work with a collection of data products such as searching, browsing, or debugging through lineage and logs.

Data product consumers and providers mainly interact with the data product experience plane to discover, learn, understand, consume, build, and maintain data products. The data product experience plane is optimized for the delivery and consumption of data products as the unit of value exchanged between the consumers and providers. To a lesser degree they may use services in the infrastructure plane, often in cases where the data product experience plane doesn't yet provide the services they need. For example, a particular data product may want to expose its output port via a graph query language, but the data product experience plan does not support this as a packaged output port implementation, yet. In this case, the data product developers may use the infrastructure services directly to provision a graph query engine and then hook it up to their output port implementation. Ideally their graph query output port implementation gets harvested later and built back into the standard output ports supported by the platform.

Data mesh planes do not impose a strict layering in accessing their services. The data product experience plane provides a set of operations on a data product and manages the complexity of provisioning its underlying infrastructure. But it does not intend to strictly stop platform users from accessing the infrastructure plane. It's just going to make it so easy to work with data products that domain teams would not have any incentive to directly work with the infrastructure services.

While the data product experience plane optimizes for the user experience, the data infrastructure utility plane makes sure that the resources' performance and utilizations are optimized. The utility plane optimizes to get the best out of what the underlying infrastructure providers offer around storage, compute, orchestration, etc. It adapts the data product experience plane to the underlying physical hosting environment. It is organized around the underlying resources and its users, the majority of which are the platform engineers who are building the other planes. Many of the data infrastructure plane services are shared with the operational systems.

In this chapter I will take you further along the design of your data mesh platform capabilities with a user-experience-centric approach. I will go through a few key journeys of data product developers and consumers and discover what interfaces the platform exposes to streamline the journeys.

Design a Platform Driven by User Journeys

The ultimate purpose of the platform is to serve the cross-functional domain teams so they can deliver or consume data products. Hence, the best way to begin the design of the platform is to understand the main journeys of your platform users and evaluate how you can make it easy for them to complete their journeys successfully using the platform.

There are a few main high-level personas in the data mesh ecosystem:

Data product developers
> This persona covers the role of a data product developer, considering a wide spectrum of skill sets—from generalist developers with general programming skills to specialist data engineers who are well-versed in the existing analytical data processing technologies.

Data product consumers
> This persona covers multiple roles that have one thing in common: they need access and use data to do their job. Their job might be:

> - Training or inferring ML models, as data scientists
> - Developing reports and dashboards, as data analysts
> - Developing new data products that consume data from existing ones, as data product developers
> - Building data-driven services and applications in the operational domain, as an application developer

> This is quite a wide range, and platform interfaces and services can vary depending on the exact role.

Data product owners
> Data product owners are responsible for delivering and evangelizing successful data products for their specific domains. The success of the data products depends on their adoption and value delivery, as well as conformance to the wider policies of the mesh and their interoperability with other data products. They use the platform to keep the pulse of their data products.

Data governance members
> Since data governance is founded on a federated structure, there is no one specific data governance role. Nonetheless, the members of the governance team have a collective set of responsibilities to assure the optimal and secure operation of the mesh as a whole. There are various roles within the governance group such as subject matter experts on security and legal issues, as well as data product owners with specific accountabilities. The platform facilitates their collective journey as well as the individual roles.

Data platform product owner

The data platform planes and their services are products whose users play all the other roles mentioned earlier. The data platform product owner is responsible for delivering the platform services as a product, with the best user experience. Based on an understanding of the platform users' needs and constraints, the data platform product owner prioritizes the services that the platform offers.

Data platform developer

The platform developers build and operate the data platform as well as use it. Data platform developers who work on the data product experience plane services are users of the utility plane services. Hence, their skillset and journey are important to the design of the utility plane services.

In this chapter I demonstrate how to approach the platform's design using two example roles: a *data product developer* as well as a *data scientist as a data product consumer*.

Data Product Developer Journey

One of the key journeys of a data product developer is to create and operate a data product. This is an end-to-end and long-term responsibility that embraces the continuous delivery principle (*https://oreil.ly/Z5lq2*) of "everyone is responsible." Building and operating a data product is not someone else's problem.

Figure 10-2 shows the high-level phases of the data product creation journey. These stages are iterative with continuous feedback loops. For simplicity of demonstration, I have drawn the journey as a linear succession of stages. The journey begins with the activities around the inception of a data product such as ideation and exploration of sources. It continues to the actual build and delivery of the data product, followed by monitoring it, continuously evolving it, and optionally retiring it.

A data product development journey interacts with other journeys. In the case of a source-aligned data product that consumes data from an operational system, the data product developers work closely with the source application developers. They co-design and implement how the application will share its operational data as an input to the data product. Note that these people belong to the same domain team. For example, development of the **play events** data product requires close collaboration with the **player** application that generates the raw data.

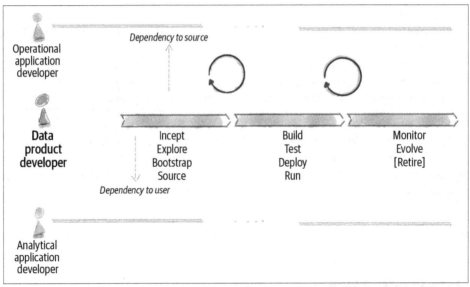

Figure 10-2. High-level example of the data product development journey

Similarly, if the data product is built for a known analytical application, in the case of a consumer-aligned data product, there is a collaboration that happens early between the data product developers and the analytical application developers. Data product developers need to understand the goals of the analytical application and its needs in terms of data fields and the guarantees that the data product must support. For example at Daff, an ML-powered **playlist recommendation** application requires data from the **music profiles** data product. The **music profiles** data product developers need to work closely with the **playlist recommendation** application team to align on the expected classifications of the profile.

Let's look at the high-level stages of data product development and how the platform interfaces are designed to support them (Figure 10-3).

The notation and phrasing of the interfaces are not representative of a final implementation. The imperative language is chosen to focus on the functionality, while in reality the declarative forms of APIs are more desirable. For example, the */deploy* interface is very likely implemented as */deployments*, the declarative resources for the deployed data products.

The interfaces are exemplary and demonstrate the semantics of the operation and not the actual syntax or mechanism of the interface, e.g., CMD, UI, API, etc.

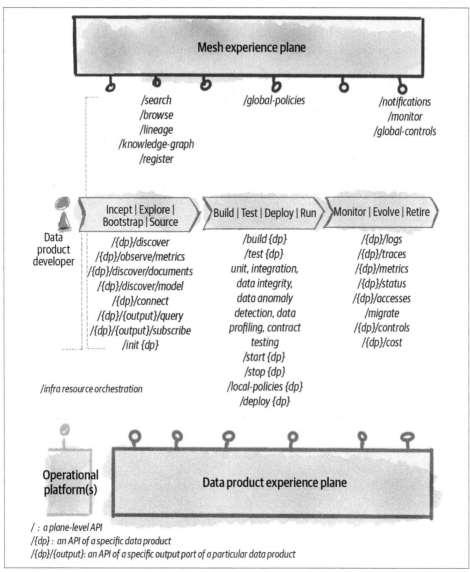

Figure 10-3. High-level example of the data product development journey using the platform

Incept, Explore, Bootstrap, and Source

Data products often come to exist because we discover one or many potential analytical use cases that need their data. While data products, particularly source-aligned ones, have many diverse use cases, some beyond our imagination today, we still need to start the inception—the creation—of them from a real use case that demonstrates the value of the data product in a real-world context. Consumer-aligned data products directly serve one or multiple specific use cases. The inception of a consumer-aligned data product always involves direct collaboration with its consumers.

During the inception of a data product, the developer is in an *exploratory* phase looking for potential sources for the data product. The source can be discovered as an upstream data product, an external system (to the organization), or an operational system (in the organization). During the exploration, the developer may study the upstream source's *discovery* information, to evaluate the source's suitability, data guarantees, documentation, data profiling, existing users, etc.

Once potential *sources* are nominated, the developer can quickly *bootstrap* a *hello world* data product. The platform provisions the necessary infrastructure. It enables the data product developer to connect to the sources and consume data—either in the form of *synthesized data*, obfuscated, or the actual data. At this point the developer has all the necessary resources to start experimenting with the source data and the data product's transformation logic.

These steps constitute the exploratory steps of incepting a data product. Rapid discovery, access to source output data, quick scaffolding of a data product, and provisioning of infrastructure are all the necessary pieces of the inception and bootstrapping phase.

For example, the **playlist** team plans to generate new playlists for holiday seasons across different countries. They need data about regional holidays and their sentiment, as well as labeled music profiles that associate different tracks with their relevant holiday. They start by searching for existing data products on the mesh with similar information. They find a few sources for music profiling and then connect to those data products and start playing with the data to assess their completeness and relevance. They quickly create a simple holiday playlist data product to see what playlists they can generate from the simplest implementation of music holiday profiling.

Table 10-1 provides a summary of platform APIs used during this phase.

Table 10-1. Example interfaces provided by the platform planes in support of a data product inception

Development phase	Platform Plane	Platform interface	Platform interface description
Incept | Explore	Mesh experience	*/search*	Search the mesh of existing data products to find suitable sources. The search can be based on various parameters such as source operational systems, domains, and types of data.
	Mesh experience	*/knowledge-graph*	Browse the mesh of related data products' semantic models. Traverse their semantic relationship to identify the desired sources of data. Example: the playlist team can browse the semantic relationship between the holiday-related music profilings they have found.
	Mesh experience	*/lineage*	Traverse the lineage of input-output data between different data products on the mesh to identify the desired sources based on the origin of the data and the transformations the data has gone through. Example: the playlist team can look at how the existing music holiday profiling is created and trace back what its sources are and what transformation has led to the classifications. This is to evaluate the suitability of the existing music holiday profiling.
Bootstrap | Source	Data product experience	*/{dp}/discover*	Once a source is identified, access all the data product discoverability information such as documentation, data model, available output ports, etc.
	Data product experience	*/{dp}/observe*	Once a source is identified, access the data product's guarantees and metrics —real-time—such as how often the data is being released, the last release date, data quality metrics, etc. Example: Once the playlist team finds a promising *holiday music profiling*, they need to evaluate how often this data is refreshed and what its completeness compared to all the music available on the platform is. This assessment gives them more trust in the data.
	Data product experience	*/init*	To get started with experimenting with the source data, this API bootstraps a barebones data product with enough of the infrastructure available to connect to the sources, access their data, run transformation on the data, and serve the output in a single access mode for verification. The scaffolding of a data product allocates the continuous delivery pipeline, early environments, provisioning of data processing clusters, and accounts to run and access infrastructure resources for the data product. This marks the beginning of the data product life cycle.
	Mesh experience	*/register*	During the initialization of a new data product, it's automatically registered with the mesh. It's given a unique global identifier and address and makes the data product visible to the mesh and the governance process.
	Data product experience	*/connect*	Once the source is discovered, the data product gets access to the source by connecting to it. This step validates the access control policies governing the source. This might trigger a request for permission to get access to the data product.

Development phase	Platform Plane	Platform interface	Platform interface description
Bootstrap | Source (*continued*)	Data product experience	/{dp}/ {output}/ query /{dp}/ {output}/ subscribe	Read data from a particular output port of the source data product, either in a pull-based querying model or subscribing to changes.

Build, Test, Deploy, and Run

Data product developers have an end-to-end responsibility of building, testing, deploying, and operating their data products. The stage I have simply called "build, test, deploy, and run" is a continuous and iterative series of activities that data product developers perform to deliver all the necessary components of a successful data product. This data product is *autonomously discoverable, understandable, trustworthy, addressable, interoperable and composable, secure, natively accessible,* and *valuable on its own* (see "Baseline Usability Attributes of a Data Product" on page 33).

Table 10-2 lists the high-level interfaces to deliver a data product.

Table 10-2. Example interfaces provided by the platform planes in support of data product development

Development phase	Platform plane	Platform interface	Platform interface description
Build	Data product experience	/build	Compile, validate, and compose all the components of a data product into a deployable artifact that can be used to run the data product in various deployment environments. See Table 10-3 for the data infrastructure plane interfaces used during this phase.
Test	Data product experience	/test	Test various aspects of a data product. Test the functionality of data transformation, the integrity of the output data, expectations of the data versioning and upgrade process, expectations of the data profile (its expected statistical characteristics), test bias, etc. Testing capabilities are offered in different deployment environments.
Deploy	Data product experience	/deploy	Deploy the built revision of a data product to an environment, including the developer's local machine, a development sandbox on the target hosting environment (e.g., a specific cloud provider), and pre-production or production environments.
Run	Data product experience	/start /stop	Run or stop running the data product instance in a particular environment.
Build/Test/ Deploy/Run	Data product experience	/local-policies	One of the main components of a data product is the policies that govern its data and function. Policies include encryption, access, retention, locality, privacy, etc. The platform facilitates configuration and authoring of these policies locally, during the development of a data product, their validation during test, and their execution during access to data.

Development phase	Platform plane	Platform interface	Platform interface description
Build/Test/ Deploy/Run	Mesh experience	/global-policies	In many organizations policies that govern a data product are authored by the global (federated) governance team. Hence, the platform enables authoring of the global policies and application of these policies by all data products.

Let's look more closely at what is involved at the data infrastructure plane.

Building a data product has many parts to it. A data product developer must configure or code all of these parts to implement an autonomous data product. The platform is a key enabler in lowering the cost and effort required to code or configure each of these components.

Figure 10-4 maps the build and execution of different components of a data product to the lower-level platform interfaces, *infrastructure plane* APIs. A data product developer, in the majority of the cases, simply interacts with the data product experience plane: building, deploying, and testing a single data quantum. The data product experience plane delegates the implementation of the data product components to the data infrastructure plane.

The developers must understand, code, and configure different aspects and components of a data product given the technologies that the data infrastructure plane offers. For example, the choice of how to code the *transformation* aspect of a data product depends on what computation engines the data infrastructure plane supports.[1] Nevertheless, data product developers focus on coding the transformation, using the technology made available to them, and leave it to the data product experience plane to manage the build, deployment, and execution of transformation along with all the other components. In this process, the data product experience plane delegates the details of transformation execution to the data infrastructure plane.

---

[1] The data infrastructure plane, for instance, may offer Apache Spark or Apache Beam tasks orchestrated with Prefect or Serverless functions.

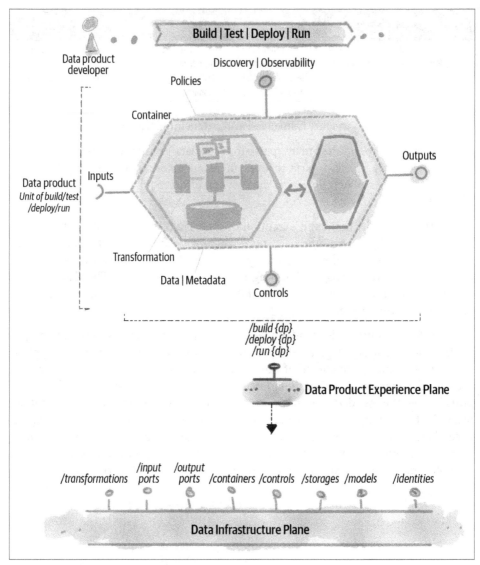

Figure 10-4. Example of data infrastructure plane interfaces to support data product delivery

Table 10-3 lists some of the data infrastructure plane capabilities utilized during the development of a data product.

Table 10-3. Example of data infrastructure plane interfaces that support data product experience plane APIs

Platform interface	Platform interface description
/input-ports	Provides different mechanisms for consuming data according to the design of data products, e.g., event streaming input, remote database queries, file read, etc. It triggers executing the transformation when data is available. The input port mechanisms keep track of consumption progress as new data becomes available.
/output-ports	Provides different mechanisms for serving data, according to the modes of access data product offers, e.g., streams, files, tables, etc.
/transformations	Provides different execution mechanisms for running all the computation necessary to transform data.
/containers	Managing the life cycle of data products and all its required infrastructure resources, as an autonomous unit.
/controls	Provides a wide range of technologies to enable configuration and execution of diverse and evolving policies such as access control, encryption, privacy, retention, locality, as code.
/storage	Input ports, output ports, and transformation all require access to permanent and temporary storage for data and their metadata (SLOs, schemas, etc.) The platform must supply access to different types of storage (blob, relational, graph, time series, etc.) and all the operational capabilities such as failover, recovery, backup, and restore.
/models	The mechanisms to describe, share, and link semantic and syntax schema models of the data.
/identities	The mechanism to identify and address a data product uniquely on the mesh.

Maintain, Evolve, and Retire

Maintenance and *evolution* of a data product involves continuous change to the data product: improving its transformation logic, evolving its data model, supporting new modes of access to its data, and enrichment of its policies. The changes to data products result in continuous iterations of *build, test, deploy, and run* ("Build, Test, Deploy, Run" on page 188), while maintaining an uninterrupted processing and sharing of data.

The platform must reduce the overhead of *how* a data product is maintained to *what* is to be maintained. For example, if the result of a new build is a change to the semantic and schema, the data product developer simply focuses on changes to the data model, and the transformation of data based on the new model. The complexity of how different versions of schemas (semantic and syntax) are managed, associated with the data, and accessed by the consumer is managed by the platform.

In some cases, the evolution of a data product has no impact on its underlying infrastructure resources. For example, a bug fix to the transformation code simply requires rebuilding and redeploying the data product and fixing the generated data. In other cases, the evolution impacts the underlying resources. For example, migrating a data product to a new environment in the case of switching storage vendors requires reallocating the storage resources and migrating the data product's underlying data.

Monitoring the operational health of each data product, and the mesh as a whole, is another key capability that the platform offers during this phase. The operational excellence of the mesh depends on monitoring various aspects of each data product: monitoring its performance, reliability, SLOs, effectiveness of its computational policies, and operational cost based on resource usage. In addition to monitoring individual data products, the mesh experience plane must gather insights and monitor the state of the mesh as a whole. For example, detect and alarm when *master data products* are detected—data products that aggregate data from too many sources and become a bottleneck as they are used by many.

During the lifetime of a data product, there will be times when mesh-level administrative controls must be invoked. For example, the right to be forgotten can be triggered through the mesh-level *global controls*, delegated to every single data product's *control* interface, and implemented through the data eviction function of their underlying storage.

Will a data product ever cease to exist? I can think of two scenarios that it would. A data product can retire in the case of migration to a new data product or in the case that all of the data records it has ever generated must be discarded and no new record is ever going to be generated. In both cases the platform enables data product developers to gracefully retire the data product so its downstream consumers can either migrate to the new source over time or themselves retire. As long as someone is using the past data, the data quantum continues to exist, though it may not execute any further transformation nor produce any new data. A dormant data product will continue to serve its old data and enforce its policies, while a fully retired data product is simply extinct.

Table 10-4 shows a few of the platform interfaces to support the maintenance, evolution, and retirement phases of data product development.

Table 10-4. Example of data platform interfaces to support data product maintenance

Platform plane	Platform interface	Platform interface description
Data product experience	/{dp}/status	Checking the status of a data product.
Data product experience	/{dp}/logs /{dp}/traces /{dp}/metrics	The mechanism for a data product to emit its runtime observability information such as logs, traces, and metrics, according to the design of the data quantum's observability ("Observability Design" on page 264). The mesh layer monitoring services utilize the data provided by these mechanisms.
Data product experience	/{dp}/accesses	The logs of all accesses to the data product.
Data product experience plane	/{dp}/controls	Ability to invoke high-privileged administrative controls such as right to be forgotten on a particular data quantum.

Platform plane	Platform interface	Platform interface description
Data product experience	/{dp}/cost	Tracking the operational cost of a data product. This can be calculated based on the resource allocation and usage.
Data product experience	/migrate	Ability to migrate a data product to a new environment. Updating the data product revision is simply a function of *build* and *deploy*.
Mesh experience	/monitor	Multiple monitoring abilities at the mesh level, logs, status, compliance, etc.
Mesh experience	/notifications	Notification and alerting in response to detected anomalies of the mesh.
Mesh experience	/global-controls	Ability to invoke high-privileged administrative controls such as right to be forgotten on a collection of data products on the mesh.

Now let's move our attention to the data consumer journey and see how platform interfaces may evolve to support such a persona.

Data Product Consumer Journey

The persona of a data consumer represents a wide range of users, with various skill sets and responsibilities. In this section, I focus on an example data scientist persona who is consuming existing data products to train an ML model and then is deploying the ML model as a data product to make inferences and generate new data. For example, Daff uses an ML model to produce a curated playlist every Monday for all of its listeners to start their week. The ML recommendation model that generates the Monday playlists is trained using data from existing data products such as **listener profiles**, **listener play events**, their recent reactions to the songs they have liked or haven't, and the **playlists** of what they have listened to recently.[2]

Once the ML model is trained, it is deployed as a data product, **monday playlists**.

If you recall from Chapter 7 data mesh creates a tightly integrated operational and analytical plane. It interconnects domain-oriented (micro)services and data products. Despite a tight integration and feedback loop between the two planes, data mesh continues to respect the differences of the responsibility and characteristics of each plane, i.e., microservices respond to online requests or events to run the business, and data products curtate, transform, and share temporal data for downstream analytical usage such as training machine learning models or generating insights. Despite the attempt in clarifying the boundary between the entities of the two planes, ML models blur this boundary.

ML models can belong to either plane. For example, an ML model can be deployed as a microservice to make inferences online as the end user makes requests. For example, during the registration of a new listener, given the information provided by

---

2 This example is inspired by the Discover Weekly (*https://oreil.ly/4h8m4*) feature of Spotify, which I personally look forward to every Monday.

the listener, a classifier ML model is called to augment the user's information with their profile classification. Alternatively, an ML model can be deployed as the transformation logic of a data product. For example, the playlist recommender ML model is deployed as a data product that makes inferences every Monday and generates new playlists. This data then can be fed into the operational service that displays the playlists to the listener. Figure 10-5 shows this example.

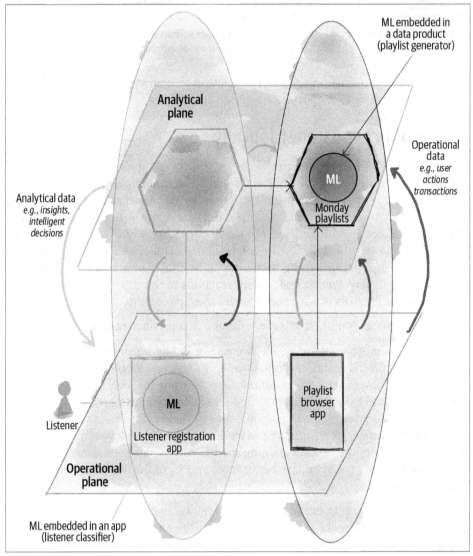

Figure 10-5. Example of a bimodal deployment of ML models

In this section, I explore the data scientist's journey for an ML model that gets deployed as a data product to demonstrate the overlap of this journey with data mesh platform capabilities. Figure 10-6 demonstrates a high-level journey to continuously deliver an ML model as a data product. This value stream follows the practice of *continuous delivery for machine learning* (CD4ML (*https://oreil.ly/fQh2I*)) to continuously hypothesize, train, deploy, monitor, and improve the model in rapid feedback loops with a repeatable process.[3]

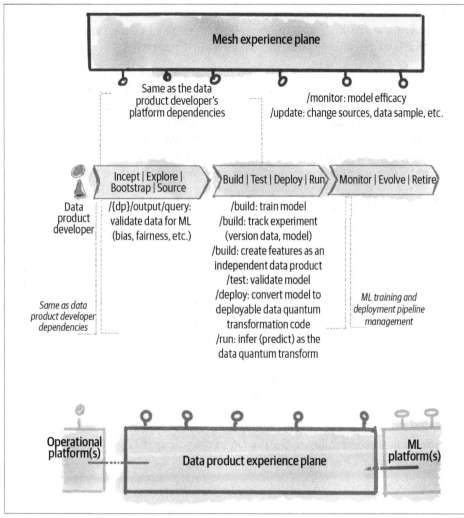

Figure 10-6. Example ML model development journey

---

3 This process is also known as MLOps; however, I use the CD4ML notation since it overlays and integrates closely with continuous delivery of software and data products.

From the data platform perspective, this journey is very similar to the "Data Product Developer Journey" on page 175 we explored earlier. There are some differences that I call out next.

Incept, Explore, Bootstrap, Source

In this example, ML model developers start their journey with the inception of the data product that will ultimately embed in their model. The inception of this data product includes the formulation of the hypothesis for an intelligent action or decision based on the existing data. For example, is it possible to curate and recommend a playlist that is played and replayed (loved) by many listeners?

To start the exploration to validate the hypothesis, the ML model developers explore and search existing data products and evaluate the sources using their discoverability APIs as well as through sampling output ports data. During this phase, the platform interfaces remain the same as what I presented earlier. The main difference here is perhaps the type of discoverability information the data scientists care about. They must evaluate whether there is bias in the data and fairness of the data. This can be evaluated by sampling and profiling the source data product output port.

Build, Test, Deploy, Run

The journey continues to build the model and train it using the upstream data product output ports. During the training, the model developer may decide that the training dataset requires change, modifying the upstream data product data into *features*. For example, the training features may only include a subset of **playlists** information joined with **song profiles**. In this case, the data transformation pipeline to generate features becomes itself a data product. For example, **monday playlist features** becomes a data product that is developed similarly to any other one.

During this phase the model developers need to keep track of the data that results in a particular revision of the model. The versioning of the source (training and test) data can use the *processing time* parameter exposed by all data products as the revision of the data—a timestamp that is unique to each state of data and indicates when a data was processed and published. This removes the need to keep a copy of the data[4] for future reuse and repeatability of the model, as the source data product always allows retrieving past data. Chapter 12 will elaborate on this.

---

4 Lack of native versioning of analytical data, today, demands usage of tools such as DVC (*https://dvc.org*) to version data used to train ML models.

The process of model training and tracking can be handled by an ML platform—a platform of technologies and tools that satisfy the unique needs of ML model training pipelines. These services work closely and integrate with the data platform.

During deployment, the model needs to be packaged into a format that can run as the transformation code of the **monday playlists** data product.[5] During the model run, the infrastructure plane transformation engine can handle the unique needs of executing ML models such as execution on targeted hardware—GPUs or TPUs (*https://oreil.ly/38Yuv*).

Maintain, Evolve, and Retire

Similar to other data products, developers continue to monitor the performance of the model and make sure the output data, the playlists, is created as expected.

One of the unique needs of model monitoring is observing the efficacy of the models and monitoring actions that the listeners take. For example, do new revisions of the model result in an increase in duration of listening to the playlist, more replays, and more listeners? Monitoring such parameters may utilize the operational plane capability of monitoring metrics. In this case, the **player** application can provide these metrics.

Recap

If you take away one thing from this chapter, I wish it to be this: there is no single entity such as a platform. There are APIs, services, SDKs, and libraries that each satisfy a step in the journey of the platform users. A platform user journey, whether the user is a data product developer or a consumer, is never isolated to the data mesh platform services. They often cross boundaries with APIs that serve the operational systems—e.g., using streaming capabilities to consume data from a microservice—or cross boundaries with ML model training capabilities such as experiment tracking or utilization of GPUs. Hence, view your platform as a set of well-integrated services that are there to satisfy a seamless experience for their users.

The second point I'd like you to take away is to respect the separation of planes so that you can choose to optimize both for the human experience and machine efficiency. For example, use the data product experience plane to optimize the user experience at the logical level of interacting with a single unit of a *data quantum*. Create a separate data infrastructure plane to optimize for the machine, e.g., separation of compute from storage to handle independent scaling of each or co-locality of all data to reduce data movement. The lower plane optimization decisions should not impair the developer experience, and vice versa.

---

5 For example, Python models are serialized into a pickle (*https://oreil.ly/M0IXy*) binary file format.

I'd like to leave you with one last point in the first step in your path to creating a data mesh platform: start with discovering and designing an optimized journey for roles such as data product developer and data product consumer, with minimal friction and maximum delight and engagement. Once you have done that, feel free to continue your search to find the right tools for various stages of their journey.

How to Design the Data Product Architecture

The *data product* is a central concept to data mesh. Architecturally, it is designed as an *architecture quantum* and called a *data quantum*. A data quantum encapsulates and implements all the necessary behavior and structural components to process and share data as a product (Chapter 3). It builds and runs with autonomy yet connects to other data quanta on the mesh. Interconnection of data quanta creates the symmetric and scale-out architecture of data mesh.

All data products share a set of common properties; e.g., they consume data from upstream sources, transform data, serve data, govern data, etc. This part of the book discusses an opinionated way of designing each of these properties.

I have organized this part of the book around the individual *affordances*[1] of a data product—the relationship between properties of a data product and how people (or systems) can interact with them. For example, how data mesh users discover, read, or manage the life cycle of data products, directly interacting with one.

Chapter 11, "Design a Data Product by Affordances", summarizes the approach to the design of a data product. Chapter 12, "Design Consuming, Transforming, and Serving Data", discusses how data products afford consuming, transforming, and serving data for a diverse set of users—programs and people. It discusses a set of necessary design constraints to make a distributed system of data sharing work.

---

1 Affordances are defined by Don Norman in his book *The Design of Everyday Things*.

Chapter 13, "Design Discovering, Understanding, and Composing Data", discusses how a data product affords its users to discover, understand, and trust it. It introduces how a data product affords data composability so that data users can create new types of aggregated data in a decentralized fashion. Chapter 14, "Design Managing, Governing, and Observing Data", touches on the remaining properties of a data product in how it affords data users to govern it, observe it, and manage its life cycle.

The objective of Part IV is to help you identify design techniques that are compatible with the vision of data mesh and separate them from those that are not. It is not attempting to be a handbook of how to implement a data product. The discussion of each affordance will cover what it is, why it is important, and what the characteristics of a data mesh approach to it are.

Similar to Part III, the discussions here will stay technology agnostic, though the design characteristics I introduce for each affordance will guide you in choosing a technology that is compatible with data mesh. For example, the principle of *dump pipes and smart filters*, equivalent to *dumb pipes and smart endpoints (https://oreil.ly/ x6Cny)* for data products, will lead you to choose a technology that does not impose data processing pipelines to control the flow of data between data products.

First, let's look at the overall approach to the design of a data product as an architecture quantum.

Design a Data Product by Affordances

> *The misconception which has haunted philosophic literature throughout the centuries is the notion of "independent existence." There is no such mode of existence; every entity is to be understood in terms of the way it is interwoven with the rest of the universe.*
> —Alfred North Whitehead

The design of the data product as an architecture quantum ("Data Product as an Architecture Quantum" on page 151) is arguably the most important aspect of the data mesh architecture. It is element of architecture that is unique to data mesh. It builds upon prior approaches and learnings and yet departs from them.

In this part of the book, I use the shorthand of *data quantum* when the focus of the conversation is on the design of a data product in the context of architecture, and I use that interchangeably with data product.

As a distributed scale-out architecture, data mesh designs its data products as self-contained, autonomous, and coequal nodes, *data quantum*, on the mesh. Each data product is designed to be self-sufficient and affords its users and developers with all the capabilities they need to do their job: discover them, understand them, use them, build them, govern them, and debug them. That is why I have dedicated a part of the book on how to approach the design of a self-sufficient data product.

Fundamentals of Software Architecture defines the constituents of architecture as:

Structure
The components and their interfaces, interactions, and integrations

Characteristics
Abilities such as extensibility, reliability, etc.

Decisions
Hard-and-fast rules that govern the design

Principles
　　Guidelines that influence decisions

In addition to these, I will introduce and focus on another element: *affordances*—the relationship between interfaces of data products and how people (or systems) can interact with them, for example, how a data product affords its users (programs) to connect to it, subscribe to its outputs, and continuously receive data from it. Another example is how data users—people or programs—can discover a data product, understand it, and explore its data.

I call this approach to the design of data product architecture *design by affordances*.

Reading through this chapter guides you through a way of designing a data product architecture that is compatible with data mesh thinking. My hope is that you take this approach and apply it to the design of data products, beyond the aspects I introduce in this part of the book. This is a way of thinking and a method to model an architecture you can take and contextualize to your unique situation.

I will show you the ropes, and it's you who will raise the sails and navigate the waters.

Data Product Affordances

In his book *The Design of Everyday Things*, Don Norman (*https://oreil.ly/cotSU*), the father of cognitive engineering, calls out *affordances* as one of the five fundamental principles of interactions. He describes:

> The term affordance refers to the relationship between a physical object and a person (or for that matter, any interacting agent, whether animal or human, or even machines and robots).

> An affordance is a relationship between the properties of an object and the capabilities of the agent that determine just how the object could possibly be used. A chair affords ("is for") support and, therefore, affords sitting. Most chairs can also be carried by a single person (they afford lifting), but some can only be lifted by a strong person or by a team of people. If young or relatively weak people cannot lift a chair, then for these people, the chair does not have that affordance, it does not afford lifting.

> The presence of an affordance is jointly determined by the qualities of the object and the abilities of the agent that is interacting. This relational definition of affordance gives considerable difficulty to many people. We are used to thinking that properties are associated with objects. But affordance is not a property. An affordance is a relationship. Whether an affordance exists depends upon the properties of both the object and the agent.

Why does this matter in the design of data product interfaces and capabilities? It is because for each of the data product properties, e.g., serve bitemporal data ("Bitemporal data" on page 208), there is an assumption made about who or what will be interacting with the property and what they are capable of, e.g., agents that are time-aware. These assumptions and constraints defined by the affordance are necessary to get a decentralized system to work with integrity and reliability. You are essentially designing a data product by inspecting the relationship of its properties and capabilities with other agents in the data mesh ecosystem—data providers, consumers, owners, governance, and other components such as services of the data platform and other data products.

For the most part you can think of each of these affordances as properties of a data product. But keep in mind who and what agents the property affords and who it doesn't.

Figure 11-1 lists affordances for a data product to *autonomously* transform and serve meaningful, understandable, trustworthy data that can be connected to other data in the ecosystem. The word *autonomously* here means that its life cycle can be managed independently without interruption to other data products. It has all the structural components to do its job. Its dependencies to other data products or platform services are through APIs with explicit contracts, creating loose coupling.

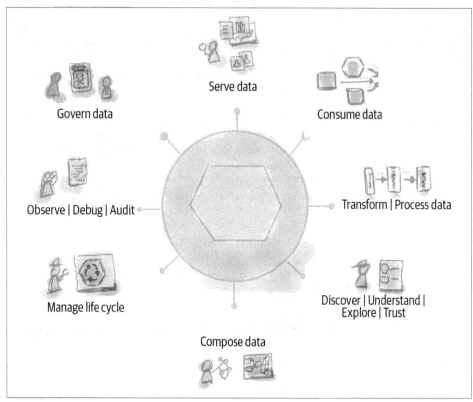

Figure 11-1. Data product affordances

The phrase *data product user* in the following context refers to all the interactive agents with a data product in a data product ecosystem. That includes people such as data product developers, data product owners, data product consumers, governance groups, etc., as well as systems such as other data products and services of the multiplane data platform.

Table 11-1 summarizes each of the affordances and gives you a reference to the chapter that discusses them further.

Table 11-1. Data product affordances

Data product affordance	Description
Serve Data ("Serve Data" on page 201 in Chapter 12)	The data product shares immutable and bitemporal data, available through clearly defined read-only interfaces supporting multiple modes of access. The data product affords a diverse set of data product users to access data for training machine learning models, generating reports, data analysis and exploration, and building data-intensive applications. It does not afford transactional and operational applications that require updating or deleting data to maintain their current state.
Consume Data ("Consume Data" on page 217 in Chapter 12)	The data product consumes data from upstream sources of a variety of types. The data product affords consuming data from its collaborating operational application, other data products, or external systems. The data product only affords consuming data from the sources it identifies and configures through the platform. It does not afford consuming data from sources it does not identify and configure.
Transform Data ("Transform Data" on page 226 in Chapter 12)	The data product processes and transforms input data into new data that it then serves. The data product affords data product developers with multiple modes of transformation computation. The transformation can be program code, a machine learning model, or a complex query running inference. The transformation can generate new data or remodel or improve the quality of input data.
Discover | Understand | Explore | Trust ("Discover, Understand, Trust, and Explore" on page 233 in Chapter 13)	The data product serves APIs and information that affords data product users to discover, explore, understand, and trust it.
Compose Data ("Compose Data" on page 244 in Chapter 13)	The data product affords data product users to compose, correlate, and join its data with other data products. The data quantum affords programmatic data composability by performing set (table or graph) operations computationally. The data product does not afford data composability to systems that demand a single and tightly coupled data schema (e.g., SQL schema) shared across multiple data products.
Manage Life Cycle ("Manage the Life Cycle" on page 255 in Chapter 14)	The data product affords data product users to manage its life cycle. It provides a set of build-time and runtime configuration and code so that data product developers can build, provision, and maintain it.

Data product affordance	Description
Observe | Debug | Audit ("Observe, Debug, and Audit" on page 262 in Chapter 14)	The data product affords data product users to monitor its behavior, debug its issues, and audit it. It provides programmatic APIs to provide the necessary information such as data processing logs, lineage, runtime metrics, and access logs.
Govern ("Govern Data" on page 258 in Chapter 14)	The data product affords data users (governance group, data product developers) and the mesh experience plane (administrative and policy controls) a set of APIs and computational policies to self-govern its data. It enables the build-time configuration of its governing policies and runtime execution of them at the point of access to data, read or write. For example, it maintains data security by controlling access to its data and protects privacy and confidentiality through encryption.

Data Product Architecture Characteristics

There are a common set of architecture characteristics that the design of all data products share. You can assess the design of your data products against these characteristics to assure the data mesh objective of "getting value from data at scale" is met:

Design for change

Changing data and its model is a must-have design characteristic of a data product. If you recall from earlier chapters, *responding gracefully to change* is an objective of data mesh and hence a characteristic supported by all data products.

For example, the design decision to front various aspects of a data product with APIs makes change more manageable. Another example, adding time as an attribute of many aspects of a data product, the snapshots of data, the snapshots of a data model, the time of SLOs, etc., makes handling the change of these parameters easier. By default, all data product artifacts and data are versioned using the notion of time.

Design for extension can be considered a subset of design for change characteristics. Data product capabilities evolve and mature over time. For example, on day one a data product may only support a single mode of access through files, and later evolve to support events and tables. This means data products have an extensible design. Loosely coupled components such as collaborating sidecars or agents improve extensibility. They can be extended with new capabilities and injected into the data product at deploy or runtime, while statically linked or shared libraries are less easily extensible as they require a rebuild of data products to become available.

Design for scale

The design of the data product must result in a scale-out mesh. The mesh should scale out while maintaining its agility to change and speed of access to data as more data products are added, as the number of sources of data increases, and as the diversity and the number of data users grow.

Any centralized point of synchronization, coordination, or access can be detrimental to this trade-off. That is why a data product is autonomous.

For example, the design decision to enforce access control or other policies in the execution context of a data product—i.e., the sidecar—is a scale-out architectural decision. Alternatively, using a central gateway in between data users and data products to control access becomes a chokepoint over time.

Design for value
The design of a data product must put delivering value to its consumers with the least amount of friction at its heart. While this might seem rather obvious and perhaps redundant, the tale of software engineering is littered with clever designs that are hardly helpful to delivering value.

The design of data product interfaces should focus on sharing easily understandable, trustworthy, and secure data with users, with the least number of steps, checks, and interventions. For example, while data bitemporality is necessary to maintain and reason about integrity and trust in data in a distributed system, many users don't care about time in their day-to-day usage. So while the data product maintains bitemporality internally, it may give shortcut APIs that reduce the notion of time, assuming "now" or "latest" by default.

Design Influenced by the Simplicity of Complex Adaptive Systems

An architecture like data mesh shares properties with complex adaptive systems (*https://oreil.ly/XUaMQ*). It is made up of a network of autonomous self-organizing agents with dynamic interconnectivity. Taking inspiration from complex adaptive systems impacts the architectural designs in two ways.

Emergent Behavior from Simple Local Rules

First, we can take inspiration from the fact that powerful group behaviors emerge from a simple and small set of rules governing every agent, locally. For example, a beautifully synchronized flock of thousands of starlings in the autumn sky emerges from every starling bird following three simple rules:[1] separation (don't run into close-by flockmates), alignment (follow the close-by lead flockmates), and cohesion (move at a similar speed as the neighboring flockmates). The birds don't need a global orchestrator or knowledge of the whole.

---

1 Craig Reynolds, "Flocks, Herds and Schools: A Distributed Behavioral Model," *SIGGRAPH '87: Proceedings of the 14th Annual Conference on Computer Graphics and Interactive Techniques,* Association for Computing Machinery, pp. 25–34, CiteSeerX 10.1.1.103.7187. (1987)

Similarly, powerful group behaviors emerge from the mesh by defining a small set of simple characteristics and behavioral rules for each data product. For example, each data product defines its input ports (where and how it consumes input data from its immediate upstream sources) and defines its output ports (what data and how it shares its output data). A data product can define its input ports to connect to other upstream data products' output ports.

The input ports and output ports define a *data flow* configuration, set locally by each data product. From this local data flow rule emerges a mesh-level graph of lineage—the graph of data flow across the mesh between all data products.

In this case, there is no centralized definition of the data flow graph or lineage. No data product has knowledge of the whole mesh. There is no central orchestrator of the pipelines, aware of a global configuration. This is different from the existing data pipelines design, when a central orchestrator is working with a central repository of all pipeline configurations.

Other examples of emergent mesh-level properties form simple and local data-product-level rules. These include a global knowledge graph emergent from the local definition of data product semantics and their relationship to their immediate nodes and the mesh-level runtime performance based on local metrics and logs provided by each data product with correlation identifiers (*https://oreil.ly/SO6JU*).

The emergent properties and behaviors can be surfaced through the data platform's *mesh experience plane* services.

No Central Orchestrator

Data mesh, like complex adaptive systems, doesn't need a central controlling architectural element. The flock of birds doesn't have an orchestrator, but what it does have is a set of biological *standards* defining how it detects speed, distance, and the leader.

Similarly, data mesh introduces a set of standards that each data product follows for interoperability and cohesion of behavior. For example, in Chapter 10 I introduced "global policies" as a service provided by the mesh experience plane. This service can conveniently configure access control rules for each data product. However, the interpretation and execution of the rules happen locally within the data product at the right time—access read or write—without the intervention of the central access control authority.

In some organizations the rule authoring itself is decentralized and delegated locally to the data products. However, the platform embeds a standardized sidecar within each data product for the uniform interpretation and execution of the rules.

Recap

By now, I hope I have established a mindset and approach to the design of the core element of the data mesh architecture, data product as an architecture quantum.

First, you are going to arrive at the right design by looking at the relationship between a data product and other components and users of a mesh, the data product affordances: serving data, consuming data, discovering data, governing data, auditing data, etc.

Second, you are going to design a scale-out architecture, creating coequal data products that can change without a fear of breaking others; they scale out without imposing centralized bottlenecks and focus their design on the outcome of delivering value.

Third, you are going to deploy the principles of complex adaptive systems where possible: design simple and local rules and behaviors in each data product that can collectively lead to the emergence of mesh-level knowledge and intelligence.

With this newly formed mindset, let's go through the design of data product affordances in the next few chapters.

CHAPTER 12

Design Consuming, Transforming, and Serving Data

A data product's primary job is to consume data from upstream sources using its *input data ports*, transform it, and serve the result as permanently accessible data via its *output data ports*.

In this chapter, I go through the design characteristics of these three basic functions that all data products implement: *consume data* ("Consume Data" on page 217), *transform data* ("Transform Data" on page 226), and *serve data* ("Serve Data" on page 201).

Let's begin with the one that has the most unique properties to a data mesh approach.

Serve Data

A data product serves domain-oriented data to a diverse set of analytical consumers. It does so through its *output data ports (interfaces)*, introduced in Chapter 9. The output data ports have *explicitly defined contracts* and APIs.

This seemingly simple affordance of "serving domain-driven data" has interesting properties when considering its relationship with the agents in the ecosystem and their capabilities and needs.

Let's look at the relationship between a data product and its data users.

The Needs of Data Users

Figure 12-1 shows the needs of data users and how a data product serves them.

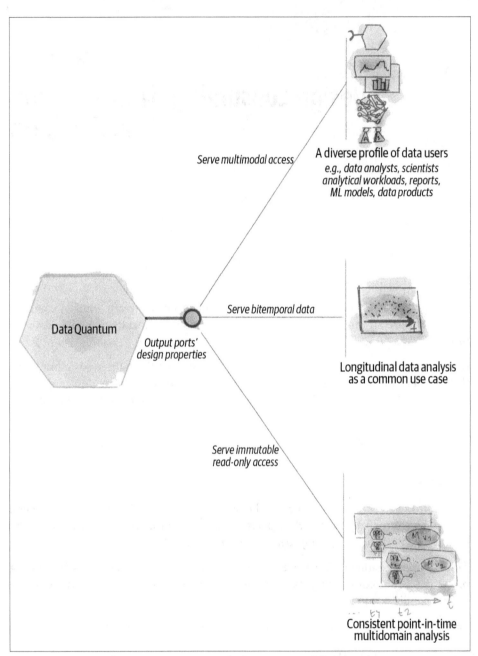

Figure 12-1. Serve data properties to satisfy data users and their needs

The requirements driven by data users impose a set of design considerations on how data products serve their data:

Analytical data users have a diverse profile

Data users—clients accessing and reading data—fall on a wide spectrum of personas and application types: people such as data analysts, data scientists, and data-driven application developers; and systems such as reports, visualizations, statistical models, and machine learning models, etc. Recalling Chapter 3, a data product serves its data in a manner that feels native to such diverse personas. We called this baseline usability characteristic of a data product *natively accessible*.

The design implication of this requirement is to serve data with multimodal access—serving the same data semantic in different formats and modes of access.

Analytical data users need longitudinal data

The mesh maintains a longitudinal view of the global state of data, wholly, for analytical use cases, and most importantly *without an off-the-mesh* data lake, warehouse, or any external system to maintain the global state.

This continuously changing global state of the data is stored and maintained by a connected graph of data products, and no other architectural elements. This is the meaning of decentralization of architecture.

Insights, retrospective or futurespective, are most powerful when they account for the passage of time. Only by having access to continuous data changes over time can we formulate trends, make predictions, and discover correlations between different events across multiple domains. Data mesh assumes time as an ever-present parameter in both presenting and querying data.

The design implication to access longitudinal data, data that represents events and state changes over time, is for each data quantum to serve bitemporal data.

Analytical data users need a consistent view of multiple domains at a point in time

The majority of the analytical use cases process data from multiple data products. Such use cases correlate multiple data products at a consistent point in time. For example, when Daff trains a machine learning model on 2021-07-01 to predict subscriber growth for the next month, it does that based on the data from the last three years, *known* and *processed* by multiple data products on 2021-07-01.

To support the repeatability of this version of the growth model, processed on 2021-07-21, the mesh maintains an unchangeable state of data across multiple data products on 2021-07-21.

Providing point-in-time consistent data across multiple data products, combined with versioning of data for repeatability, introduces multiple design considerations for serving data: bitemporality, immutability, and read-only access.

Serve Data Design Properties

Let's go a bit deeper in each of the properties we discovered earlier: *multimodal*, *immutable*, *bitemporal*, and *read-only access*. These characteristics are integral to the working of data mesh.

Multimodal data

The job of a data product is to serve the analytical data of a particular *domain* with a specific and unique domain *semantic*. However, for a data product to serve its diverse consumers *natively*, it must share the same domain *semantic*, in different *syntaxes*; the semantic can be served as *columnar files*, as *relational database tables*, as *events* or in other formats. The same semantic is served without compromising the experience of the data consumer. People who write reports consume the data as relational tables. People who train machine learning models consume data in columnar files, and real-time app developers consume the events.

I personally find it helpful to visualize the nature of analytical data as the dimensions of *space* and *time(s)*. I use the space dimension to represent the different *syntactic materialization* of the data, the *formats* of data. Any data product may present its data with *multiple formats*, or in a *multimodal form*, for example:

- Semi-structured files, e.g., columnar files
- Entity relationships, e.g., relational tables
- Graph, e.g., property graph
- Events

When a data user accesses a data product, using its top-level data product discovery API ("Discover, Understand, Trust, and Explore" on page 233), it first gets to learn about the data product's semantic—what domain information the product is serving e.g., **podcasts, podcast listeners**, etc.—and then it accesses one of the data product's output APIs ("Output data ports" on page 159) for a particular mode of access to the data. How the data is served depends on the underlying (physical) technology: subscribing to an event log, reading distributed columnar files, running SQL queries over relational tables. Domain-oriented semantics is the top-level concern, while formats and the mode of access are second-class concerns. This is an inverse model to existing architectures, where the storage and encoding technology dictates how the data is organized first and then it is served.

Figure 12-2 shows the diverse modes of access with an example. The **play events** data product provides access to its play events data through three modes of access: subscribing to its "play events" topic (capturing the state changes of listeners as they log in, play a podcast, stop playing, etc.), accessing the same play events through SQL

---

queries (over tables with rows of attributes of events), and columnar object files (a file for each attribute of all events).

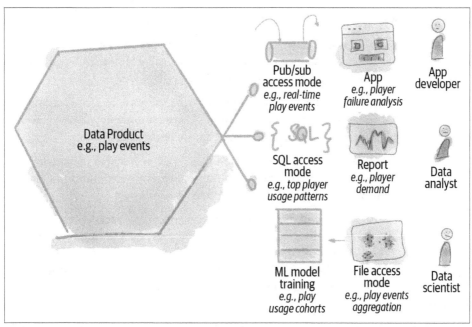

Figure 12-2. Example of a data product's multimodal access

These three modes of access and topologies of the data can satisfy diverse personas of consumers: a data-intensive app developer watching for error events to improve the quality of the player, the data analyst using the synchronous SQL access model to create a daily report of top player usage patterns, and a data scientist using the file access mode to train its ML model discovering classification of play patterns.[1]

All this is enabled by the same data product, **play events**, through its individual *output data ports*.

Today, the complexity of supporting multimodal access is the symptom of the absence of higher-order and abstraction APIs to present and query data semantically and agnostic to its underlying encoding and format.

---

1 A single data topology may have multiple modes of access. For example, data formatted as a stream of events can be used by SQL and publisher/subscriber access modes.

Immutable data

> No man can cross the same river twice.
>
> —Heraclitus

Immutable data, once it is created, doesn't change. Data products serve their data in a way that once a piece of data is processed and made available to the data users, that specific piece of data does not change; it cannot be deleted or updated.

Changing data often leads to complexities and errors, something that is known by any experienced programmer. This is why there's considerable interest in functional programming, which holds as a key axiom that data is never changed.

This is particularly relevant to analytical use cases. With immutable data, data users can rerun analytics in a repeatable way; retraining models or regenerating reports on a particular point-in-time dataset gives the same repeatable result.

Repeatability is needed because often results yield a striking observation that requires the analyst to dig deeper. If the data they are using changes, then they may not be able to reproduce the striking result and may wonder if this is due to a data change or a programming error. If there is a bug in the analysis, it's much harder to track down when working with an unstable data source, where the analyst cannot get the same answers from repeated runs of the same code.

The confusion and complexity of mutable data is made worse in data mesh, where source data can be used by multiple data products, and multiple data products can be the sources of a particular analysis where multiple data products each keep a slice of truth contributing to the larger understanding of a state of business. The distributed nature of data mesh demands immutability to give confidence to data users that (1) there is consistency between multiple data products for a *point-in-time* piece of data and (2) once they read data at a point in time, that data doesn't change and they can reliably repeat the reads and processing.

Figure 12-3 shows a simple example: a **listener demographics** data product provides geographic demographics of the listeners on a daily basis, where the listeners connect. It has two downstream data products, **artists regional popularity** (where most listeners for an artist are located) and **regional market size** (number of listeners in different regions). These two data products are part of the source for **regional marketing** data product, which recommends regional targeted marketing activities. It uses **regional market size** to identify low-risk countries with the least market impact to do A/B testing or experiments, and **artists regional popularity** to promote artists based on their popularity.

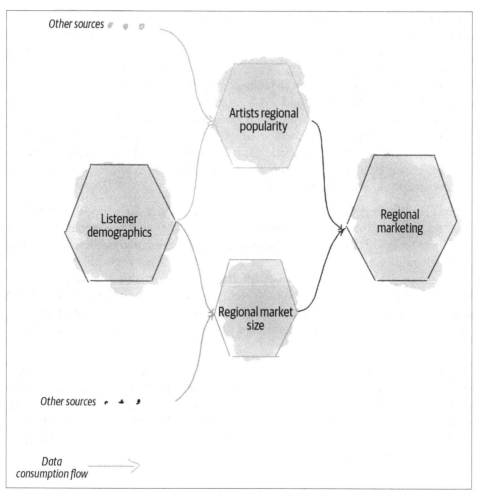

Figure 12-3. Example of correlating inconsistent data

Each of these data products has its own cadence in processing and serving data. Hence, there is no way to guarantee that all their data updates at the same time. This can lead to a deadly diamond. If **listener demographics** updates its data at the time that **regional marketing** runs its analysis, it can consume inconsistent data because **listener demographics** could serve data before the update, and regional market size after. Worse, **regional marketing** doesn't even know about this inconsistency.

Data mesh addresses this problem by removing the possibility of updated data going undetected by data users. Changes to data are always presented as new pieces of data with identifying time-variant attributes so data users never get to correlate inconsistent pieces of data, each coming from a different data product. The most general way to do this is to use bitemporal data, which I cover in the next section.

For example, **listener demographics** shares its data as tuples like {listener_id: '123', location: 'San Francisco', connection_time: '2021-08-12T14:23:00, processing_time: '2021-08-13T01:00'}. Each piece of information has two time-variant identifying fields, the "connection_time," e.g., when the listener connected to listen to music, and the "processing_time," when **listener demographics** processed this information. Once this tuple is processed and made available to data users, it never changes. Of course, the same listener may listen to content the next day from a different location, and that would manifest itself as an appendance of a new data entity {listener_id: '123', location:'New York', connection_time: '2021-08-13T10:00', processing_time: '2021-08-14T01:00'}. These are two different pieces of time, while they still convey an update, a new location of the listener.

More generally, immutability of data reduces opportunity for incidental complexities, complexity in dealing with the side effects of shared states' updates across a distributed mesh of consumers and solving the intractable computer science problem of distributed transactions. Imagine the complexity that goes into the code of each downstream data reader on the mesh if the mesh allows that the data they have already consumed keeps changing, or replaying the same reads yields a different result. Immutability is another key enabler of *design for change* and maintaining the *eventual consistency*[2] of the mesh through the propagation of new processing times and their immutable states.

Keeping data immutable is important any time but is particularly vital for the data mesh. But it's also true that past data changes as new information becomes available or data processing bugs are fixed; hence, we need to be able to make retracted changes to data. Let's look at bitemporality to see how data mesh implements immutability and retracted changes and how it allows for data to change even though it must remain immutable.

Bitemporal data

> It seems that change and time are inseparable: changes take time; are located and ordered in time; and they are separated by time. The inseparability of time and change is a kind of logical truth.
>
> —Raymond Tallis

Bitemporal data is a way of modeling data so that every piece of data records two timestamps: "when an event has actually occurred or a state actually was," *actual time*, in combination with "when the data was processed," *processing time*.

---

2 Eventual consistency means that at some point the mesh will become consistent once a data product's newly processed data propagates to its downstream consumers.

Bitemporal data modeling makes it possible to serve data as immutable entities, i.e., as tuples of {*data product fields, actual time, processing time*}, where processing time monotonically increases every time a new data entity is processed,[3] and to perform temporal analysis and time travel, i.e., look at past trends and predict future possibilities. Both of these outcomes are essential to data mesh.

For example, consider a typical temporal analytical use case that predicts the growth of Daff's business: a growth prediction model. This model uses subscription changes over a long period of time to discover patterns and trends. It uses the *actual time* of the **subscriptions** data product—the time when subscribers actually join or leave their memberships—correlated with other *actual times* of other related events from the **marketing activities, calendar,** and **support issues** data products. These data products process and serve data with a different cadence. To train a repeatable version of the model, using consistent data from different data products, **growth prediction** selects a common *processing time*—when the data products have processed and become aware of an event. For example, the version of the model trained on 2022-01-02T12:00 uses the subscriber information, support issues, and marketing events of the last three years (actual time), known and processed, as of 2022-01-02T12:00 (processing time).

Actual time and processing time are the two entangled axes of time that a data product preserves and serves:

Flux of actual time
> To represent the data in a form that meets the needs of analytical use cases, the data product captures and shares the state (or events) of the domain over time, over an infinite[4] span of time. For example, the **podcast listeners** data product can share "daily podcast listeners information from a year ago to now."
>
> The *actual time* is the time when an event occurs or the time when a particular state exists. For example, 2021-07-15 is the *actual time* of podcast listeners (data) who actually listened to Daff's podcasts on this date. The presence of actual time matters, as predictive or diagnostic analysis is sensitive to the time when something actually happens. This is not the case for many of the operational functions. Most of the time the operational functions deal with the *current state* of the data, e.g., "give me the current address of present podcast listeners to send them printed marketing material."

---

3 Reprocessing previous data, e.g., fixing a past error, results in a new data entity and a new processing time. The data product's obsolete record policy can decide whether the past (error) data entity is retained or not.

4 The definition of infinite depends on the data retention policy of the data quantum.

Actual times fluctuate. A data product can observe out-of-order actual times or receive new data about the same actual time after a correction is made on the source data.

Continuum of processing time

The *processing time* is the time at which a data product observes, processes, records, and serves its knowledge or understanding of the state or event, for a particular *actual time*. For example, on 2021-08-12T01:00, the **podcast listeners** data product processes all data about people who listened to podcasts on 2021-08-11 and gains an understanding of the state of the world then. 2021-08-12T01:00 is the *processing time*.

Providing *processing time* as a mandatory attribute of data is the key to *design for change*. Our understanding of the past changes; either we fix errors that occurred in the past or become aware of new pieces of information that improve our understanding of the past. We can't change the past, but what we can change is the *processing time* of the present. We serve a new piece of data with a new processing time that reflects fixes of the past actual times.

Processing time is the only time that can be trusted to move forward monotonically.

I use *processing time* to collapse four different times into one:

Observation time
When a data product becomes aware of the event or state

Processing time
When the data product processes and transforms the data observed

Record time
When a data product stores the processed data

Publish time
When the data becomes available to data users for access

These subtle time differences are most relevant to the internals of a data product and not the data users. Hence, I have collapsed them into one *processing time* that matters most to the data users.

Martin Fowler presents this bitemporality in a simple and brilliant post, "Bitemporal History" (*https://oreil.ly/0HKiC*). In this section, I summarize how data products adopt this concept, in a unified model, agnostic to the latency of the processing and the shape of the data (events or snapshots).

Impact of bitemporality.   Let's briefly discuss the positive impact of bitemporality in a few scenarios:

Retractions

Our understanding of the world continuously evolves. Our understanding of the world can have errors or missing information. In this case at a later processing time, we fix our misunderstandings. For example, at 2021-08-12T1:00 we process all the information about "People who listened to podcasts on 2021-08-11," but we make a mistake in counting the number of listeners and calculate 3,000. The next time we process the information at 2021-08-13T10:00, we fix the error and create a new count, 2,005 listeners on 2021-08-11. 3,000 and 2,005 become two different *values*, for the same *identity*, "Podcast listeners count on 2021-08-11," captured and shared as *two* separate *states*, the state processed at 2021-08-12T10:00 and the state processed at 2021-08-13T10:00.

Using bitemporality builds in *change*, change in the state of data, its data model, SLO metrics, etc. The continuous processing of change becomes a default behavior built into all consumers and the mesh as a whole.

This greatly simplifies the logic of data users. Updates to the past are no longer a special case and a surprise. They are just newly processed data that tell a new story about the past. The consumers can keep track and pin the data they have processed at a point in time in the past and travel back to it to access a past revision of data. Of course, building such a system is no easy engineering task.

Skew between processing time and actual time

Skew is the time difference between actual time and processing time. Only true real-time systems have a negligible skew: the event gets processed, and our understanding of the world gets formed, almost exactly when an event happens. This is very rare in data processing systems, particularly in analytical data processing with a chain of data products, each processing data multiple hops away from the actual source of an event. The presence of the two times informs the data users of the skew so that they can make a decision on how to process the data based on their timeliness needs. The further away from the source-aligned data product, the larger the skew can become.

Windowing

It is common for a data product to aggregate upstream data over a window of time. For example, **play sessions** aggregates all the events during an engagement of a listener with the player device—e.g., a series of play events when the listener navigates from one podcast to another, finally picks one, and then drops out after a few minutes of listening and puts the player away. It helps with the behavioral analysis of the listeners engaging with the player. In this case, the actual times of play events can span multiple minutes, a time window. Data users with the knowledge of the window can perform time-aware operations on the data.

Reactive processing of continuous change

Data mesh assumes a world in constant change. This constant change can be in the form of new data arriving or our understanding of past data evolving, marked by the *processing time*. Data products can continuously process change by reacting to the event that their upstream data product has changed: a new *processing time* has become available.

Processing time becomes a primitive mechanism for creating reactive and asynchronous data processing between connected data products.

Temporality versions all aspects of a data product

Processing time, a data product's notion of time, is built into all attributes and properties of a data product that change over time: data schema, data semantic, relationships between data, SLOs, and other meta. They automatically become versioned by time.

Processing time becomes a primitive for versioning permanent properties of a data product, i.e., data schema. The processing time becomes a parameter to correlate time-variant information such as SLOs of the data products.

Example. Let's look at the previous example, visually. Figure 12-4 shows the two dimensions of time and their relationships to each other, for a single data product.

There are a few notable pieces demonstrated in Figure 12-4:

Skew

It is inevitable that the data quantum processes an event and gains and formulates its understanding of the state of its data, later than the point in time when an event actually occurs. For example, the state of the daily listeners during 2021-08-11 is known by the system later than its occurrence time at 2021-08-12T01:00. There is a skew of at least 1 hour to know the daily state of podcast listeners, and up to 25 hours.

Processing error

The total listeners processed at 2021-08-12T01:00 had an error in its calculation and captured the total daily listeners of 2021-08-11 as 3,000 people instead of 2,005, a bit more optimistic.

Retractions

The error that occurred on 2021-08-12T01:00 was caught by the data product developers, a fix was applied to the processing code, and on the next processing interval at 2021-08-13T01:00 the correct value of 2,005 is reported. Hence, the data served at processing time 2021-08-13T01:00 includes data for daily podcast listeners of 2021-08-11 and 2021-08-12.

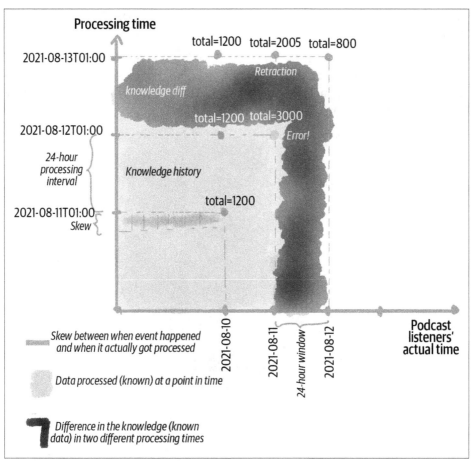

Figure 12-4. Actual time and record time relationship

What Figure 12-4 shows is that the data serving interface and APIs are a function with two time parameters, a processing time and an actual time. For simplicity of use, they can take special and default parameters like *latest* for data users who are only interested in the latest state of the data.

In this example, I have used a low-resolution wall time for simplicity. The governance standardizes how time is standardized, and the platform implements that consistently. The *processing time* guarantees ordered reads. It can be implemented as an internal *system time*, an incremental counter since an epoch, or a monotonically increasing number. Data consumers use the processing time as an index to know what data they have consumed.[5] The *actual time* can follow a DateTime standard like ISO 8601.

The data users of analytical data can perform time travel and go back and forward in time when accessing data. The upper bound of how far they can travel back can vary: to the first data ever processed or just to the latest one. This depends on the data product's retention policy.

Figure 12-5 demonstrates a simple visualization of this time travel across the axis of processing time.

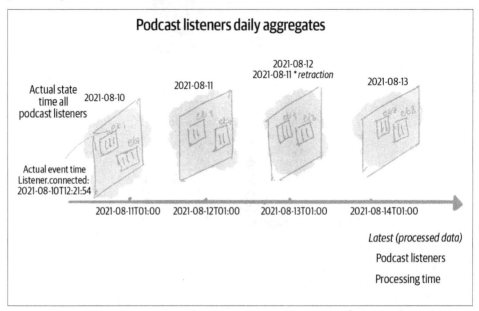

Figure 12-5. Serving data on the axis of processing time

States, events, or both. How systems encode and process data falls into two camps: states and events.[6] *State* captures the condition of a system at a point in time, e.g., "number of podcast listeners today." *Event* captures the occurrence of a particular change of state, e.g., "a new podcast listener connected." While *state* or (*change*) *events* require two very different ways of storing or serving data, I consider that an orthogonal concern to the time dimensions we discussed here. It's up to the data product's logic whether it makes sense to capture or serve a stream of change events, or the stream of inferred states of the system as snapshots, or do both. It's likely that

---

5 Often an underlying technology like Kafka provides this mechanism.

6 The duality of data processing can be observed in many systems: streams versus table (e.g., Confluent (*https://oreil.ly/Y9va4*)), snapshots versus deltas (e.g., Databricks Delta Lake (*https://delta.io*)).

---

data readers would like to see both. Nevertheless, the presence of the two time axes remains.

Reduce the opportunity for retracted changes.   As discussed early, changing past data (retractions)—due to fixes or arrival of new data—is handled like any other newly processed data. Fixed data is presented as a new data entity with an actual time that belongs to the past, but with a new processing time. Additionally, in the next section, "Read-only access" on page 216, I will present a special-case handling of data updates such as exercising the right to be forgotten at the mesh level.

Despite the methods to handle retractions, data products must strive to reduce errors and the need for retractions. Here are some strategies for reducing the need for fixes:

Increase the processing time interval to introduce quality control
Imagine the **play events** data product. It captures the signals coming from **player devices**. The data product can occasionally miss events or receive delayed ones. This is due to network interruptions, no access to the on-device cache, etc. However, the data product transformation code can introduce a processing delay to correct the missing signals through synthetically predicted/generated ones, or aggregate the signals to a median or other statistical representation of the same data. This means that the data product is introducing a longer skew between the actual time and the processing time to have an opportunity to fix the errors in time and avoid retractions. This is often a suitable technique for business processes that have an inherent need for reconciliation. For example, while receiving payments transactions near real time, there is a daily dump of corrected and reconciled payment accounts that get served later. This would require increasing the processing interval. In the case of payments, the correctness of accounts is preferred over the timeliness of transactions.

Adjust the data product's SLOs to reflect the expected errors
If we continue the preceding example, some consumers might be perfectly tolerant of the errors in the near-real-time data. For example, an app detecting **player errors**, on best effort, doesn't care if there are missing events here and there. In this case, the **play events** data product can publish the data without reconciliation for a category of consumers like the "player error detection" app. However in this case, the data product communicates its quality objectives according to the expected range of errors that may occur in terms of missing signal.

Read-only access

Unlike other analytical data management paradigms, data mesh does not embrace the concept of the mythical *single source of truth*. Every data product provides a truthful *portion* of the reality—for a particular domain—to the best of its ability, *a single slice of truth*. Data can be read from one data product, morphed and transformed, and then served by the next. The mesh maintains its integrity through the propagation of change as *appends* of *bitemporal immutable data* from an upstream data product to the downstream consumers, automatically. As such, the mesh maintains a state of eventual consistency as new data propagates through the graph.

By now, it might seem obvious that the mesh or individual data products do not present a direct *update* function; updates are the indirect result of the data product processing its input. Change to a data product, in the form of appends of newly processed data, is only carried out by the transformation code of a data product. This guarantees immutability and also maintains the eventual consistency of the mesh.

However, there are cases such as the global governance administrative functions executing the *right to be forgotten*, in accordance with regulations such as GDPR, that change the data.

You can think of these as a specific administrative function, triggered by the mesh experience plane, on all data products' control ports ("Control Port" on page 167), executing the command, in this case a crypto shredding (*https://oreil.ly/eg5u7*). Data products always encode the user information encrypted; by destroying the encryption keys—which live on the platform and not in the data product—the user information is essentially rendered unreadable. If you do find yourself with other special-case operations that require updating data that is already processed, this operation is implemented as a *global control port* function, and not a function of an output port. Keep the output ports for data users to just read data.

Serve Data Design

Let's bring it together and look at the design of the data product to serve data. Figure 12-6 shows a likely logical architecture, where data products own and maintain a core representation of their domain and serve that in multiple spatial modalities, using the concept of output data port adapters. Each port, always, provides data in a bitemporal, immutable, and read-only mode. The data retention's duration depends on the policy of the data product. It may retain and make data accessible for many observations (processing times), just the latest, or somewhere in between.

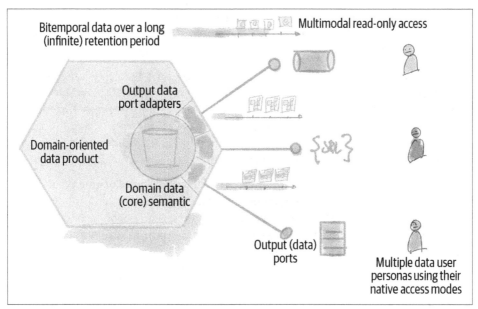

Figure 12-6. Data product's high-level components to design serve data

Table 12-1 summarizes the data product components involved in serving data.

Table 12-1. High-level data product components to serve data

Serve data component	Description
Output data port	Interface (API) to serve data according to a specific mode of access for a particular spatial format of data (syntax). This implementation could simply be an API that redirects access to a particular physical technology, e.g., a bitemporal table in a warehouse storage, a file in a lake storage, or a topic of an event log.
Output (data) port adapter	The code responsible for presenting the data for a particular output port. The implementation could simply be a step in the data product's transformation code that stores data in a particular syntax, or as sophisticated as a runtime gateway for adapting core data stored to many modes of access on read.
Core data semantic	Expression of the data semantic—agnostic to the modes of access or its spatial syntax.

Consume Data

In the majority of cases, data in organizations originates from the internal or external operational systems, in interaction with people or other operational agents, such as devices. In some cases, data is received as purchased or freely downloaded archives. For example, the operational data in Daff is generated by listeners subscribing and listening to different content, content providers publishing music, and the artist management team paying and handling the affairs of the artists, and so on.

Data products *consume* this data and transform and serve it in a manner suitable for analytical use cases. Hence, in the majority of the cases, data products consume data from one or multiple sources.

Architecturally, *input data ports* ("Input data ports" on page 159) implement the mechanisms necessary for a data product to define and execute the consumption of its source data. The input data port is a logical architectural construct that allows a data product to *connect to a data source, execute queries,* and *receive data—events or snapshots—as a continuous stream or a one-off payload.* The choice of the underlying technology is an implementation-specific concern and is left to the data platform.

Figure 12-7 shows a high-level picture of how data products consume data. A data product consumes data from one or multiple sources. The sources could be a collaborating operational system or other data products. The consumed data is then transformed into the core data model and served in multiple modalities via its output ports.

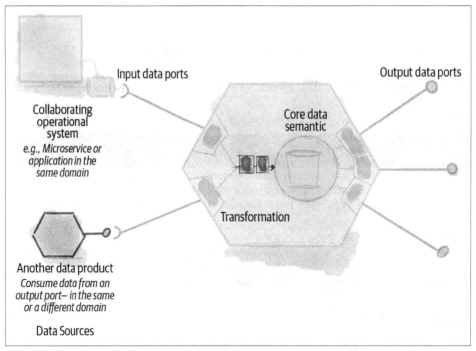

Figure 12-7. Data product's design to consume data

Each data product can have one or multiple sources. Source-aligned data products ("Source-Aligned Domain Data" on page 21) mostly consume their data from the operational system. As we get into aggregate data products ("Aggregate Domain Data" on page 23) we see other data products becoming the source, and consumer-aligned data products ("Consumer-Aligned Domain Data" on page 24) often include smart logic or machine learning models to provide locally sourced data for particular use cases.

Let's dive into some of the notable characteristics that impact the design of a data product's input data.

Archetypes of Data Sources

The design of data input capability must support multiple archetypes of sources. Here are a few top-level categories:

- Collaborating operational systems
- Other data products
- Self

Collaborating operational systems as data sources

Source-aligned data products consume data from their collaborating operational systems, one or multiple applications that generate data as a byproduct of running the domain's business. They consume data optimized for the operational system and transform it to a format suitable for analytical usage. They decouple downstream analytics use cases from the internal details of the operational application.

The phrase *collaborating* here implies a tight coupling between the data product and its source operational system. They both must belong to the same domain. The operational data contract between the source application and the data product is often tightly coupled; changes to the operational system's data and model impact the data product's data and model.

That's why I highly encourage keeping the collaborating operational system sources and their collaborating data products in the same domain. This allows the domain team in charge of the changes to the operational systems to collaborate closely with the data product developers to keep the two in sync.

There are cases where an operational system is not aligned to a single domain, e.g., CRM COTS (customer relationship management as a commercial off-the-shelf) products encapsulate multiple domains of products, customers, sales, etc., into one. In this case the COTS system can expose multiple domain-aligned interfaces, each for a particular source-aligned data product.

Figure 12-8 shows an example of a source-aligned data product input. The **listener subscriptions** data product consumes data from a microservice in its domain, **listener subscription service**. It receives the changes in listener subscriptions as near-real-time events published on an event log. The **subscription events** log is controlled and maintained by the operational system, as a short-retention medium. The data product consumes the events, performs transformations on them, and ultimately serves them as a long-retention temporal view of listener subscription information.

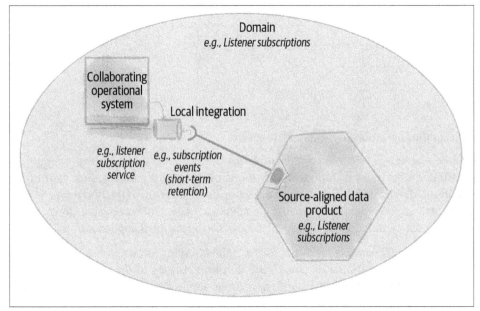

Figure 12-8. Example of a data product with input from a collaborating operational system

Common mechanisms for implementing the input port for consuming data from collaborating operational systems include asynchronous *event-driven* data sharing in the case of modern systems, and *change data capture* (*https://oreil.ly/EB8m8*) for legacy systems that are difficult to change. Modern operational systems sharing their *domain events* is increasingly becoming a common practice and is a great model for feeding data to a collaborative data product. Change data capture is a set of integration patterns to discover and track changes to an application database, which then can be sourced as the input to the data product. This is the least desirable way to receive data from a collaborating operational system. It exposes the internal implementation of a database transaction and doesn't correspond to a business domain. But sometimes it is the only available option in the case of legacy systems.

How a data product consumes data from an operational system is heavily influenced by the ability of the team to extend the operational system. The design ultimately depends on the agreement within the domain's team on how to integrate their operational system with their data product.

Other data products as data sources

Data products can consume data from other data products on the mesh. For example, the **podcast demographics** data product receives attributes about the listeners from **listener profiles** and **podcast listeners** data products. It correlates the listener profile information with the podcast listeners and applies classification transformation to these sources. It then serves information about the **podcast demographics**. This example is depicted in Figure 12-9.

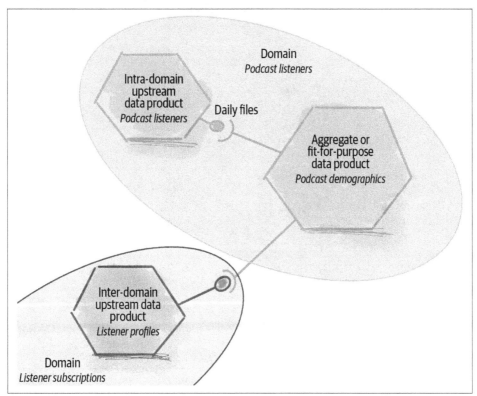

Figure 12-9. Example of a data product with input from other data products

In this case, the input port consumes data from another data product's output ports. The source data product can belong to either the same domain or other domains. Nevertheless, the implementation of input data ports and how they consume data from other data product's output ports is standardized.

A data product utilizes its upstream output's *actual time* and *processing time* to select its desired data. In the case of a streaming input, the input port mechanism will keep track of the processing time in the source data to process new data as it arrives.

Self as a data source

In some cases, a data product's local computation can be the source of data. For example, a local transformation such as a machine learning model inference generates new data. Consider the **artists** data product as shown in Figure 12-10. Its transformation runs a machine learning model that adds new data, such as "emerging" or "declining" data for artist classification, to the information it receives from the **artist onboarding** microservices. Additionally, the data product uses locally stored data such as a list of possible classifications as its input.

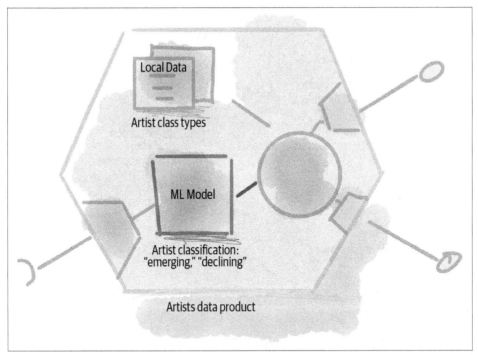

Figure 12-10. Example of a data product with local input

Locality of Data Consumption

Data mesh leaves many of the implementation decisions to the underlying technology. Data mesh architecture is agnostic of the underlying technology and infrastructure—as much as possible.

For example, where the data is *physically located* and whether a consuming data product *physically copies* data from one location to another are implementation details built by the platform. However, data mesh architecture components such as input and output ports are great interfaces to abstract the internal implementation of data or processing movement across physical boundaries. A simple set of APIs that connect a data product's input port to another's output port can hide the physical movement of data from one physical storage and trust boundary to another. Similarly, executing the data consumption request can execute a remote query issued from one computational environment to another.

The implication of this design is that a mesh can *span one or multiple physical infrastructures, multiple clouds*, and *on-prem hosting environments*. This means that when a data product consumes data from its source, in that process, it can physically move data from one underlying hosting environment to another. This seemingly simple capability can have a profound impact on *data migration to the cloud* and a *multicloud data platform*.

For example, Daff is moving all their analytical data and processing to a cloud environment. Today, the podcast service runs on an on-prem infrastructure, along with its underlying operational database. The **podcast listeners** data product runs on the cloud. It consumes data through an asynchronous input data port interface. Once a new podcast listener is registered, the **podcast listeners** data product essentially copies that information from an on-prem stream to its cloud storage and then makes it available through its cloud-based output data interfaces.

This implements a continuous data migration through data products from one environment to another, without a big bang data migration strategy. The same mechanism can move data from one cloud provider to another. For example, if a company has a multicloud strategy and they want to keep data across multiple cloud providers, implementation of the input port can move data from the source's cloud provider to the consumer's. Of course, for this to become a reality, the underlying platform infrastructure must support a few key features such as internet-compatible addressability of data products, identity authentication and authorization across trust boundaries, and internet-accessible endpoints for output data ports.

Figure 12-11 demonstrates data consumption between two different data products across two environments.

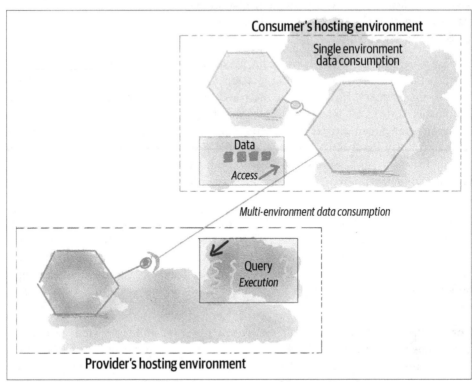

Figure 12-11. Multi-environment data consumption model

Data Consumption Design

Data products intentionally specify what data, from which sources, and how they consume data. The data product specifically defines and controls the capability to consume data. This is contrary to other data architecture where sources dump data on the processors without knowledge of where and how the data gets to them. For example, in previous architectures an external directed acyclic graph (DAG) specification defines how the processors get connected to each other centrally, rather than each processor defining how it receives data and serves it.

Figure 12-12 demonstrates the data product's high-level design components to consume data through input data ports.

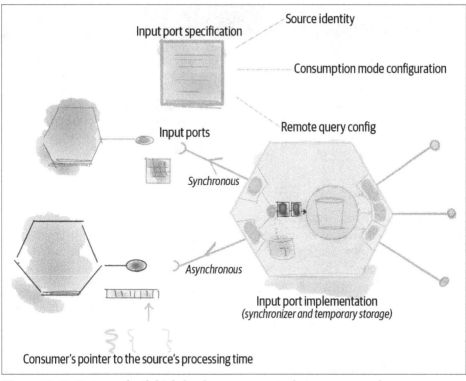

Figure 12-12. Data product's high-level components to design consume data

Table 12-2 summarizes a data product's high-level components to design consuming data.

Table 12-2. Summary of data product's high-level components to design consume data

Consume data component	Description
Input data port(s)	The mechanism by which a data product receives its source data and makes it available for further internal transformation.
Input data port(s) specification	A declarative specification of input data ports that configures from where and how data is consumed.
Asynchronous input data port	Asynchronous input port implementation reactively calls the transformation code when the necessary source data becomes available. Subscription to event streams or asynchronous I/O read on files are examples of async input ports. An asynchronous input port keeps track of the source data product's *processing time* pointer and when it receives data for a new processing time it reactively executes the transformation.
Synchronous input data port	Synchronous input ports pull data from the source and call the transformation code when the data is fetched. For example, "Daily podcasts summary" pulls data from **podcast listeners** synchronously and calculates the count and other summaries when the data is fetched. It pulls data daily at midnight.

Consume data component	Description
Remote query	An input port specification can include the query executed on the source to receive the desired data. This capability reduces the amount of data that is otherwise fetched redundantly. The query is expressed in a query language that the source understands, such as SQL, GraphQL, Flux, etc., and is defined by the input port specification.
Input port synchronizer and temporary storage	Input ports often interdependently consume data. For example, the **artist classification** transformation code can't start running until data from two independent sources of **artists** and **listeners** becomes available. Temporary storage is necessary to keep track of observed and unprocessed data, until all observations needed become available for processing.

Transform Data

Almost all data products perform a transformation, no matter how minimal. We create a data product because we see value in sharing a new analytical model of existing data. Creating this new model requires transformation. Creating and maintaining the transformation code is what a data product developer pays most attention to.

Traditionally this transformation has occurred in the data pipelines moving data from an input source to an output sink. In data mesh design, the transformation—whether implemented as a pipeline or not—is encoded in and abstracted by the data product.

The transformation is an *internal implementation* of a data product and is controlled by it. Since it's an internal concern, I don't intend to be specific in how it must be designed. In my opinion, it's up to the taste, capabilities, and needs of the data product developer to choose how to implement the transformation.

It is helpful to look at a few different ways of implementing the data product's transformation.

Programmatic Versus Nonprogrammatic Transformation

Data processing and transformation falls into two main camps: *nonprogrammatic transformations* (e.g., SQL, Flux, GraphQL) and *programmatic data processing* (e.g., Apache Beam, Apache Spark, Metaflow).

Nonprogrammatic approaches either use relational algebra performing set operations such as SQL, or flow-based functions such as Flux. Either way, the idea is that we can capture the intent of how data is transformed from one set to another with a statement. It is simple and approachable for many data product developers, but also limited to the features of the statement. For more complex transformations the statements become difficult to understand, hard to modularize, and challenging to test automatically.

In practice we should not find many data products that simply perform nonprogrammatic transformations. Any other downstream data product can run the same remote queries themselves, and there is no need for intermediary data products.

Figure 12-13 demonstrates an example of a nonprogrammatic transformation. The intention is to create demographic information for top listeners. The **top listeners** data product uses its input ports on **played songs** and **listener profiles** to capture the profile information of listeners who have listened to songs today. Then it produces various statistics on demographics of listeners, e.g., age groups who have listened most or least today, countries that have listeners most or least today, etc.

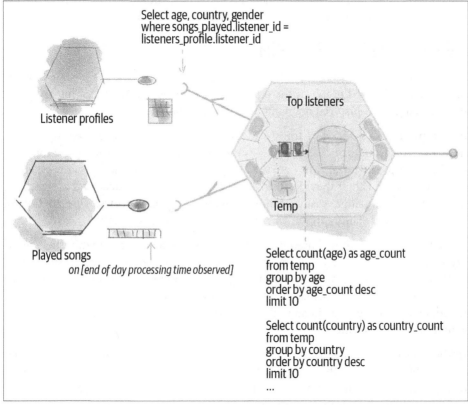

Figure 12-13. Example of a nonprogrammatic transformation

On the other hand, programmatic data processing uses code logic, conditions, and statements to transform data. Programmatic data processing libraries such as Apache Beam or Apache Spark can be used in different programming languages such as Python, Java, etc. The transformation code has access to the full power of the hosting programming language, imperative or declarative. It can be modularized and tested. This approach is more complex for noncoding data product developers but more extensible. The advantage of this approach is that the statistics can be calculated incrementally as more records about **played songs** arrive.

Data mesh doesn't take a position on what approach a data product adopts for its transformation and relies on common sense: use programmatic approaches for more complex use cases, and use a nonprogrammatic approach when the transformation is trivial and simple. Or even better, if the transformation is trivial and nonprogrammatic, do nothing and don't create an intermediate data product. Just leave the end consumers to run the queries themselves. Note that, even in the case of programmatic transformations, the input port may evoke a nonprogrammatic query on the source before processing it. This reduces the amount of data moved to the transformation code and pushes the processing to where upstream data resides.

Dataflow-Based Transformation

The dataflow programming paradigm, introduced in the 1960s, defines a computer program as a directed graph of the data flowing between operations. This programming paradigm has inspired many modern data pipeline designs.

A data pipeline is a series of transformation steps (functions) executed as the data flows from one step to another. Data mesh refrains from using pipelines as a top-level architectural paradigm and in between data products. The challenge with pipelines as currently used is that they don't create clear interfaces, contracts, and abstractions that can be maintained easily as the pipeline complexity grows. Due to lack of abstractions, single failure in the pipeline causes cascading failures.

The pipeline—or dataflow-based programming model in general—within the boundary of a data product is a natural paradigm for implementing the transformation code. In this scenario, pipelines tend to get less complex, since they are bounded by the context and transformation of a single data product. They also get upgraded, tested, and deployed as a single unit with a data product. Hence, pipeline stage tight coupling is less of a concern.

In short, using data pipelines within the boundary of a data product for transformation is OK, as long as the pipeline stages don't extend beyond the boundary of a data product. No transformation occurs between data products, beyond providing and consuming data through read-only output and input data ports. I call this the principle of *dumb pipes and smart filters*.

Figure 12-14 shows the high-level components involved in a pipeline transformation.

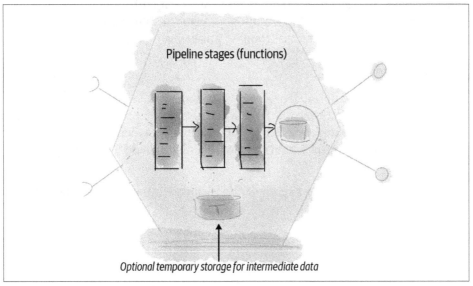

Figure 12-14. Pipeline transformation

ML as Transformation

The third transformation category is model based; deploying and running a machine learning or statistical model as a data product's transformation. For example, imagine Daff using a TensorFlow (*https://www.tensorflow.org/*) recommender to recommend songs to extend the listener's existing playlists. The TensorFlow model can be serialized and deployed as the **playlist recommender** data product. The data product consumes the listeners' playlists, makes predictions on what songs are recommended next, and stores those as playlist extension recommendations that are read and used when the listeners play their lists. The recommender model is executed within a program and a desired programming language, but its computation is mainly performed by the model.

ML models can be deployed in many different contexts such as microservices and applications, as well as data products.

Time-Variant Transformation

The common characteristic of all transformations is respecting the axes of time—*processing time* and *actual time*. The transformation code is aware of the time parameters when it processes the input and when it generates output with the respective times.

The input port mechanism keeps track of the processing time of each source. The transformation code generates the actual time of its output based on the calculation performed on the source data. The output port serves the transformed data accompanied with the data product's internal count of processing time.

Transformation Design

The design of the transformation—build-time definition, deployment, and execution—is heavily dependent on the framework of choice and the underlying technology. Whether the transformation is implemented by a declarative statement or programming code, platform capabilities are required to build, test, deploy, and run the transformation.

Figure 12-15 shows a few high-level design elements involved in a data product's transformation.

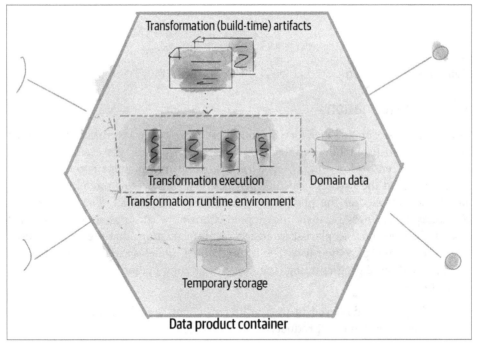

Figure 12-15. High-level components to design transformation for data products

Table 12-3 summarizes the high-level components involved in designing the data product transformation affordance.

Table 12-3. Summary of high-level components to transform data for a data product

Transform data component	Description
Transformation artifact(s)	The code, configuration, statement, or model that defines the transformation. This artifact is executed on the input data to produce the output, for a particular *record time*.
Transformation runtime environment	Transformations are invoked based on the configuration of the transformation, for example on a regular time basis or availability of the necessary input data. Once invoked they require a computational environment to execute, bounded by the data product container. The underlying platform provides this environment.
Temporary storage	Steps of a transformation code may require access to temporary storage that persists state across different phases of transformation. This is provided by the underlying platform.

Recap

In this chapter I presented a few core design elements and characteristics of data products as an architecture quantum, to autonomously consume, transform, and serve data.

To serve data in a distributed mesh architecture, I identified a few properties for the data products' output ports: serve *bitemporal, immutable* data via *read-only* and *multimodal APIs*. These constraints were driven by the objectives and assumptions of data mesh:

- Data products serve their domain-oriented data natively to a wide set of data users (multimodal access).
- Data products can be used in temporal analytics use cases (bitemporal).
- Data products can safely consume data from other data products, as well as transform and serve it, while maintaining a global state of eventual consistency at a point in time (bitemporal).
- Data product users process data for analytics and ML (read-only).

Data products have control over where and how they receive their upstream data. They use their input ports to get data from collaborating operational systems in the same domain or upstream data products. The input ports can implement data movement between different hosting environments in support of a multicloud deployment or an incremental cloud migration.

Data products almost always perform some kind of transformation in order to serve higher-value data. The transformation implementation can have multiple forms, including data pipeline functions, a sophisticated query, or ML model inference.

This chapter sets a high-level frame of thinking and approach to the design of data products in their core function of data sharing. I expect that future data mesh implementations evaluate and refine this.

CHAPTER 13

Design Discovering, Understanding, and Composing Data

Discovering, understanding, and trusting data is a necessary step of data journeys. What makes data mesh's approach unique is how to discover, understand, and trust data in a decentralized mesh of interconnected and autonomous data products, without creating centralized bottlenecks.

Similarly, composing new data from intersections and aggregations of multiple existing data is a basic function necessary for all data work. Data mesh introduces the ability to compose multiple data products in a decentralized fashion without creating tightly coupled data models that become bottlenecks for change.

This chapter introduces each affordance of data discoverability and composability briefly. I describe data mesh's position and introduce the design considerations so that each individual data product plays a part, locally, in its discoverability, understandability, and composability. I discuss how these local affordances of a data product surface mesh-level capabilities across many data products without creating tightly coupled synchronization points.

This chapter describes the boundaries of a data mesh approach, what is compatible with the objectives of data mesh, and what is not. The exact specifications are yet to be defined and tested and are outside of the scope of this book.

Discover, Understand, Trust, and Explore

Data mesh defines *discoverability*, *understandability*, *trustworthiness*, and *explorability* as some of the intrinsic characteristics of a data product. I briefly introduced these in Chapter 3 as data products' basic usability characteristics. These properties are key in enabling the journey of a data user—to find the right data, understand it, trust it, and explore its suitability for the analytical use case at hand. These properties answer questions such as: Is there any data product that tells me something about listeners? What information is actually provided by a data product about listeners? Can I trust it? Can I use it for my specific use case with a particular set of data requirements? How can I get access to it for early experimentations? And so on.

I don't think there is any dispute about this so far. Where data mesh differs from the majority of data discoverability approaches today, i.e., data catalog services, is in how to achieve these affordances.

At the time of writing there are two established approaches: I call the first approach *a posteriori curation and consolidation*. In this approach, data stewards or members of the governance team are tasked with identification, tagging, documenting, and consolidating information about data that is already generated by the domains, after the fact. Then this curated information becomes the source for discovery. The other approach I call *a posteriori investigative intelligence*. This approach applies intelligent machine observations, unleashed after the fact on the data that is already generated, to extract metadata. For example, one could run algorithms over a large body of operational data to decide the trustworthiness of a table by analyzing who has accessed it, how widely it is used, and how it is being used. This information creates a layer of knowledge about the data that is useful for discoverability.

 While intelligent and investigative algorithms are helpful to bootstrap data mesh, discovering what data is available to an organization prior to implementing data mesh or helping observability of the mesh by adding additional information to each data product, they are insufficient.

Data mesh's main difference with both approaches is that it *shifts discoverability left*. Data discoverability, understandability, etc., *starts with the data product* itself, when the data product is created and throughout its life cycle. It's the responsibility of a data product to share the information needed to make itself discoverable, understandable, trustworthy, and explorable.

Data mesh designs discoverability for *machine* and *human access*—people can discover, understand, trust, and explore data products, and machines can automate these functions and build high-order capabilities on top. For example, the *mesh experience plane* can automate search of data products, using the discovery data provided by each data product.

The concept of a *discovery (port) API*, the mechanism through which a data product is discovered, was briefly introduced in Chapter 9. In this section, I discuss a few design elements in implementing discovery ports and focus on what is different in data mesh compared to other approaches.

Discovery and understanding aren't limited only to what I cover in this chapter. I will discuss it further in the "Observe, Debug, and Audit" section in Chapter 14.

Figure 13-1 shows the high-level interactions involved in the discovery process.

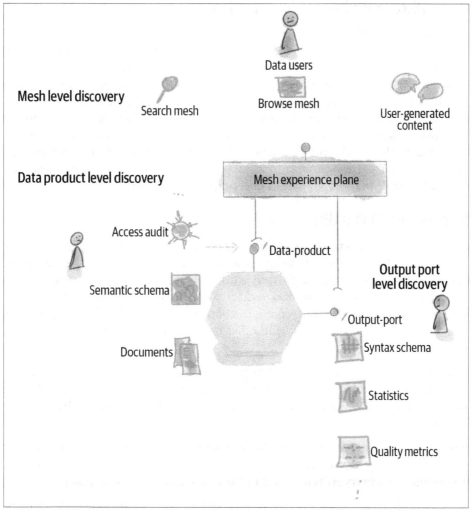

Figure 13-1. Example of a high-level design for a data product's discoverability, under-standability, trustworthiness, and explorability

The *mesh experience plane* plays an important role in surface mesh-level discovera-bility, such as search and browse functions. The mesh-level operations are enabled through data-product-provided data and APIs. Some of the discoverability information is scoped to the data product (e.g., its semantic specification and documentation), and some is scoped to each of its output ports (e.g., data format specification, statistical properties and shape of data, and quality metrics and SLOs).

Let's look a bit closer.

Begin Discovery with Self-Registration

Discovery of an entity begins with awareness of the entity's existence and the ability to locate and address it. In data mesh, discovery begins with a data product making its existence known to the wider ecosystem, particularly the mesh experience plane services of the data platform, such as search or browse. Allocation of various pieces of information such as name, address, and location can be done at different stages of the build, deployment, or runtime of a data product. There is prior art in the operational platforms such as a service mesh to register, address, and locate services. Similar technology and approaches can be deployed here. The minimum information required to enable a data product to kickstart discovery is a unique *name (identifier) as an addressable endpoint* for further querying of information.

Discover the Global URI

Ideally, all data products have a standard interface to describe themselves: a globally accessible URI[1] that is the root to access all other discovery facets of the data product. The information supplied by such a discovery API includes data-product-level information such as the core data semantic specification, overall documentation, the access logs, as well as deeper information specific to each of its output ports such as their specific data syntax and other metadata such as privacy levels, quality guarantees, etc.

The information supplied by the data product's discovery API can be updated at different stages of the life cycle. Some, including the schema specifications, are known at build time, and others, such as statistics describing the shape of the data, are created at runtime.

The data product developers maintain the data product discoverability information along with the data product's data. They use data platform components such as standardized discovery APIs provided by the *data product experience plane*.

Data users often begin their discovery and search through the mesh experience plane and can quickly deep dive into a specific data product's discovery information.

---

1 In this book I have used URI for the familiarity of the term; however, the implementations will use IRI (Internationalized Resource Identifier), which is similar to a URI but with the extended character set.

Understand Semantic and Syntax Models

All models are wrong, but some are useful.

—George Box

Data is a collection of facts put together according to a *model*. The data model is an *approximation* of reality, good enough for the (analytical) tasks at hand. Over time the approach to data modeling has evolved. At the time of writing, there are multiple common practices: relational tables (SQL data stores), flattened relations into nested tree structures (JSON structures) stored as columns or rows, property graphs—where entities and relationships both have properties (graph databases)—semantic graphs (Semantic Web), time-series data modeling, etc. Some modeling styles are more expressive and closer to intuitive human understanding of the world, and some are lossy and optimized for machine processing. For example, property graphs can model the world more intuitively as they describe the entities, their types, their properties, and the entities' relationships with each other. Most importantly, they can model the type and property of relationships explicitly. This is in contrast to nested tabular structures, where we have to make assumptions about the nature of the relationships based on the attribute values. Figure 13-2 shows a high-level modeling of the **playlist** domain as a property graph.

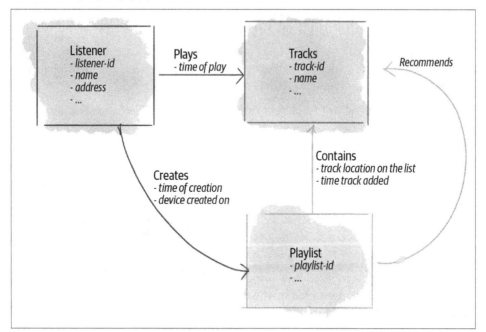

*Figure 13-2. Example semantic modeling of the **playlist** domain as a property graph*

Ideally, a data product models its business domain data as close to the reality of the business as possible. I call this the data product's *semantic model*: a machine and human-readable model definition that captures the *domain model* of the data: how the data product models the domain, what types of entities the data includes, the properties of the entities, the relationships between the entities, etc.

In addition to the *semantic model*, a data product encodes its semantic according to the access models supported by its output ports. I call this the *syntax model*. Every output port will have its own syntax model. For example, the playlist *file output port* will model the playlists as a nested table, stored as columnar files and defined according to the JSON schema (*https://json-schema.org*). This modeling is optimized for machine learning training using features (columns across all records).

The *semantic model*[2] is helpful for both machine and human understanding of what the data intends to capture without making hidden assumptions just by looking at the *syntax model*. It helps with the automated validation of data against its intended model. It also participates in the creation of a larger knowledge graph.

In addition to syntax and semantic modeling, coded data *expectations*[3]—the tests that articulate the expected values and distribution of data—defined by data product users and developers are greatly helpful to understanding data.

Establish Trust with Data Guarantees

In their quest to find the right data, data users need to assess certain *essential characteristics* of data in order to assess whether the data meets the guarantees that their particular use case requires.

These characteristics fall into different categories, such as *objective measures of data quality, levels of maturity, conformance to standards, temporal characteristics*, and so on.

A data product calculates and shares these objective metrics. For some of these metrics, it defines and maintains guarantees (SLOs). For example, the **play events** data product defines the timeliness of its events as a metric with a guarantee of 10–30 ms (delay range). It serves the latest timeliness metrics as it processes data and strives to meet its guarantee. These metrics are the means of informing and establishing trust, as well as a *contract* to set expectations with the data users.

The definition of these metrics, how to calculate them and present them, is a concern of global governance and enabled by the underlying *data product experience plane* in a standardized way.

---

2 The semantic model helps the data users to find meaning in data, but it does not convey the meaning by itself.

3 See Great Expectations (*https://oreil.ly/y0Tes*) as an example of a tool for expressing expectations of data.

Following is a list of categories of guarantees. This list is only intended to be an example and by no means complete. These measures are continuously updated as a data product processes new data. Similar to other metadata, the metrics are temporal, i.e., dependent on the data product's processing and actual times (or time windows):

Data quality metrics

There are a set of characteristics that can be grouped together as quality. These attributes aren't intended to define whether a data product is *good* or *bad*. They just communicate the threshold of guarantees the data product expects to meet, which may be well within an acceptable range for certain use cases. For example, the **player** domain may provide two different data products: a **play events** data product with near-real-time data and a lower level of consistency, including missing or duplicate events, and a **play sessions** data product with longer delays but a higher level of data consistency. Each can be considered trustworthy for their respective use cases. Here are a few examples in this category:[4]

Accuracy

The degree of how closely the data represents the true value of the attribute in the real-world context

Completeness

The degree of data representing all properties and instances of the real-world context

Consistency

The degree of data being free of contradictions

Precision

The degree of attribute fidelity

Data maturity metrics

In my opinion, data maturity is defined subjectively by an organization based on their roadmap and aspirations toward a data-driven operating model. For example, an organization can define a maturity model based on a few factors such as *degree of usage* (how widely the data is being used), *life cycle* (whether the data product under development and actively evolving and being optimized or dormant), *diversity* (number of modes of access and use cases they support), *linkage* (degree of linking to other data products in the form of reusing types and data), etc.

Data products calculate and share their maturity according to the organization's standard model.

---

4 At the time of writing, ISO/IEC 25012 (*https://oreil.ly/eOTU7*) standardizes 15 characteristics of data quality.

Data standards conformance

There are existing domain-specific data models that a data product may adhere to in order to increase its interoperability level. For example, in the healthcare domain, FHIR HL7 (*https://oreil.ly/H99gH*) resource definitions can increase the level of interoperability with a larger number of data consumers internal and external to the organization. The decision to adhere to industry standards must factor in the advantages (e.g., external interoperability) and disadvantages (e.g., transformation cost of fitting to a one-size-fit-all model).

Data products can express what standards their data model adheres to.

Temporality metrics

Data products intrinsically provide temporal data. Parameters illustrating the temporal shape of the data are helpful in assessing the suitability of data. Here are a few examples:

Epoch (actual and processing)

The earliest actual and processing times for which data is available. This indicates how far back in history a data user can time travel to access data. It illustrates the data product's duration of data retention.

Processing interval

A data product can report how often the data is processed, if there is such a pattern. In the absence of a specific interval, data products can provide statistics around mean, max, and min intervals. This sets the expectation for the data consumer as to how frequently they can expect to read and process new data.

Last processing time

Most recent data's processing time.

Last actual time (window)

Most recent data's actual time (or window).

Actual window

The window of actual times over which input data is processed and new data is created, if the data is aggregated over windows of time.

Timeliness

The degree to which the actual time and processing time are separated. The timelier the data is, the smaller the gap is between actual time and record time. In the previous chapter, I used the term *skew* for this property.

User-driven metrics

So far, all the categories mentioned earlier are provided by the data product—the provider of data.

Data users often establish trust based on the experience of their fellow data users using the data. Hence, the data product must capture and present the perception and experience of its consumers as a set of quality metrics. For example, the company may develop a *recognition system* such as allocating stars that data users can assign to data products based on their experience (e.g., reduced lead time in understanding and using the data, the perceived quality of data, the responsiveness of the data product development team, etc.).

I've provided the preceding list to give you an idea of the kind of information a data product is best placed to calculate and capture, right in the flow of its data processing, and provide autonomously to consumers to increase their level of trust.

Today, an overly populated landscape of metadata management technologies attempts to define and expose such information. The data mesh approach is agnostic to these tools and expects that all data products provide and manage the trust metrics consistently. There are two notable past open source standards to consult in establishing a consistent set for trust metrics: Data on the Web Best Practices: Data Quality Vocabulary (*https://oreil.ly/SZTWx*) and, relatedly, Data Catalog Vocabulary (*https://oreil.ly/DQDBK*). They attempted to create a consistent vocabulary with the mission of establishing best practices in providing an open data ecosystem on the web.

Explore the Shape of Data

Exploring data and understanding its statistically significant properties are critical to learning and trusting data for a particular use case. Data mesh recognizes data exploration as a critical step in the journey of data users, even if they ultimately choose not to use the data.

In scenarios where data users already have access to the data, they can run various queries—using the data product's output port—to explore individual records.

However, in many scenarios, where individuals cannot access individual records, often due to lack of access, they must be able to explore the shape of the data and evaluate whether it is fit for their particular use case. The data product is responsible for providing information that lets consumers explore the shape of the data without processing individual records.

For example, a data product's discovery interface can include functions that examine the distribution of data fields, value ranges, value frequencies, percentiles, etc. For example, to evaluate whether the existing **social media mentions** data product is a reliable source for identifying trends, the discovery interface can examine the "distribution of the sources of individual mentions." Is only a small group of people skewing the outcome, or is there a bell curve distribution of sources that can be reliably used?

More generally, data products can provide access to their data with *differential privacy* (*https://oreil.ly/eCl3A*) applied, to enable a host of explorations without providing access to individual sensitive records. Differential privacy is a technique that improves privacy while retaining the ability to perform useful analytics on large numbers of data, for example, by introducing tolerable noise in the data. "Differential privacy lets you gain insights from large datasets, but with a mathematical proof that no one can learn about a single individual."[5]

Learn with Documentation

Human-readable documentation is a wonderfully powerful tool to help a data user understand the data product, its ports' syntax, and its underlying data. Most importantly it helps a data product developer to tell a data story. Computational notebooks, originally introduced by Wolfram Mathematica, have been a trusty companion for scientists in support of scientific research, exploration, and educational processes. More recently, they are being extensively used in data science. They give a simple, document-based, intuitive, and interactive interface to explore data.

Data products can offer and maintain a set of computational notebooks that essentially communicate how the data can be used and show its properties in action. They combine human-readable documentation, code, and data visualization all in one place to tell a compelling story about the data. Additionally, the underlying platform can facilitate the sharing of data users' computational notebooks to capture other novel ways of using the data, expressed by others.

Computational notebooks are a great way to document, educate, and share use cases about a data product. However, I do not advocate the production application of notebooks. As they grow, a lack of programming support to create modular, testable, and scalable code makes maintaining them as long-lived production code difficult.

Discover, Explore, and Understand Design

Almost all the discoverability information I have listed in this section needs to be standardized across all data products to enable a seamless experience with the mesh, as well as a fair evaluation and comparison between different data products. This implies that the platform must be closely involved in providing the standardized approach in calculating, capturing, and sharing the information. For that, the data product sidecar ("Data Product Sidecar" on page 165) is best positioned to be extended with discoverability capabilities. If you recall from Chapter 9, the data product sidecar is a platform-provided agent that runs within the computational context

---

5 Cynthia Dwork and Aaron Roth. 2014. "The Algorithmic Foundations of Differential Privacy," *Foundations and Trends in Theoretical Computer Science*, 9(3-4): 211-407.

of a data quantum and is responsible for cross-cutting concerns that intend to be standardized across all data products.

Figure 13-3 demonstrates the data product sidecar's interactions in support of discoverability. It is not intended to be a listing of all the capabilities discussed here.

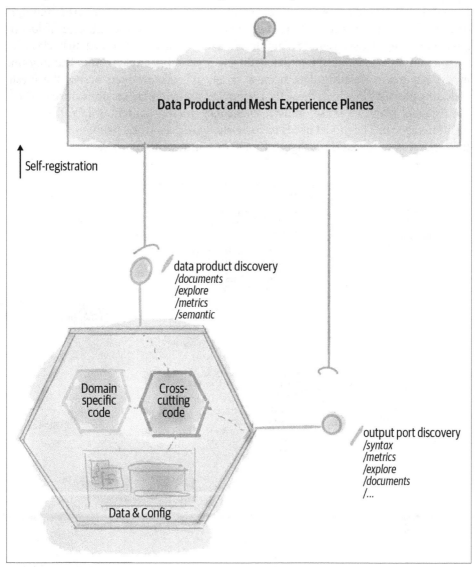

Figure 13-3. A data product sidecar provides a unified model of discoverability for all data products

Compose Data

> Learn how to see. Realize that everything connects to everything else.
>
> —Leonardo da Vinci

Powerful analytical use cases require *correlating* and *connecting* data across multiple data products and between different domains. For example, the use case of identifying **emerging artists** requires training a machine learning model that classifies whether an artist is gaining popularity during a period of time or not. Training this model requires correlating data from a variety of data products across the mesh, including **playlists** in which the artists' songs are present, **play sessions** during which the listeners play the artists' music, and **social media** content where the artists' mentions appear. The model needs to correlate these data products for each artist and for a specific window of time. Figure 13-4 demonstrates this example.

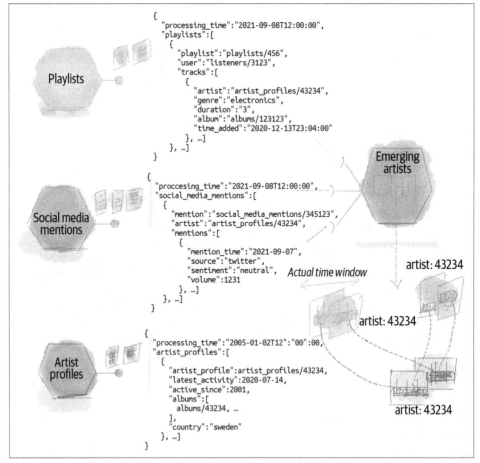

Figure 13-4. Example of data product composability

Data users who need to connect data across the mesh are either an on-the-mesh data product that is performing transformation on multiple sources or an off-the-mesh analytical application like an analytics report.

I use the generic term of correlation or composition as a placeholder for operations that can be performed on two or more data products such as join, union, filter, intersection, search (traverse), etc.

Consume Data Design Properties

Decentralization of data products imposes the following requirements on how data composability is designed in a data mesh implementation.

Ability to compose data across different modes of access and topologies
Recalling the previous affordances of consuming, transforming, and serving data in Chapter 12, data can be served in different modes—e.g., files, database tables, streams, etc. Hence, the ability to compose data needs to be agnostic to the syntax of data, underlying storage type, and mode of access to it.

For example, if we add **play events** to the previous example, the training of the **emerging artists** model needs to be able to compose information about artists across data served as a stream of events and columnar files.

As a result, many of the existing composability techniques that assume homogeneous data, such as defining primary and foreign key relationships between tables of a single schema, won't work.

Ability to discover and learn what is relatable, decentrally
Before composing data across different data products, a data user needs to discover what information across different data products is relatable. In our previous example, the **emerging artists** data product's developer needs to have the knowledge that information about an artist is present and relatable across the **playlists**, **social media mentions**, and **artist profiles** data products.

Traditionally, this is achieved through shared and centralized type systems or schemas. In contrast, data mesh needs to adopt a distributed data modeling approach.

Ability to seamlessly link relatable data
Once data users discover that the artist information is present in **social media mentions**, **playlists**, and **artist profiles**, they need to be able to map and correlate individual entities of the same artist across these data products. They need to know which field(s) in each data product is representing the artist, and how they can be mapped, for example, mapping a globally unique **artist identifier** that all data products consistently use to identify artists.

Ability to relate data temporally

Data products serve data across two time dimensions, processing time and actual time (or time windows). Inherently, times are the parameters of relating two data entities. For example, when discovering the emerging artists, the code (or query) transforming and correlating data across social media mentions and playlists includes the actual times when mentions of the artist happened or the artist was added to the playlist. The beauty of incorporating time by default is that all other operations naturally become a function of time.

In order to discuss data mesh data composability design, let's briefly look at some of the existing approaches to data composability and assess how they align with data mesh or not.

Traditional Approaches to Data Composability

Looking at the existing data technology landscape, we find a few notable approaches to data composability. At the time of writing, these approaches don't work for data mesh as is, but there are interesting lessons to learn.

In all these approaches, composability is enabled through the *explicit* definition of relationships and a shared type system. Using explicitly defined relationships, the system infers what can be related to what other information and how:

Relations defined in fact tables

Relational schemas, particularly star and snowflake schemas[6] adopted by data warehousing systems, define explicit relations between different types of data. For example, to access data for the **emerging artist** model training, a schema defines three dimension tables for **artist profiles**, **social media mentions**, and **playlists**. To compose and relate these data products for each artist, a fourth table—a fact table—is created with foreign keys of artists pointing to each of these tables.

Figure 13-5 shows the example of a fact table and its foreign key links to dimension tables.

This method of data composability, while performant and flexible for running queries in a centralized system, does not suit data mesh. It creates tight and fragile coupling between data products. Each data product's schema cannot change independently as they tightly link in the same schema to others. It assumes a homogeneous data syntax (tabular) across data products, and internal storage system identifiers create tight coupling to a specific implementation.

---

6 A snowflake schema is a multidimensional database schema that normalizes all entities into dimension tables and defines their relationships in a separate table, a fact table that holds foreign keys to dimension tables. The star schema is a special case of the snowflake schema.

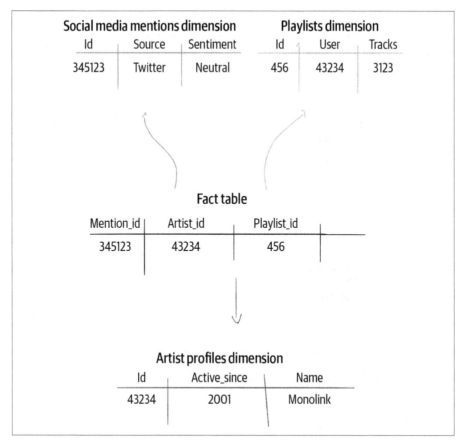

Figure 13-5. Example of composability enabled via fact and dimension tables

Data mesh moves away from explicitly defining facts or joining tables.

Relations defined using a distributed type system

Another approach to discovering relatable data is using a type system. For example, GraphQL's Apollo federation (*https://oreil.ly/CQLsu*) allows individual services to define a subgraph, a schema for a set of data types that the services can in turn resolve and provide data for. Each subgraph has its own schema and defines a set of types, objects, and their properties. Each subgraph schema can refer to other types defined in other subgraph schemas and can extend them. A gateway is then responsible for composing different subgraphs. The gateway uses the federated type system to correlate subgraphs and create a supergraph.

The relationships are presented through nested (tree-like) types. For example, in our example, the `Playlist` schema (type definition) will have a nested member field representing the `artist`, whose type refers to the `artist` type defined in the `ArtistProfile` schema:

```
// Artist Profile Schema
type ArtistProfile {
    artist: Artist
    active_since: Date
    ...
}
type Artist {
    id : ID!
    name : String
}
---------------------------

// Playlist Schema
type Playlist {
    user: String
    tracks : [Tracks]
...
}
// Using a shared type, Artist, defined in the Artist Profiles schema
type Track {
    artist: Artist
    duration: Int
    ...
}
```

A distributed type system is suitable for data mesh as it respects loose coupling and clear ownership of reusable types. However, it requires further refinement to account for change of the types (schemas) independently, and the dimension of time (versions of type), while allowing for type reuse.

Relations defined using hyperlinks and a centralized type system

Another method of defining relatable data is to use explicit HTTP hyperlinks in schemas to shared data types, whose schemas are often available through a centralized and shared schema registry, e.g., schema.org (*https://schema.org*). The direct hyperlink to schemas is often accompanied by direct hyperlinks to individual data instances across different sets.

For example, this approach is adopted by Linked Data (*https://oreil.ly/nSQOj*) and the standardizations that have been developed around the Semantic Web—a Web of Data at a global scale. While Linked Data adoption hasn't widely infiltrated enterprises' analytical data management, it's an interesting source of inspiration as it has tried to address distributed data linking and composability at a global scale, with an emphasis on linking related data through web links.

The following is a simple (and incomplete) example in JSON-LD, demonstrating data linking and schema links:

```
// Sample data provided in a (partial) JSON-LD format
// Defining the terms used by referring to their explicit
// definitions in a centralized schema
{
    "@context": {
        "@vocab": "https://schemas.daff.com/playlist#",
        "listeners": "https://schema.org/Person#",
        "artist": "https://schemas.daff.com/artist#",
        "album": "https://schemas.daff.com/album#",
        "track": "https://schemas.daff.com/track#",
        "track:id": {"@type": "@id"},
    },
    "@id": "https://daff.com/playlist/19378",
    "@type": "Playlist",
    "name": "Indie Playlist",
    "genre": ["Indie Rock"],
    "tracks": [{
        "@id": "https://daff.com/playlist/19378/1",
        "@type": "PlaylistElement",
        "artist:name": "Sonic Youth",
        "album:name": "Daydream Nation",
        "track:name": "Teen Age Riot",
        "track:id": "https://daff.com/tracks/39438434"
    },{
        "@id": "https://daff.com/playlist/19378/2",
        "@type": "PlaylistElement",
        "artist:name": "Thurston Moore",
        "album:name": "The Best Day",
        "track:name": "Speak to the Wild",
        "track:id": "https://daff.com/tracks/1275756"
    }
    ]
}
```

In this model, every single entity and data type has an explicitly defined schema, identified with a schema URI, and it can link to other schemas by defined ontologies and vocabularies (*https://oreil.ly/m2XzY*). Ontologies are explicit and formal specifications of terms in a domain and the relations among them and to other domains. For example, a playlist contains tracks, which contain links to definitions of tracks and artists. We are able to refer to these ontologies using the @context section of this JSON-LD Document. Each of these individual concepts has a schema with a unique URI that is often registered and available from a centralized repository of schemas.[7]

---

7 For more on developing ontologies, see Ontology Development 101 (*https://oreil.ly/ZodOD*).

Additionally, every single identifiable entity has a unique URI. For example, each artist in the `artist profiles` has a unique URI that other relatable entities can link to it. This data linking creates a graph, where new relationships can be inferred (*https://oreil.ly/eC71a*) by traversing the existing relationships.

This model suits distributed data modeling and composability, but it requires further refinement to avoid using shared centrally managed schemas that will be difficult to maintain and change over time.

Compose Data Design

The previous section contrasted the existing composability approaches to data mesh. With that, let's summarize data mesh's design of data composability and some of its key design elements.

The design prioritizes *loose coupling*, between data products, and minimizing *centralized synchronization points*. Data composability across the mesh relies on a *distributed type system (schemas)*, where each data product owns and controls the life cycle of its own schema. One data product can use and refer to other data products' schemas and data and use the mappings from one data product to its neighboring ones to identify what is relatable and how.

Note that at the time of writing, data mesh's approach to composability is an area of development.

Let's look at the design elements a bit more closely:

Distributed type system
Each data product, independently, defines the semantic types of the data it serves. Such a semantic definition, a schema, can be uniquely addressed by data users. A data product's semantic can refer to types defined in other data products' semantics and extend them—*semantic linking*. If the referencing system uses the internet addressing scheme of a URI, it simply enables a distributed type system that extends the scope to multiple hosting environments and organizations.

It is likely that the mesh experience plane creates a centralized index of all types defined by all data products on the mesh. The index is simply a read-only redirection mechanism to individual data products. It can continuously get updated as new data products get created or existing ones are updated or deleted.

Data product global URI
Each data product has a unique address, ideally in the form of a URI, that can be accessed programmatically within and across different data mesh instances. This address is the root to access all other sharable properties of the data product, such as its semantic schema, output ports, data entities, etc.

Data entity URI

Entities that appear in multiple data products must be identified with globally unique identifiers. The identifiers can be in the form of a URI to a particular data product that can ultimately resolve the address to a particular entity. In the example shared earlier, the concept of an "artist" is a polyseme that appears in multiple data products, like **playlists** and **artist profiles**. A data product becomes the source for generating these URIs. In this example, **artist profiles** allocates the URI at the time of artist onboarding.

How the global identifier is allocated, and how a data product resolves that to point to the information about a particular artist, requires sophisticated search and pattern matching capabilities. For example, the **social media mentions** data product finds certain names mentioned in Twitter comments. How it goes about mapping those mentions to known artists and artist URIs is a sophisticated pattern matching that looks at many different contextual parameters such as a mention of albums, tracks, events, etc. The **artist** domain might provide an artist resolution service for this purpose, using an ML model.

Machine optimization

Data product design is optimized for both humans and the organization as well as the machine at the logical level. For example, using loosely coupled hyperlinks over tightly coupled foreign key–primary key tabular relationships, data mesh favors the organization's optimization over the machine's. For example, URIs can remain the same while data products might change over time and get deployed to a different location.

If the platform demands query speed optimization, federated query engines can create internal indices to data served across different data products. These internal indices, which are more tightly coupled, continuously get refreshed and hidden away from data product developers. They are used internally by query engines. An analogous scenario is the web indices that Google maintains traversing web links. As search users, we just deal with human-accessible URIs, while Google search engines internally will use their optimized hashed indices.

In summary, at the logical level the representation of data is more sympathetic to the users, and at the physical level it is more sympathetic to machine operation.

The human element

While it's important that there are technical measures to support composition, such as agreed-upon ID schemes and standardized data formats and modeling, data composition also requires a human element. Data product owners need to be aware of related data and be motivated to make it easier for data users to build meaningful relationships. Like any product owner, they need to listen to their customers' needs and look for ways to facilitate compositions.

Figure 13-6 shows the high-level components important to the design of data composability of data products.

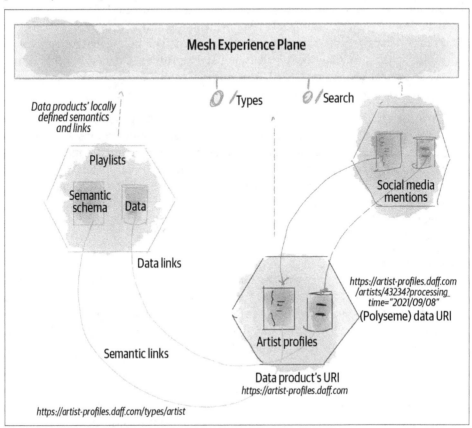

Figure 13-6. Data product's high-level components to design data composability

Recap

Data products are responsible for bridging the gap between the known and the unknown so data users trust them. The discovery, understanding, trust, and exploration of data begins with the data product, with the intentional design of interfaces and behaviors to share information about a data product's data semantic, data formats, usage documentations, statistical properties, expected quality, timeliness, and other metrics. Once these basic functions and metadata sharing is built into each data product, more sophisticated and ML-based discovery functions can be built for the mesh of connected data products to search, browse, examine, and get meaning from the mesh.

To drive higher-order intelligence and knowledge from individual data products, data users need to correlate and compose them. While the ability to stitch data together is fairly simple in a centralized model, a schema can define all the entities and their relationships. For data mesh this requires a few design considerations. These design considerations stem from one main objective: define a system of distributed data models that enables data composability that can rapidly evolve, without creating tightly coupled or centralized models. I introduced design concepts such as a data product's ownership of a time-variant, sharable, and referenceable semantic data model, semantic model linking, a global identification system to map data across data products, and most importantly the responsibility of data product owners to continuously look for opportunities to discover and create meaningful relationships with other data products.

I hope that this chapter inspires future data mesh implementers to create an open data modeling and composability language, agnostic to the underlying data storage and formatting technology.

CHAPTER 14

Design Managing, Governing, and Observing Data

Data products are long-lived, and with that comes the need to manage their state and govern, debug, and audit them over their lifetime.

This chapter concludes the design of the data product architecture, with a look at the final three affordances that enable managing a data product over the course of its lifetime.

In this chapter I discuss the design of how a data product affords:

- Data product developers to manage its life cycle from inception through many iterations of change, fixes, and evolution
- Being governed and in compliance with global policies
- Being monitored, debugged, and audited

Manage the Life Cycle

> Never tell people how to do things. Tell them what to do and they will surprise you with their ingenuity.
>
> —George S. Patton

Data mesh's promise of scale can be fulfilled only if the life cycle of a data product can be managed autonomously, when a data product can be built, tested, deployed, and run without friction and with limited impact on other data products. This promise must remain true while there is interconnectivity between data products—through their input and output data ports, sharing data, or schemas.

In Chapter 10 we looked at the journey of a data product developer in managing the life cycle of a data product with a focus on the use of platform services. It was then evident that the majority of the work around provisioning and managing infrastructure resources or complex mechanisms such as managing change and revisions is done by the underlying platform, the *data product experience plane*.

What remains to discuss here is the capabilities a data product provides to create and evolve it.

Manage Life-Cycle Design

One of the key capabilities of a data product in its life-cycle management is to define the specification of its *target state*—the resources it demands and the configurations required to do its job. I call this specification *a data product's manifest*. Data product developers configure and maintain the data product manifest and present it to the platform alongside other artifacts such as the data product's transformation code, tests, semantic definition, etc.

Figure 14-1 shows the interactions of managing the life cycle of a data product, with a focus on the capability expected from the data product: providing its manifest and other artifacts. A data product team develops two groups of artifacts: source artifacts such as transformation code and semantic definitions, and the data quantum manifest, the declaration of the target (runtime) state of the data product and resources it would require. The platform will use these artifacts to generate the build and runtime artifacts, provision necessary resources, and run the data product container.

As discussed in Chapter 4, the declarative modeling ("Abstract complexity through declarative modeling" on page 60) of a data product hides complexity. A data product declares its desired target state in its manifest. The manifest can change and evolve during the data product's lifetime.

Using the manifest declaration, a data product developer can communicate various facets and properties of a data product, in a standard fashion and ideally agnostic to the underlying physical implementation. The developer can change the declaration over time, create new revisions, and retire old ones.

The name *data product manifest* is inspired by other declarative infrastructure provisioning and orchestration systems like Kubernetes and Istio.

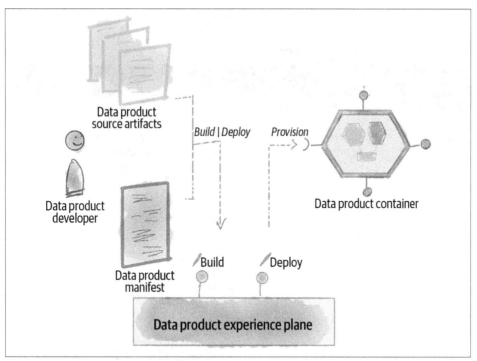

Data product
source artifacts

Build | Deploy

Provision

Data product
developer

Data product container

Data product
manifest

/Build   /Deploy

Data product experience plane

Figure 14-1. High-level interactions to manage the life cycle of a data product

Let's look a bit more closely at what a data product manifest can contain.

Data Product Manifest Components

Data mesh adopts a developer-experience-centric approach to the definition of the manifest. This means the data product developer focuses on aspects of the data product, rather than on the internals of the platform and how the platform physically provisions the data product. Additionally, a manifest does not lock in the data product to a physical implementation and ideally will be agnostic to the underlying platform and, hence, portable.

Table 14-1 lists a few examples of the components that a manifest defines.

Table 14-1. Data product manifest components

Manifest component	Description
Data product's URI	Data product's globally unique identifier. This was first introduced in Chapter 13 as the key identifier ("Discover the Global URI" on page 236) to discover and address a data product.
Output ports	Declaration of each output port, its supported mode of access, and any required guarantees. Using this declaration, the platform provisions resources such as storage and stream topics.
Output port SLOs	Declaration of what service level agreements each output port guarantees.
Input ports	Declaration of each input port and its structural characteristics, where the data comes from, and how it's retrieved.
Local policies	Configuration of local policies such as locality, confidentiality, privacy, retention, etc.
Source artifacts	Description of what other source artifacts are part of the data product, including its transformation code and input ports queries.

Over time, the design of the manifest language should allow for extensibility and addition of new facets over time, as the platform evolves to support new types of resources, or data products' dependencies and capabilities evolve.

The aspects of a data product that are best defined (imperatively) as code are not included here. For example, the data transformation logic, the input port queries, output port custom adapters, and code to enforce custom aspects of the policies are best implemented as code and maintained as data product source artifacts.

Govern Data

> I think Computation is destined to be the defining idea of our future.
>
> —Stephen Wolfram

Data mesh's position on governance and compliance with policies, introduced in Chapter 5 is to implement the policies that govern the data products as *code* and *embed* them in each and every data product. Embedded policies are validated and imposed at the right time through a data product's life cycle, and right in the flow of data. For example, if the policy demands in-memory encryption of certain types of data, articulation of this *policy as code*, embedded in the data product, allows the data product to test and enforce this policy at many different points in its life cycle: enforcing the policy at build and deploy time by validating that data product has access to a secure enclave,[1] using the secure enclave during the access and transformation of the data, and so on.

---

1 A trusted execution environment (TEE) that isolates an environment—processor, memory, and storage—with a higher level of security than the main application's execution context.

The idea of treating policies as code means that the policies are versioned, tested and executed, and observed like any other code. Policies, similar to data and data schema, are time-variant and change over time.

Govern Data Design

In Chapter 9 I introduced a data product's architectural components that enable *configuration* and *execution* of the policies embedded in each and every data product; I introduced the concept of a control port ("Control Port" on page 167), a set of interfaces that allow configuration of policies (e.g., setting access control rules for a data product) and calling high-privilege governance functions (e.g., executing the right to be forgotten and performing other data fixes). The concept of a *data product sidecar* ("Data Product Sidecar" on page 165) was introduced as a homogeneous execution engine accompanying all data products, to carry out the cross-functional needs of all data products such as *policy execution*. A sidecar is simply a logical placeholder for potentially multiple execution mechanisms for different policies, incrementally decorating[2] the data product over time. Lastly, I introduced the concept of the *data product container* ("Data Product Computational Container" on page 166) as a way of encapsulating the runtime instantiation of a data product's resources.

Since governance is a global concern and policies need to be applied to data products consistently, I proposed that the platform provide these components, container, sidecar, etc. These components work in collaboration with the *mesh experience plane*. The mesh experience plane provides capabilities for governance processes such as configuring policies and the right to be forgotten globally across the mesh, for all data products. This is depicted in Figure 14-2.

In addition to configuration and execution, governance of policies requires observability of their state of adoption. I will cover the observability aspect in the next section.

Policies can be domain-specific or agnostic. For example, a data product serving healthcare domain data must adhere to HIPAA—the Health Insurance Portability and Accountability Act in the United States—to assure the security and privacy of patients' health records. Domain-agnostically, all data products must adhere to their guaranteed data accuracy levels.

Whether policies are domain-specific or domain-agnostic, here are a few design characteristics that underpin a successful implementation of data mesh governance.

---

2 In object-oriented programming, the decorator pattern is a design pattern that allows behavior to be added to an individual object over time. Erich Gamma et al., *Design Patterns: Elements of Reusable Object-Oriented Software*, 1st ed., (Boston, MA: Addison-Wesley Professional, 1994).

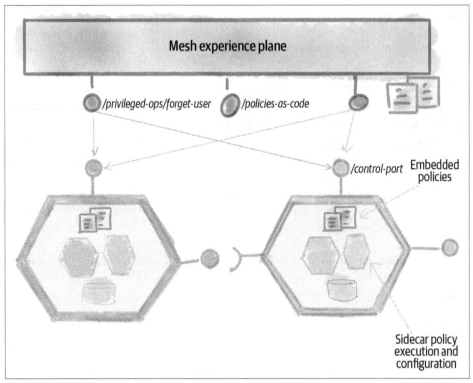

Figure 14-2. High-level design of embedded policies as code

Standardize Policies

It's critical to have a consistent way to express, configure, and enforce policies for all data products across the mesh. Policies are an element of every data product and part of its interface—e.g., control ports. Hence, standardizing what they are and how they are expressed and enforced will remove unnecessary complexity.

Let's look at a simple policy: *access control*, how we define and enforce who can access what data. The basic construct required to get access control work is the notion of *identity* of data users: how we confidently identify users—humans or systems— whether they are on the mesh and off the mesh. If we can't have a standardized way of specifying and recognizing identity, it's almost impossible to get data sharing across multiple data products. The more diversified the approach in designing identity is, the higher the friction and cost of sharing data. While this simple example must seem obvious and intuitive, you might be surprised that data management systems have not yet agreed on standardized identity and access control. Many storage and data management technologies have their own proprietary way of identifying the accounts of consumers and defining and enforcing their access control.

Here are a few examples of policies that benefit greatly from standardization.

Encryption

Depending on a data product's security policy, data is encrypted in transit, at rest, and more recently in memory with the progress of confidential computing (*https:// oreil.ly/DQ2Gj*). Today, encryption methods are fairly well standardized, naturally because there are two parties or more involved in encryption and decryption and they both need to agree on the protocol. Data mesh design can extend this standardization by including the expression of what is encrypted, at what level and with what method, in a data product's discovery interfaces and schemas.

Access control and identity

In a distributed architecture like data mesh to share data across the boundaries of a single platform, or an organization, there must be universal agreement in how we define and verify identity and access control rules. Most importantly, how do we do this in a technology-agnostic way? Independent of where data is stored or what cloud provider manages it, we need a standardized way to identify data users and manage their access.

While we are reaching agreements around identity in accessing operational APIs and services, we are far from that in analytical data access. In the operational world, the movement toward distributed APIs led to the standardization of identity—end user applications or other services—with the OpenID Connect protocol, usage of JSON Web Token (JWT) validation, X.509 certificates for services, and more recent standardization protocols such as SPIFFE (*https://spiffe.io*). The motivation of API sharing has been a big driver for establishing identity standards.

In the analytical data space, data remains locked up by technology vendors. There are not many incentives to share data across vendors, which results in lack of interest in creating access control standardization. I hope that data mesh's main motivation, *sharing data* beyond a technology silo, becomes a catalyst to change this.

Privacy and consent

The recent decade's regional privacy laws[3] aim to protect personally identifiable information of individuals, whose data is being captured and controlled by organizations. These laws have led to some level of standardization,[4] mostly in operating models and processes involved in managing data. However, due to the lack of standardization and incentives in data sharing, we find very limited effort behind the standardization of

---

3 Examples include GDPR (EU), CCPA (CA, USA), and Australia's Privacy Principles (Australia).

4 ISO/IEC 27701:2019 (*https://oreil.ly/ib7LD*), Security techniques.

privacy and consent. We are far from a consistent way of recognizing what data must be protected as private information, and how data owners' consent is expressed and shared along with their data, how they can consistently grant or revoke consent in how their data being used, and most importantly how transparently they can view the usage of their data.

As a distributed data sharing and management architecture, data mesh demands a consistent way of managing privacy and consent across all data products. The consents are a type of computational policy that each data product can embed.

Data and Policy Integration

The concept of a data product as an architecture quantum attempts to integrate data, code, and policy as one maintainable unit. This self-contained unit liberates us from many governance issues, including struggling to manage privacy and consent outside of the bounds of a specific technical storage. For example, the separation of consent policy from data makes it difficult to track or even respect the consent of the user, once the data is shared beyond the boundary of a particular technical system where consent is being managed. Data mesh links the policy and its configuration with the data it is trying to govern.

Linking Policies

Similarly to linking to data semantics and data entities across different data products, as discussed in Chapter 13, data products' policies can link to each other across data products so that when data leaves a particular data product to get processed by others, it maintains its link to the original policy that governs it. If the data transformation morphs it in a way that it no longer has a link to the original data and schema, the policy link is naturally broken too. Policy linking is helpful to multiple data products to retain access to the latest state of the policy, as maintained by the source data product.

This is an area that requires further development; however, data mesh enables the foundation to build distributed and ever-present policy sharing along with the data, a *data quantum*.

Observe, Debug, and Audit

> Don't control, but observe.
>
> —Gregor Hohpe

Let's look at the final and indispensable capability of a data product: *observability*. Data product observability is the ability to infer the internal state of data products, and consequently the mesh, by observing their external outputs. Observability intends to answer questions such as: Are data products performing their jobs successfully? Are they meeting their guarantees? Are data products conforming to the policies? Does processed data meet its statistical properties, volume, frequencies, ranges, distribution, etc.? Has there been any undesired access to a data product? Have there been any issues with data products, and if so what is the root cause? Are there any anticipated problems on the horizon? Observability answers these questions at the level of individual data products and their collection as a mesh.

The distributed architecture of data mesh—a loosely coupled mesh of data products, linked with each other to share their data, data models, and policies—creates complexity in observability. There are many moving parts that can each fail, there is a large number of data products and interconnections to monitor, and failures may go unnoticed. In a monolithic and tightly coupled system, a single failure often results in the failure of an overall system, which is easy to detect. In data mesh, the loose coupling of data products limits the failures as locally as possible; hence, it requires automated and comprehensive observability to detect and debug such failures.

The use cases for data product observability can be summarized as follows:

Monitor the operational health of the mesh
> Are data products receiving the data they expect, running their transformations successfully, and serving their data in compliance with their SLO guarantees and with the expected statistical properties? Observability detects if there are any interruptions to these processes, automatically self-heals and fixes the issues, and notifies the relevant people.

Debug and perform postmortem analysis
> When something goes wrong, when data is not matching our expectation, or there is an error in receiving, transforming, or serving data, data product observability helps data product developers and owners to assess the impact of the failure and discover the root cause.

Perform audits
> Data products enable third parties to perform audits—regulatory, risk, compliance, or security; for example, a service could continuously and automatically audit the access logs for security assurance—who is accessing what data, when, and how.

Understand data lineage
> Data lineage—understanding where data has originated from and what transformations it has gone through—remains an element of understanding and trusting data and is necessary for debugging issues with data. This is particularly helpful in machine learning where the quality of the model largely depends on the quality of the training data. Data scientists demanding a deeper understanding and trust in the training data often evaluate the data lineage. The lineage coupled

with contextual (runtime) metrics about data and the model are must-haves to understand and spot the real issues underlying an ML model deviation.

Observability Design

Data mesh observability begins with each data product, by design, sharing its external output and reporting its status. Each data product shares its *logs*, *traces*, and *metrics* while consuming, transforming, and sharing data. Building on these outputs, the mesh experience plane can then observe and monitor the mesh-level status.

The role of a data product in its observability is the key difference between the existing data observability and data mesh. Existing approaches monitor the state of data by an external party—the data team—inspecting the data after the fact in a lake or warehouse.

In data mesh, many of these after-the-fact data checks become part of the implementation of the data product's transformation, the tests and controls, articulated as computational expectations of data.

Let's discuss a few notable design characteristics of how data products enable observability.

Observable outputs

In the operational plane, distributed architectures like microservices have converged on three kinds of external output that collectively enable observability: *logs*, *traces*, and *metrics*. These are often referred to as observability pillars:

Logs
> Logs are immutable, timestamped, and often structured events that are produced as a result of processing and the execution of a particular task. They are often a great source of information in *debugging* and *root cause analysis*. In the case of a data product, the act of consuming, validating, transforming, and serving data can produce logs. For example, the **artist profiles** data product's log can capture when new data is received by the input port from the **artist onboarding service**, a summary of steps taken to productionize the data through a series of transformations, and when data for a particular processing time becomes available to data users.
>
> For logs to be useful and secure, it is important to standardize the structure, define the mandatory elements that all logs must consistently provide, and implement the right level of privacy measures to prevent overexposing information in the logs. This will allow for automated and ML-based analysis of the logs for insights on the operational health of the mesh. Collecting logs without setting up automated analysis is often futile, similar to collecting any other kinds of large-volume data without the ability to analyze it.

Traces

Traces are records of causally related distributed events. The trace records are structured in a way that can encode an end-to-end flow of actions and events. Traces, similarly to logs, are immutable, timestamped, and structured events. In the analytical data plane, the main usage of a trace is to create *data lineage:* how data flows through the data products and how data gets transformed by each product. Similar to logs, data products adopt a single standard to model the structure of their traces.

Note that traces in the operational plane often capture a tree of calls and transactions that get executed as a consequence of a request. For example, a web request to fetch a list of artists may result in calls into various microservices. Traces in data mesh represent the flow of data or data requests through a graph of input and output ports—from the source data product to the origin of the data to the final data consumers.

Metrics

Metrics are objectively quantifiable parameters that continue to communicate build-time and runtime characteristics of data products. In "Establish Trust with Data Guarantees" on page 238 in Chapter 13, I introduced a few categories of metrics that each data product continuously shares, e.g., timeline, completeness, accuracy, etc. Metrics similar to the logs and traces are immutable, timestamped (often numerical) events that can be tracked over a period of time.

These pillars are a great starting point for adapting a distributed observability model to data products. In Chapter 9, I introduced the observability APIs ("Data Discovery and Observability APIs" on page 159) as a standard interface for data products to share their external observability outputs, shown in Figure 14-3.

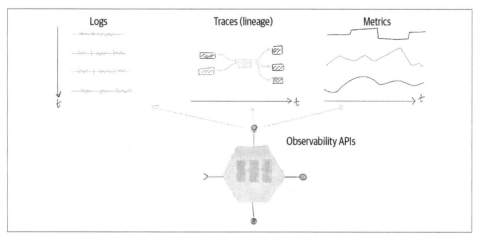

Figure 14-3. Three types of data product outputs shared by observability APIs

Traceability across operational and data planes

Many data products originate from operational systems. Specifically, source-aligned data products get their data from their collaborating operational system. For example, the **artist profiles** data product begins its existence by the act of an artist onboarding using the artist onboarding microservice application.

Hence, to provide a complete picture of data lineage, or the ability to debug issues and perform root cause analysis, the observability of data must extend beyond the data products to the operational systems. Observability data must be traceable to the operational systems.

Structured and standardized observability data

To facilitate creation of higher-order intelligence and insights from data products' observability data, the metrics, logs, and traces must have a structured format and ideally be standardized. They must model specific fields such as the data product's global URI, actual and processing timestamps, output port URIs, etc. Any structured information can have an unstructured element such as plain text for free-format messages. At the time of writing there is a need to create open industry standards for data product metrics, logs, and traces.[5]

Domain-oriented observability data

One way to scale and extend observability over time is to apply domain-oriented design to the observability itself, e.g., create domains of observability such as **data quality**, **data shape**, **data conformance**, etc.

One can imagine that the mesh-level observability information can itself be managed as data products; e.g., the **data quality** data product can provide metrics and a complementary set of insights on the data quality of the mesh.

 I have always felt uneasy with the generalization of all data about data into a catchall bucket of metadata. This approach removes intentionality in designing different classes of metadata. In fact, in my writing I have refrained from using the term *metadata* as much as possible. It's my personal belief that all data is data, there are correlations and relationships between different types of data, and all data can be designed as domain concepts, ranging from business domains (e.g., **artist profiles**) to observability domains (e.g., **data quality metrics**). The reusable concept of the data product caters to all analytical data.

---

5 At the time of writing, OpenLineage is in early development and can be mapped to data products' traces.

Recap

Man muss immer umkehren. (One must invert, always invert.)

—Carl Jacobi

If I could leave you with one takeaway from this chapter, it would be to invert your perspective on whose responsibility it is to manage, govern, and observe data; shift the responsibility from an external party getting engaged after the fact to the data product itself.

Data paired with computational capabilities and policies, in the quantum of a data product, can afford its users with basic capabilities: managing its life cycle with the help of a manifest, governing its data with execution of its embedded policies, and observing its state with its logs, metrics, and trace outputs.

There is a common thread present in the design characteristics of all data product capabilities introduced in this chapter:

Standardization
> Standardization of the data product's interfaces for mesh-level interoperability, e.g., adopting a common structure for logs

Emergence
> Emergence of mesh-level capabilities from individual data products, e.g., discovering lineage by observing each data product's input, transformation, and output traces

Agency
> Agency of each data product to share its observability outputs, error logs, metrics, etc.

Extensibility
> So that new competencies over time can be enabled over time, e.g., adhering to new policies

This chapter concludes the discussion of data mesh with regard to the capabilities and affordances of data products. Next, I will zoom out to the big picture of strategy, execution, and organizational change toward data mesh.

PART V

How to Get Started

A journey of a thousand miles begins with a single step.
—Lao Tzu

We have both made it to the last part of this book. Well done!

Are you considering adopting data mesh for your organization or helping others to do so? Are you in a position to influence, lead, or manage the execution of data mesh? Do you need some help on how to approach such a transformation organizationally and where to get started?

If you answered yes to these questions, this part is for you.

I assume that you have a solid understanding of data mesh foundational principles from Part I and understand the motivation and objectives of data mesh from Part II.

Scope

Data mesh is an element of a data strategy that fosters a data-driven organization to get value from data at scale.

Execution of this strategy has multiple facets. It affects the teams, their accountability structure, and delineation of responsibilities between domains and platform teams. It influences the culture, how organizations value and measure their data-oriented success. It changes the operating model and how local and global decisions around data availability, security, and interoperability are made. It introduces a new architecture that supports a decentralized model of data sharing.

In this part of the book, I describe a high-level approach to start and guide the execution of this multifaceted change. In Chapter 15, "Strategy and Execution", I introduce an *evolutionary* approach to adopt data mesh incrementally, generating value from an increasing number of data products while maturing the platform capabilities. In Chapter 16, "Organization and Culture", I cover some of the key changes to teams, roles, and performance metrics to create long-term ownership of data products and peer-to-peer data sharing.

At the time of writing this book, we are in the early years of adopting data mesh and beginning to create a decentralized organizational model where data sharing and analytics are becoming embedded into business-technology domains.

The approach suggested in these chapters is the adaptation of an evolutionary and large-scale transformation model that has been successfully applied in scenarios such as building domain-oriented operational teams and digital platforms.

I will share my experience of blockers and enablers specific to data mesh. This is just a starting point, and we have years ahead of us to refine a transformation approach unique to data mesh.

CHAPTER 15

Strategy and Execution

The essence of strategy is choosing to perform activities differently than rivals do.
—Michael E. Porter

Is your organization adopting a data-oriented strategy? Is it planning to offer distinct value to its customers and partners using data and insights? Does your organization have a vision to use data to perform a different set of activities or its current activities differently? Is your organization curious about data mesh as a foundation for implementing this strategy?

If you answered yes to these questions, this chapter is for you.

In this chapter I describe the relationship between data mesh and an overall data strategy, and how to approach its execution through an iterative, value-driven, and evolutionary approach.

But first, a quick self-assessment.

Should You Adopt Data Mesh Today?

Before you proceed to the rest of this chapter, you may ask yourself, is data mesh the right choice for my organization? Or more importantly, is data mesh the right choice now?[1]

Figure 15-1 depicts my perspective on these questions. I suggest that organizations that fall in the colored section of the spider graph—scoring medium or high on each of the assessment axes—are best positioned to adopt data mesh successfully at this

---

[1] "Now" is when this book is published and implies an early state of maturity for technologies that natively support data mesh.

point in time. You can use the following criteria to self-assess whether data mesh is the right choice for your organization now.

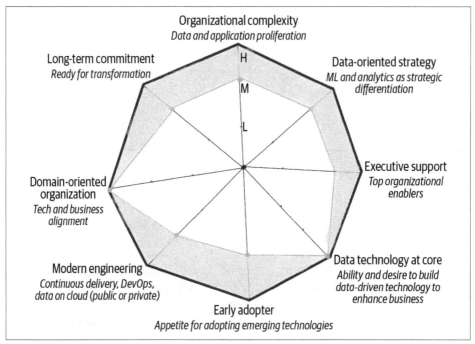

Figure 15-1. Criteria to self-assess readiness for data mesh adoption

Organizational complexity

Data mesh is a solution for organizations that experience scale and complexity, where existing data warehouse or lake solutions have become blockers in their ability to get value from data at scale and across many functions of their business, in a timely fashion and with less friction.

If your organization has not reached such a level of complexity and the existing data and analytics architectures meet your needs, data mesh will not offer you much value.

Organizations with a large proliferation of data sources and use cases that score moderate or high on data complexity benefit from data mesh. For example, enterprises or scaleups—fast-growing startups—whose business encapsulates many different data domains and a large proliferation of data types collected from many sources and that have a business strategic differentiator heavily dependent on ML and analytical use cases are great candidates for data mesh. Enterprises or scaleups in industries such as retail, banking and finance, insurance, and large tech services fall into this category.

For example, consider a healthcare provider or payer. There is an inherent complexity in the diversity of data. It ranges from clinical visits to patient profiles, lab results, pharmaceuticals, and clinical claims. Each of these categories of data can be sourced from multiple parties in an ecosystem of business domains or independent organizations, hospitals, pharmacies, clinics, labs, etc. The data is being used for many use cases: optimized and personalized care models, intelligent insurance authorization, and value-based care.

The primary criteria for adopting data mesh are the intrinsic business complexity and proliferation of data sources and data use cases.

Data-oriented strategy

Data mesh is a solution for an organization planning to get value from data at scale. It requires the commitment of product teams and business units to imagine using intelligent decision making and actions in their applications and services. Such a commitment is possible only when the organization identifies data enabling ML and analytics as a strategic differentiator.

A data-oriented strategy then translates down to data-driven applications and services, which then turns into teams' commitment to data.

Without a strategic vision around data usage, it would be difficult to motivate domain teams and business domains to take on the extra responsibility of data sharing.

Executive support

Data mesh introduces change, and with that comes resistance to change. Any change of such scale experiences detractors and blockers. It will be necessary to make tough decisions between the progress of the platform versus building point solutions to meet a deadline. It demands motivating the organization to change how people work.

All this calls for executive support and top-down engagement of leaders. In my experience, the most successful data mesh implementations have had the backing of C-level executives.

Data technology at core

Implementing data mesh builds on a new relationship between technology and business. It builds on the pervasive application of data in each business domain. Organizations that have data technology at their core use data and AI as a competitive advantage, as the means to expand and reshape their business and not merely as an enabler.

Such organizations have the desire and ability to build and create the technology needed to embed data sharing and consumption at the core of each business function.

In contrast, organizations that see technology as a supporter of the business and not at the core often delegate and externalize technology capabilities to external vendors and expect to buy and plug in a ready-made solution for their business needs. Such organizations are not yet positioned to adopt data mesh.

Early adopter

At the time of writing this book, data mesh is enjoying its early years of adoption by innovators and lead adopters. Early adopters of new innovations must have certain characteristics: they are venturesome opinion leaders[2] in their industry. They have an appetite for adopting emerging technologies, such as data mesh.

Early adopters of a novel approach, particularly one as multidimensional and pervasive as data mesh, demand a spirit of experimentation, taking risks, failing fast, learning, and evolving. Companies that adopt data mesh at this point in time must be willing to begin from the first principles, adapt them to their context, and learn and evolve.

On the contrary, organizations that don't take risks and like to only adopt well-tested, refined, and prescribed playbooks and fall into the late adopter category may need to just wait for some time.

Modern engineering

Data mesh builds on a foundation grounded in modern software engineering practices. Continuous and automated delivery (*https://oreil.ly/d2bkH*) of software, DevOps practices, distributed architecture, computational policies, and availability of modern data storage and processing stacks—on private or public clouds. Without solid engineering practices and access to open and modern data tooling, it will be challenging to bootstrap data mesh from the ground up. Data mesh shares prerequisites for microservices[3] and requires modern data and analytics technology and practices.

Additionally, data mesh works with modern technology stacks that are API driven and easy to integrate and aim to enable many smaller teams, as opposed to one large, centralized team. Technologies that enforce centralized data modeling, centralized control of data, and centralized storage of data don't lend themselves to a successful data mesh implementation. They become a bottleneck and conflict with the distributed nature of data mesh.

Domain-oriented organization

Data mesh assumes that the adopters either are modern digital businesses with a level of technology and business alignment or are on the journey toward it. It

---

2 Everett M. Rogers, *Diffusion of Innovations*, 1.

3 Martin Fowler, "Microservice Prerequisites" (*https://oreil.ly/lqBAy*), (2014).

assumes that organizations are designed based on their business domains, where each business domain has dedicated technical teams who build and support the digital assets and products that serve the business domain. It assumes that technology and business teams are in close collaboration to use technology to enable, reshape, and expand the business.

For example, a modern bank has dedicated technology groups for digital core banking, digital processing of loans, digital commercial and personal banking, digital credit and risk, etc. There is a close alignment between technology, technical teams, and the business domains.

In contrast, organizations with a centralized IT unit that shares people (resources) based on projects across all business units, without continuous and long-term ownership of technical assets for each business domain, are not a good fit for data mesh.

Domain-oriented data sharing scales only if there is a domain-oriented tech and business alignment in place.

Long-term commitment
As you will see in upcoming chapters, the adoption of data mesh is a transformation and a journey. While it can be started with a limited scope and an organizational footprint of a small number of domains, the benefits are compounded when exploited at scale. Hence, you need to be able to create an organizational commitment to the vision and embark on a transformation journey.

Data mesh cannot be implemented as one or two one-off projects.

If you see yourself aligned with the previous criteria, let's go ahead and look at how to execute a data strategy using data mesh.

Data Mesh as an Element of Data Strategy

To understand how data mesh fits into a larger data strategy, let's look at our hypothetical company, Daff, Inc.

Daff's data strategy is to create an *intelligent platform* that connects artists and listeners through an immersive artistic experience. This experience is *continuously* and *rapidly improved* using data and ML embedded in each and every interaction of the listeners and artists on the platform. This implies capturing data from every single touchpoint on the platform and augmenting every platform feature using ML derived from the engagement data. For example, the platform's better playlist predictions lead to more listeners with higher engagement, which then leads to more data and hence better predictions—creating a positive self-reinforcing loop for the business.

Daff's ambitious strategy is executed through an organizational-wide data mesh implementation, where the nodes on the mesh can represent data collected and curated from various activities on their platform and the intelligence inferred by machine learning models trained on such data.

Figure 15-2 shows the relationship between the data strategy and data mesh.

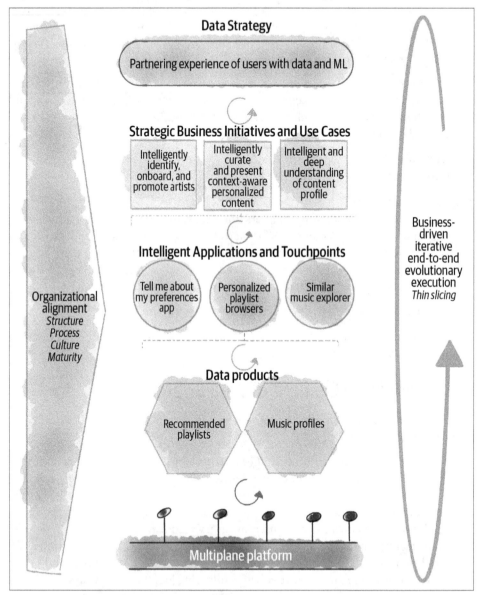

Figure 15-2. The big picture. connecting data mesh execution to the overall data strategy

As Figure 15-2 shows, data strategy drives the execution of data mesh. Let's explore the diagram top down and go through the implementation of data mesh from strategy to the platform, with continuous feedback loops.

Data strategy

Data strategy defines how uniquely a company takes advantage of data and creates a roadmap of strategic initiatives.

For example, Daff's strategy is based on partnering every content producer's, artist's, and listener's experience with data and ML.

Strategic business initiatives and use cases

Following the strategy, a set of business initiatives, use cases, and experiments are defined to utilize data and ML.

One such business initiative is the curation and presentation of ML-based content—music, podcasts, radio—to the listener. The ML models exploit multidomain data such as the user's context—location, time of day, latest activities, and the user's preferences matched with the content's profile.

These initiatives then lead to the implementation of one or multiple intelligent user touchpoints and applications.

Intelligent applications and touchpoints

Ultimately the user's experience needs to be enhanced through their touchpoints and the applications they use. Each intelligent business initiative can lead to the augmentation of existing or new user applications with ML.

For example, the initiative of "Intelligently curate and present context-aware and personalized content" can lead to changes to multiple applications. It can be offered with a new application such as "Tell me about my preferences" that helps users grasp a deeper understanding of their preferences matched with music profiles and other environmental factors. It can lead to creation of multiple playlists through the "Personalized playlist browser" app that each provide a playlist intelligently curated based on calendar events and holidays, based on the day of the week, based on different genres, based on time of day, etc. It can lead to the creation of a new intelligent exploration tool, "Similar music explorer," that allows the user to traverse a graph of related music content, based on their profiling and user preferences.

Development of these intelligent applications leads to the identification and development of data products that provide the necessary data and insights.

Data products

One of the core components of data mesh is a set of interconnected data products. Intelligent applications drive the identification and development of the data products on the mesh. While real-world applications initiate the creation of data products, not all data products get directly used by them. Consumer-aligned data products are directly used by the applications, while aggregate or source-aligned ones are likely used by those data products. Over time, a mesh of data products gets created that get reused for new and novel intelligent applications.

For example, the "Personalized playlist browser" app depends on various recommended playlist data products, such as the **monday playlists**, **sunday morning playlists**, or **focus playlists** data products that in turn rely on **music profiles** data product, among others.

Multiplane platform
The creation and consumption of data products and intelligent applications drive prioritization and development of platform capabilities. As the number and diversity of the data products, data users, and providers grow on the mesh, so do the features and maturity of the platform.

The platform features are developed in parallel and sometimes ahead of the data product and intelligent application development. However, the platform value is demonstrated and measured based on its usage through the frictionless and reliable delivery of data products.

Over time, platform features and services create a foundation for reuse in the delivery of new data products.

Organizational alignment
As the organization executes its data strategy, it implements the organizational and social aspect of the data mesh.

The formation of a federated governance operating model, formation of cross-functional—business, dev, data, ops—teams, and establishment of the data product ownership role are all organizational aspects of data mesh that require the care and attention of the change management discipline.

Organizational alignment happens concurrently and as part of the delivery and execution of data business initiatives, however with explicit intention and organizational planning.

I will cover these aspects in Chapter 16.

Business-driven, iterative, end-to-end, and evolutionary execution
The overall process described in the preceding establishes the high-level steps of the execution. However, these steps are executed iteratively, with built-in feedback and monitoring so that the organization can measure and monitor its progress toward the target state in an evolutionary fashion. Iterations continuously deliver value and execute all the steps involved end to end. See the section "Data Mesh Execution Framework" on page 279 for more on this.

In the rest of this chapter, I share some practical guidelines to use this high-level execution framework. In the next chapter, I cover the cultural and organizational aspect of data mesh implementation.

Data Mesh Execution Framework

> Brilliant strategy puts you on the competitive map, but only a solid execution keeps you there.
>
> —Gary L. Neilson, Karla L. Martin, and Elizabeth Powers, "The Secrets to Successful Strategy Execution" (*https://oreil.ly/Gf4Ff*) (Harvard Business Review)

To get started with a data mesh execution, we first need to acknowledge that it's likely going to create transformational change—culture, organizational structure, and technology. I understand the word *transformation* carries quite a bit of weight, as if we need a great deal of potential energy to get it into motion. What I want to share with you here is a high-level framework that can help you get started. This framework helps you move forward and make progress one iteration at a time, delivering value and outcomes while maturing the foundation—the platform, the policies, and the operating mode. It allows using the kinetic energy of moving forward to keep going, instead of delaying the execution to gather all the will and energy needed for a big bang push to change.

Figure 15-3 shows the high-level elements of the data mesh execution framework, *business-driven, end to end, iterative, and evolutionary.*

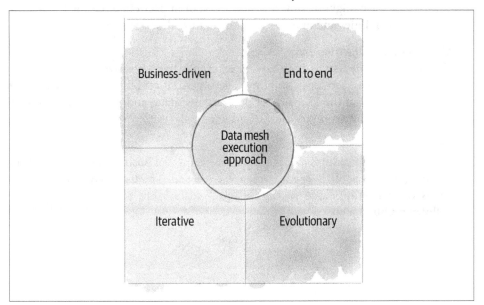

Figure 15-3. A high-level data mesh execution framework

Let's look into how these aspects impact the activities, outcomes, and measurements involved in executing a data mesh implementation.

Business-Driven Execution

Data mesh is a component of a larger data strategy, and as demonstrated in Figure 15-2, its execution is driven by the strategic business cases and user scenarios that require ML or analytics, which then drive the identification and delivery of the data products and the components of the platform to build, manage, and consume them.

This flows similar to how Amazon approaches building their major products and initiatives. "Start with the customer and work backwards—harder than it sounds, but a clear path to innovating and delighting customers. A useful Working Backwards tool: writing the press release and FAQ before you build the product."[4]

While there are many benefits to this approach, a few challenges need to be managed.

Benefits of business-driven execution

These are a few key benefits to a business-driven execution:

Continuous delivery and demonstration of value and outcome
Showing results during a long transformation has a positive impact on morale, getting buy-in, increased commitment, and assuring continuation of investment.

A business-driven execution is continuously delivering business value, though initially the pace might be slower or the scope of impact might be smaller. As the platform capabilities and operating model mature, the pace and scope improve.

Rapid feedback from the consumers
Engaging with the users—internal and external—has a positive influence on the platform and data products' usability. The organization builds and evolves what is needed based on the feedback of the business, data, and platform consumers. The feedback is incorporated earlier and iteratively.

Reducing waste
Developing data products and platforms based on real business use cases leads to building what is actually needed when it is needed. The technology investments focus on delivering value to the business, sustainably, in contrast to merely following a build plan.

---

4 Colin Bryan and Bill Carr, *Working Backwards*, (New York: St. Martin's Press, 2021), 98.

Challenges of business-driven execution

There are a few challenges to this approach that need to be closely managed:

Building point-in-time solutions
A narrow focus on delivering solutions to a single business use case at a time may lead to developing platform capabilities and data products that are not extensible to meet future use cases. This is a possible negative outcome of business-case-driven development. If we only focus on a particular business application, and not beyond that, we likely end up building point solutions narrowly designed for one particular use case, which do not extend to be reused and evolved for future use cases.

This is particularly problematic for *platform* services as well as *source-aligned* and *aggregate data products*. The purpose of the platform services and data products on the mesh is to serve and enable a wide set of use cases.

How to remediate point-in-time solution building?

Product thinking is the key to finding the right balance between point-in-time solutioning and the YAGNI (*https://oreil.ly/w9K5e*) principle—building something ahead of time when "You Aren't Gonna Need It." Applying product ownership techniques to the platform services and the data products can deliver value for customers today, with an eye on the horizon for future and upcoming use cases. Data product owners understand the unbounded nature of analytical use cases. Future use cases that we are likely unaware of today will need to reach into past data to discover patterns and trends. Hence, data products need to capture data beyond the exact need of known use cases. This is particularly true for source-aligned data products ("Source-Aligned Domain Data" on page 21), where they need to capture the reality of the business and the facts as closely as possible and as they occur.

Delivering to tight business deadlines
A business-driven execution subjects the development of platform and data products to business deadlines. Business deadlines are often hard to change as they require coordination across many parties inside the organization and sometimes with partners and customers outside. To meet these deadlines, the lower layers of the stack such the platform services can incur technical debt (*https://oreil.ly/1eiKE*), cutting corners in quality in order to meet the deadline of the business case.

This is not a new phenomenon in software development. We almost never build software in a vacuum and almost always are faced with external deadlines, drivers, and unforeseen environmental circumstances that change the priority of features and how they are built.

How to remediate incurring technical debt in the face of deadlines?

Long-term product ownership of the platform and data products and evergreen *engineering practices* (*https://oreil.ly/Ye6MX*) can assure that there is a continuous improvement process in place to address technical debts that may occur along with new feature delivery. The *long-standing* platform and data product teams have the knowledge and incentives to maintain their systems and data beyond a particular project delivery. This balances between the extensibility and long-term design of the platform and short-term project delivery. In short, the essence of the *product mode of working* (*https://oreil.ly/z2OI0*) strikes a balance between short-term technical debt to meet deadlines versus long-term product quality.

For example, long-term product owners of platform services or data products know that getting the APIs and interfaces right is a priority, even when in a pinch for time. Often it is easier to fix the tech debt incurred in implementation details than make changes to the interfaces. API changes likely have a higher cost of change as they impact a number of consumers.

Project-based budgeting

Delivery of business initiatives is often organized as time-bound projects with a fixed allocated budget. Executing a data mesh implementation through business initiatives can have a negative impact on budget and resource allocation for long-standing digital components of the mesh—data products and the platform.

When the budget is allocated to a time-bound business initiative, it becomes the sole source of investment for building the platform services or data products. As a result, their long-term ownership, continuous improvement, and maturity suffers.

How to remediate project-based budgeting?

Business projects are great vehicles for execution of the long-standing platform and data products. But they cannot be their sole funding mechanism. The platform and data products need to have their own allocated long-term resources and budget.

The project mentality is at odds with platform and product thinking where product teams are never done. They continue to mature, maintain, and evolve the product in the face of new requirements and support many projects.

Guidelines for business-driven execution

Here are a few guidelines and practices when starting with a business-driven data mesh execution:

Start with complementary use cases

Picking a couple of complementary use cases at a time, over a single use, avoids building point solutions. Building the reusable components of the mesh through complementary and concurrent use cases can be a forcing function to avoid the pitfall of point solutioning.

For example, the early use cases can be taken from different yet complementary areas such as analytics and reporting, complementing ML-based solutions. This forces the design of the data product to cater to two different modes of access, ML and reporting, over solutioning for one mode in a way that is not extensible to others.

Know and prioritize the data consumer and provider personas

Focusing on both types of data mesh user personas—data providers and data users—helps prioritize the platform capabilities fairly and for the most end-to-end impact.

Get to know the people involved in building the intelligent solutions, the application developers, data product providers, and data product consumers. Understand their native tooling and skill, and then prioritize the work based on this information.

For example, an early project is ideally done by the population of developers who are considered advanced users of the platform. They can work with missing features and be part of creating the required platform features.

In my experience, many data mesh executions begin with an emphasis on data product creation. As a result, the data consumer experience suffers, and the end-to-end outcome is compromised.

Start with use cases that have minimal dependencies on the platform's missing features

The platform evolves in response to its users. It cannot simply satisfy all the features needed by all the use cases at any point in time. In the early phases of execution, it is important that the use cases are carefully selected. The early use cases have just enough dependencies to the platform, so they drive the prioritization and build of necessary platform services without getting completely blocked.

Start with use cases and developer personas that don't get completely blocked by the missing platform capabilities. This creates momentum. As for the missing platform capabilities, they can be custom developed by the domain teams and later get harvested and generalized into the platform.

Create long-term ownership and budgeting for platform services and data products
> While business initiatives and individual use cases can provide investment to develop the mesh, the mesh must be considered a long-standing digital investment and an internal product of the company.
>
> It is expected to continue to deliver value beyond its inception. Hence, it requires its own allocated resources and investment to sustain its long-term evolution and operation.

Example of business-driven execution

Let's have a closer look at the example I introduced in the opening of this chapter and see how business initiatives can drive the execution of data mesh components.

Daff has a strategic initiative to "Intelligently curate and present context-aware personalized content." This initiative embodies a program of work using ML and insights to present and suggest different types of content such as music, podcasts, and radio channels to listeners. The program is planning to exploit data including users' interactions, profiles, preferences, their network, locations, and local social events to continuously improve the relevance of the recommendations and curated content.

This business initiative leads to the development of a few ML-based applications such as "Tell me about my preferences," "Personalized playlist browser," and "Similar music explorer." These applications depend on curated playlists and music, recommended based on many data dimensions such as mood, activities, time of day, holidays, music genre, etc.

To provide the data for these curated playlists, multiple data products must be developed. The list of data products includes consumer-aligned recommended playlists such as **monday playlists**, **sunday morning playlists**, **sports playlists**, etc., that utilize ML. To build these data products, a few source-aligned and aggregate data products are needed, such as **listener profiles**, **music profiles**, **listener play events**, **calendar**, etc.

Depending on the maturity and availability of the platform capabilities, the platform prioritizes the needs of data product developers and consumers. For example, given the growth of the number of data products, the platform may prioritize *data product automated life-cycle management*, or due to ML-based transformations it will support *ML-model transformation* and *flow-based transformation* engines.

Given the privacy concerns of users' profiles and information, the governance and the platform prioritize establishing, codifying, and automating encryption and access to personally identifiable information (PII) for all the data products.

This process repeats with the introduction of new business initiatives, e.g., "Intelligently identity, onboard, and promote artists."

End-to-End and Iterative Execution

The only thing a Big Bang re-architecture guarantees is a Big Bang!

—Martin Fowler

Continuous iterations of end-to-end delivery of intelligent business value enriches the mesh. It builds up the number of data products. It enhances the platform services. It increases the coverage and effectiveness of the automated policies.

Figure 15-4 visualizes an end-to-end iteration of data mesh execution based on the previous example. At any point in time, there are multiple iterations executing concurrently.

Through iterations of delivering use cases, such as the one mentioned earlier, more data products get created, more applications become intelligently augmented, more domains become part of the mesh, further platform services mature, and more of the policies become computationally enabled.

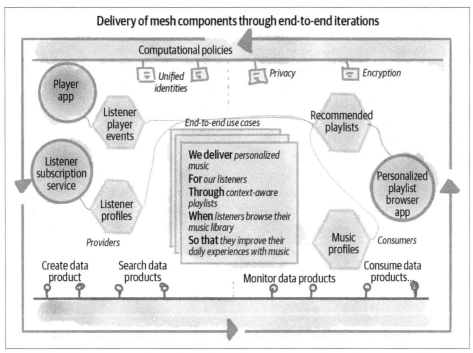

Figure 15-4. Maturing and enriching the mesh components through iterations of business use cases

Evolutionary Execution

The proposed execution model for creating a data mesh operational model and architecture is incremental and iterative, where with each iteration the organization learns, refines the next steps, and incrementally moves toward the target state.

I don't recommend a rigid up-front plan of carefully designed tasks and milestones. From experience, I simply don't believe such a plan will survive the first encounter with the execution and volatile environment of a large-scale business. Having said that, frameworks such as EDGE (*https://oreil.ly/mb069*)—a value-driven digital transformation—that prioritize getting outcomes, lightweight planning, continuous learning, and experimentation founded on agile principles (*https://oreil.ly/xzTLI*) can be very helpful in defining the operational model of the transformation.

Regardless of the transformation framework you choose, the process of executing data mesh is treated as an evolutionary one. An evolutionary process recognizes and caters for different stages of maturity of the implementation and has a set of tests and metrics that continuously guide the execution toward the optimal outcome and higher levels of maturity.

In this section, I share two tools that help you navigate an evolutionary execution: a multiphase adoption model that guides the execution at the macro level looking at the long-horizon milestones, and a set of objective functions that guide the evolution at the micro level of each iteration.

A multiphase evolution model

I have found the s-curve of innovation adoption[5] is quite a useful tool to frame the evolution of data mesh components. While the shape of the curve might be different in different organizations, some with a steeper or slower slope, or a shorter or a longer tail, the general phases of the curve can be successfully used to guide the approach to evolution. This is useful in guiding the long-horizon evolutionary milestones.

Figure 15-5 shows the s-curve of growth for data mesh. Each phase of the curve is mapped to a different population of adopters—*innovators, early adopters, majority adopters, late adopters, and laggards*—in the organization. Then, each phase of the curve is mapped to a corresponding mode of development—*exploration when bootstrapping, expanding when scaling, and extracting[6] when sustaining operation at scale.*

---

5 Rogers, *Diffusion of Innovations*, p. 1.

6 Kent Beck has named the three phases of product delivery, "Explore, Expand, and Extract, 3X" (*https://oreil.ly/UMXuN*). He has identified different techniques and attitudes toward product development during each of these phases. I have adapted them to data mesh execution.

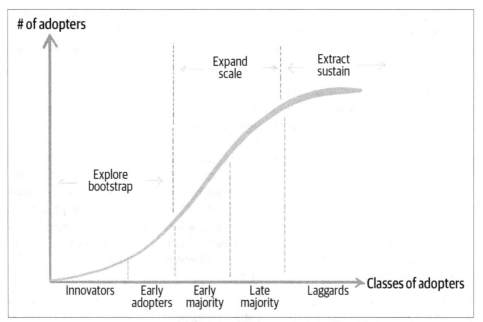

Figure 15-5. Evolutionary adoption of data mesh in an organization

This is a de facto model for adopting a new innovation, and it can be adapted to guide the evolutionary phases of the data mesh components and principles.

For example, let's see how this can be applied to the execution of the platform component. The platform implementation will go through phases of *bootstrapping with* an *exploration mindset* where the early features of the platform are built in service of the innovator and early adopters—the risk takers and expert users. As the platform matures, it expands and extends its self-serve capabilities to serve a larger population of users, the population of generalist technologists in domains without hand-holding. During the expansion phase, the platform matures its support services to reduce the friction of using the platform and satisfy a more diverse persona of late platform adopters. Once the majority of users and their needs are addressed, platform changes remain minimal, and the organization *extracts* and exploits the features that are currently in place, at scale. During this phase, the platform APIs and services get reused by new data products and use cases.

With the arrival of a major industry innovation in data management, an organization's attempt to use the platform in new and novel ways, and the vendors' shifts in the underlying technologies, the platform will go into the next s-curve of evolution, and the process repeats.

Similarly, you can use this curve to plan the execution of domain ownership. Depending on the phase of the evolution, identify the corresponding class of domains—innovators, lead adopters, late adopters, and laggards—and prioritize which ones join the mesh first. For example, pick the domains that have more data expertise as the innovator adopter before moving to the majority adopter domains. Use the early adopter domains to pave the path for others. For each phase of the evolution, be intentional about the different capabilities developed and the behavior of the teams. For example, in the early phases, the teams should adopt a more exploratory attitude to establishing policies, the platform, and data products, with a tolerable level of manual intervention. In the expand phase, the mesh needs to mature to minimize manual activities, have extensive observability in place to monitor the load, and scale usage with great policy coverage.

Let's look at the adaptation of the s-curve to each of the data mesh components and establish their characteristics for each evolution phase.

Domain ownership evolution phases. Figure 15-6 shows an example of dimensions of domain ownership as it evolves through the adoption phases.

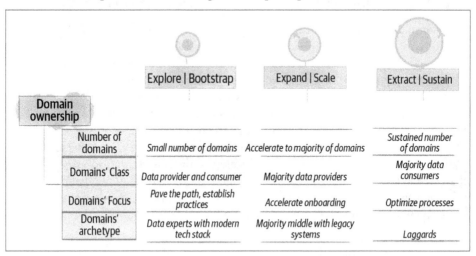

Figure 15-6. Example of domain ownership characteristics through phases of evolution

During the *exploration and bootstrapping phase*, only a small number of domains are involved in the execution of data mesh. These early domains often act both as the provider of the data and as the consumer in order to participate in end-to-end value delivery with minimal dependencies. Nevertheless, both roles are necessary to be part of this phase. In this phase the domains focus on exploration and setting up a foundation for growth. The early adopter domains are setting sensible practices in terms of defining the data product owner role and setting up the domain team structure. They pave the path by creating tooling and processes to integrate operational data from applications to source-aligned data products. The early domains are among the most advanced in their data and analytics capabilities with a modern technology stack. At this stage, value comes from unblocking a *small number of high-value use cases*.

During the *expand and scale phase*, in rapid increments, an increasing number of domains join the mesh, the majority middle. The early majority continue to pave the path and establish a set of repeatable patterns, technically and organizationally, so that the execution can rapidly scale out to the majority of the domains. New domains contribute to source- and consumer-aligned data products and aggregate data products. The need for aggregate data products and pure data domains arises with the increased number of domains. Domains have a diverse set of technology stacks, very likely with older and legacy systems that need to be integrated or migrated to the mesh. They introduce a new set of practices and tooling to handle legacy integration. At this stage, value comes from the *positive network effect*.

During the *extract and sustain* phase, most of the domains have moved to an autonomous data ownership model, and the number of domains stabilizes. Fluctuations to the domains are expected due to optimization of the data ownership model. Domains that have become bottlenecks due to the large number of data products may break up into multiple domains, and domains that users are minimally dependent on may merge with others. In this phase provider domains continue to modify, evolve, and optimize their data products, but the majority of activities are happening in consumer domains taking advantage of the large set of data products available for reuse and building new scenarios. Domains that have been technologically misaligned with the mesh, due to the location of their data or the age of their systems and data technology, may choose to join the mesh at this point where most of the capabilities and organizational practices are well established. At this stage, value comes from *consistency and completeness effects across the organization*.

Data as a product evolution phases. Figure 15-7 shows an example of dimensions of data product development as they progress through the phases of evolution.

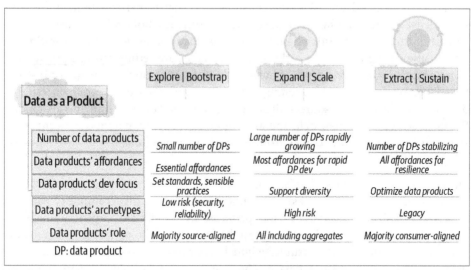

Figure 15-7. Example of data product characteristics through phases of evolution

During the *explore and bootstrap* phase, only a small set of data products is created. The early data products support an essential subset of affordances introduced in Chapter 11. For example, only a subset of output port modes may be available, with a limited retention period of sharing just the latest snapshot, or limited discoverability capabilities. In this phase, data product development has an exploratory nature in order to identify the best approach to implement each of the data product affordances. Data product developers are actively establishing patterns and sensible practices. Early data product developers work collaboratively to share knowledge and learnings. Data product development actively influences the platform features, based on experimentation and early learnings. Data products developed during this phase may not have a standard blueprint and don't yet fully utilize the platform capabilities. During this phase the chosen data products are among the low-risk ones from the security and reliability perspective, and they are tolerant of minimal standardization. The early data products are selected to be different but complementary in terms of their development model and technology requirements. This keeps the platform dependencies focused. At this time, the majority of data products are source-aligned, with a smaller number of consumer-aligned data products addressing the needs of specific use cases that are bootstrapping the mesh.

During the *expand and scale* phase, a large number of data products are being added to the mesh, at a rapid rate. With early adopters having established the standardized patterns of data product development, the data products can be developed rapidly. The data products create the necessary affordances required to be observed, discovered, and used at scale by a large number of the users without hand-holding. Data products support a diverse set of transformations such as running ML models or stream-based data processing. Data product development is focused on supporting a diversity of sources and consumers. Data products developed during this phase can be of a higher risk category with regard to privacy, uptime, resilience, etc. A diverse class of data products, with an increasing number of aggregate data products get created in this phase.

During the *extract and sustain* phase, the number of data products is likely to stabilize with a slower pace of change. The optimization of data products or new business needs may create new data products or change the existing ones. The data products continue to evolve. Data products continue to optimize for more rapid access to data, higher performance of data sharing, and other cross-functional concerns to address the large scale of usage. They also continue to optimize their life-cycle management and increase the speed of applying changes. Data products with a longer lead time to change, due to transformation complexity, are broken down into smaller and more efficient data products. During this phase the focus of data product development is to generate large-scale returns on the prior investments of data product development. Many intelligent business initiatives can use the existing data products as is. During this phase, laggard legacy data storage or systems are converted to data products.

Self-serve platform evolution phases.   Figure 15-8 shows an example of self-serve platform characteristics as they change through the evolution of data mesh.

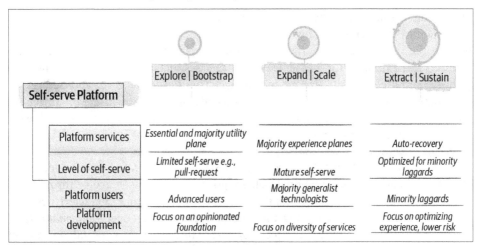

Figure 15-8. Example of data platform characteristics through phases of evolution

During the *bootstrap and explore* phase, the platform is establishing its essential foundational capabilities, mainly in the utility plane—storage, compute, accounts, access control, transformation. A primitive set of data product experience services are developed, such as basic data product life cycle management and global addressability. There are very few mesh experience plane capabilities such as basic discoverability. In this phase, the platform self-serve implementation is premature and can be as simple as pull-request-based script sharing. The platform users are expert data product developers and consumers that can get by with minimal self-serve capabilities. The platform supports a smaller number of users. The platform team is working closely with early domains to provide their needs without blocking them and harvesting the cross-functional features the domain teams are building back to the platform. In the early phases, the platform is opinionated and has a limited set of supported technologies to focus on what is necessary to get momentum.

During the *scale and expand* phase, the platform supports automatic data product generation, with all affordances in place, though some might have limited functionality. For example, the automatic data metrics sharing foundation is in place, but the metrics set may not include all possible temporal, quality, or volume information. The platform is mainly used through the data product experience plane or the mesh experience plane. Platform self-serve abilities mature rapidly to support a larger portion of the population with common requirements. Automated processes and tools are established. The persona of the platform target users skew toward majority generalist technologists. The platform focuses on serving the majority middle population of users without requiring hand-holding. Teams who wish to use a different set of technologies that the platform offers remain off the platform and will have the end-to-end responsibility of meeting the mesh governance and compatibility requirements. Only a small number of teams should fall into this category.

During the *extract and sustain* phase, the platform has a mature state of automatic observability, automatic healing, and a high degree of resiliency at scale. Any downtime in the mesh can have large-scale consequences. The platform capabilities are matured and exploited for a diverse set of use cases, data products, and teams. The platform continues to optimize the self-serve capabilities for laggards and outliers. In this phase, the platform is utilized by the majority of the teams in the organization. Platform development focuses on optimizing the experience of the mesh and lowering the risk of downtime or security breaches.

Federated computational governance evolution phases. The federated governance operating model and the computational policies governing the mesh evolve through the adoption phases. Figure 15-9 shows the evolution of governance characteristics such as the *number of domains* joining the federated governance operation, *maturity of the federated operating model*, the *focus of governance development*, and *coverage of computational policies*.

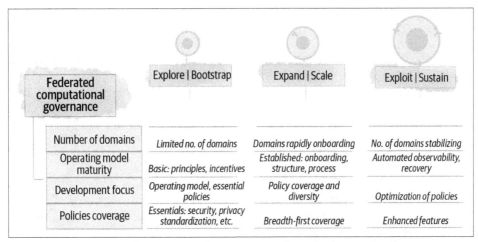

Federated computational governance	Explore | Bootstrap	Expand | Scale	Exploit | Sustain
Number of domains	Limited no. of domains	Domains rapidly onboarding	No. of domains stabilizing
Operating model maturity	Basic: principles, incentives	Established: onboarding, structure, process	Automated observability, recovery
Development focus	Operating model, essential policies	Policy coverage and diversity	Optimization of policies
Policies coverage	Essentials: security, privacy standardization, etc.	Breadth-first coverage	Enhanced features

Figure 15-9. Example of governance characteristics through phases of evolution

During the *explore and bootstrap* phase, the new governance model forms with only a few early domains that are participating in the federated governance. The governance operation establishes the principles that guide the decision-making process and decide what policies the organization must implement globally and what can be left to domains. The global incentives of domain data product teams are defined, augmenting their local domain incentives. During this phase, the existing governance structure reshapes into a federated model. The members of the existing governance group are either taking a subject matter expert role, joining the platform team to help with product management of cross-functional policy automation, or joining the domains as data product owners. The governance is focusing on setting the foundation. Data product developers in the early days may build their own implementation of policies, and the platform harvests them later into its self-serve capabilities, a form of crowdsourcing for some of the early policy implementations. The early governance and domain teams pave the path in establishing the operating model, decision making, and policy automation. The governance function establishes the essential policies relevant to early data products and domains. Only a subset of essential policies might be implemented automatically by the platform and enforced consistently in all data products, such as security and privacy.

During the *expand and scale* phase, with the basic operating model and approach to automating policies having been established by early domains and governance teams, the road is paved for scaled governance with a majority of domains joining the mesh. The process of onboarding new domains on the mesh is frictionless. The number of members of the federated governance team increases to include the majority of the domains in the organization. The team focuses on increasing the coverage and diversity of the policies and maturing the operating model for rapid onboarding of new domains. During this time, the majority of policies are automated to support a mesh with a large number of interoperable and secure data products. Basic monitoring of policies is in place.

During the *extract and sustain* phase, all data products on the mesh are embedding automated policies. There is an automated process in place to detect policy risk and lack of conformance to notify data product teams to address concerns with automated tools provided by the platform. The team focuses on optimizing the governance process and enhancing the supported features of automated policies. The mesh is monitoring and optimizing the performance of the policies.

Guided evolution with fitness functions

While the adoption phases guide the execution of data mesh at a macro level, during a large time scale of months or years, continuous measurement and tracking of a set of objective *fitness functions* guide the small increments and short iterative execution cycles.

Fitness Functions

A *fitness function* is an objective function used to summarize how close a prospective design solution is to achieving its set aims. In evolutionary computing, the fitness function determines whether an algorithm has improved over time. In *Building Evolutionary Architectures*, fitness functions objectively guide the iterations of an architecture toward its set objectives across multiple dimensions such as performance, security, extensibility, etc.

Fitness functions is a concept borrowed from evolutionary computing, which is an objective measure used to assess whether the system as a whole is moving toward its intended design target and is improving over time, or not.

In the context of data mesh, these objective functions can determine how "fit" the mesh implementation is at any point in time, and whether every iteration is moving it closer or further from its optimal state of delivering value at scale.

Data mesh's ultimate objective is increasing the ability of organizations to utilize data for analytical purposes and get value from their data at scale, aligned with organizational growth and complexity. Each of the data mesh principles contributes to this high-level outcome. Hence, fitness functions can target the outcomes expected from each principle.

Coming up with numerical fitness functions, particularly when we are still figuring out what good looks like, is very hard. Even in the case of well-established DevOps engineering practices, the book *Accelerate: Building and Scaling High Performing Technology Organizations*,[7] after years of running quantitative research and measuring 24 key metrics, demonstrates that only a small number of metrics, 4, had a direct link to the organization's performance and the majority were simply vanity measurements.

The objective measures proposed here are examples and a starting point. They need to be experimented with, quantitatively measured, and compared across organizations to prove that they are in fact just the right ones.

You might have noticed that I have used the concept of fitness function over key performance indicators (KPIs). While both concepts are essentially about objective metrics and giving visibility to the state and trend of data mesh execution progress, the fitness function tells you how "fit" the data mesh design and implementation are at any point of time and guides you through the changes to make the right ones and revert the ones with negative impact, with a focus on behaviors and outcomes that really matter.

For example, a KPI related to the "number of data products" might sound appealing to many leaders as an indicator of success and growth of the mesh. This is in fact not the right measure, as it does not indicate the "fitness" of the mesh. The target of the mesh is a design to "deliver value." This is not directly related to the number of data products but related to the "number of links to data products" as a measure of usage. The more links and interconnectivity, the more data products are being used to generate value.

Data mesh execution requires automated instrumentation, collection, and tracking of these metrics. The platform services play a key part in tracking and externalizing many of these metrics. For example, to measure the "acceleration of policy adoption" as a function of effectiveness of automated policies as code, the platform can measure the "lead time of a data product to adopt a new policy." This can be collected as instrumentation of the data products' continuous delivery pipeline.

Data product and mesh experience plane services enable the domain and global governance teams to measure, report, and track these execution metrics. Detecting trends in the wrong direction can trigger a set of actions to investigate the root cause and prioritize the fixes to nudge the evolution of the mesh toward its objective outcomes.

---

7 Nicole Forsgren, Jez Humble, and Gene Kim, *Accelerate: Building and Scaling High Performing Technology Organizations*, (Portland, OR: IT Revolution Press, 2018).

I suggest that you define a set of objective fitness functions for your data mesh execution. Automate their implementation as much as possible, and continuously monitor their trends. They can guide you through the execution of data mesh and take the next best step.

The fitness functions I have introduced in the following are only examples. I have demonstrated how they are derived from the expected outcomes of each data mesh principle. You can adopt the same approach and come up with your own fitness functions to test and evolve.

Domain ownership fitness functions. Figure 15-10 shows an example set of fitness functions that measure the progress of domain data ownership. These fitness functions measure a set of objectives that tell us whether the evolution is moving in alignment with the outcome of domain data ownership.

Is the implementation generating more value through data sharing in step with organizational growth?

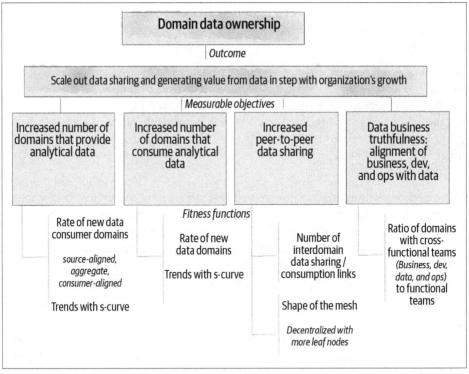

Figure 15-10. Example of domain data ownership fitness functions

Data as a product fitness functions. Figure 15-11 introduces an example set of fitness functions that measure whether the data mesh implementation is objectively progressing toward data as a product outcome.

Is the effectiveness and efficiency of data sharing across domains increasing with organizational growth or not?

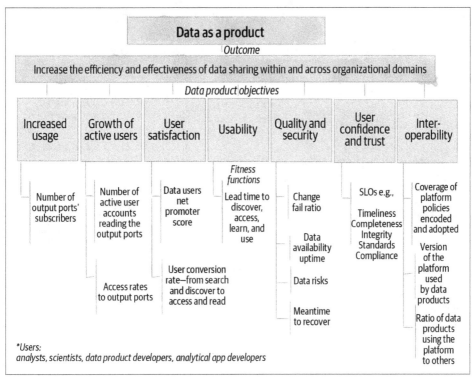

Figure 15-11. Example of data as a product fitness functions

Self-serve platform fitness functions. Figure 15-12 introduces an example set of fitness functions that measure whether the data mesh implementation is objectively progressing toward the self-serve platform outcome.

Is the platform increasing domains' autonomy in producing and consuming data products and lowering their cost of data ownership?

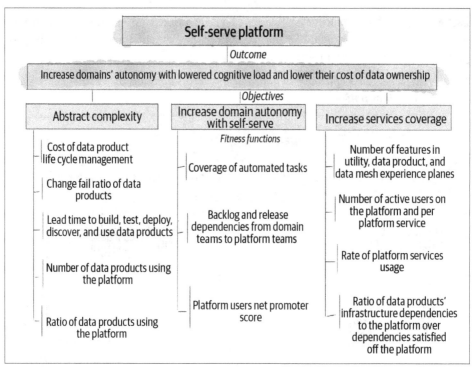

Figure 15-12. Example of self-serve platform fitness functions

Federated computational governance fitness functions.   Figure 15-13 introduces an example set of fitness functions that measure whether the data mesh implementation is objectively progressing toward the governance outcome.

Is the mesh generating higher-order intelligence—securely and consistently—through efficient joins and correlations of data products, in step with organizational growth?

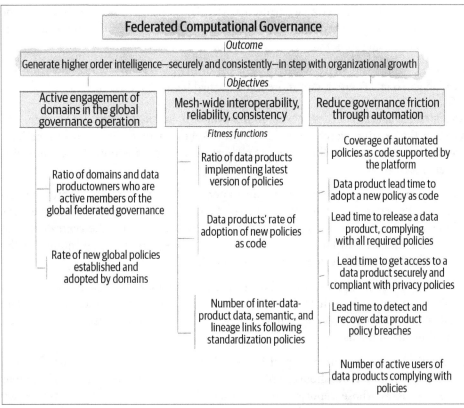

Figure 15-13. Example of governance fitness functions

Migration from legacy

We can't talk about an evolutionary execution of data mesh without talking about legacy. The majority of the organizations adopting data mesh likely have one or multiple implementations of past data architectures such as data warehouses, data lakes, or data lakehouses, and a centralized governance structure with a centralized data team.

Data mesh execution must incorporate migration from such legacy organization structures, architecture, and technology in its incremental and evolutionary journey. However, it is difficult to generalize migration from legacy, as the path highly depends on many variables specific to the organization such as the time constraint on migrating to the new infrastructure in the case that establishing the mesh coincides with migration to a new environment, e.g., a new cloud provider; the scale and number of early adopter domains; the available investment for the platform; and so on.

Laying out a migration strategy from a particular state to data mesh is out of the scope of this book and requires close collaboration with an organization and understanding its unique context.

However, what I can share with you is a list of high-level lessons learned from my experience so far. There is a lot more to be learned here.

No centralized data architecture coexists with data mesh, unless in transition. I often get asked if the existing warehouses, lakes, and lakehouses that the organizations have created can coexist with the mesh. The short answer is transitionally yes, but ultimately no.

Any incremental migration would require a period of time where the old and the new coexist at the same time. However, the goal of data mesh is to remove the bottlenecks of the lake and warehouse. Decentralized data products replace the *centralized* and *shared* warehouses and lakes. Hence, the target architecture does not intend for the centralized bottlenecks to coexist with data mesh.

For example, retaining a centralized data warehouse or a lake and then feeding a data mesh downstream from it is an antipattern. In this case, the introduction of data mesh is an added complexity, while the bottleneck of a warehouse collecting data from domains remains.

Alternatively, as a transitory step, it is possible to have a data mesh implementation that feeds data into a warehouse, which in turn serves a controlled and small number of legacy users whose reports are still using the warehouse. Until all the legacy warehouse users are migrated to the mesh, the mesh and the warehouse coexist. The migration continues, and it reduces the level of centralization of the warehouse bottleneck.

The ultimate goal of the architecture is to remove and reduce the overall level of *centralization*. Hence, ultimately a mesh implementation and a *central* data warehouse or lake should not coexist.

Centralized data technologies can be used with data mesh. At the time of writing this book, no data-mesh-native technologies have been created. We are at a stage of evolution when adopters utilize the existing technologies, with custom configurations and solutions built on top.

Today, my advice is to utilize the elements of the existing technologies in a way that they don't get in the way of building and running autonomous and distributed data products. I suggest configuring and operating the existing technologies in a multitenant way. For example, use the basic elements of lake-oriented technologies such as object storage and configure the allocation and access to the storage based on the boundary of each data product. Similarly, you can utilize data warehousing technologies as an underlying storage and SQL access mode but allocate a separate schema to each data product.

Not all existing technologies lend themselves to such configuration. You can utilize the ones that do.

Bypass the lake and warehouse and go to directly to the source. When migrating from an existing lake or warehouse, the path of least resistance is to put the warehouse or lake upstream to the mesh and implement the data products with input ports consuming data from the existing warehouse tables. My advice would be to not take this path and instead discover the existing consumers of the lake or warehouse, recognize their needs and use cases, and directly connect them to new data products that consume data from the source domain systems. Discover the domain owners early, develop the data products according to the domain's truthful representation of the data, and update the consumers if need be. Creating artificial data products that represent the lake files or warehouse tables does not achieve the outcomes of the mesh, scaling through ownership by domains and closing the gap between the source and consumer. It only adds further technical debt, creates another layer between the source and consumer, and increases the distance between them.

Use the data warehouse as the consuming edge node. Assessing the consumers of an existing warehouse, you may decide to keep some of them in the warehouse and never migrate them to the mesh. There are multiple reasons for this decision. For example, reports such as financial reports that don't change that often, rely on a small and specific set of tables, and are defined with complex business logic that are hard to reverse engineer and re-create may remain dependent on the warehouse. In this case, you want the warehouse to act as a consumer of the mesh and become an edge consuming node, with limited reports accessing a small set of its remaining tables.

Migrate from a warehouse or lake in atomic evolutionary steps. It's likely that migration from the data warehouse or lake takes many evolutionary iterations and possibly months or years depending on the size of the organization. I strongly suggest executing your migration in *atomic evolutionary steps* where the state of the system is left with less technical debt and architectural entropy when the step is completed. While this might sound logical and seemingly obvious, it's often ignored. The teams often keep adding new infrastructure and new data products while leaving the old pipelines or lake files behind. Over time they just add to the architectural complexity and total cost of ownership to maintain the new and leftover old systems. The main reason behind this coexistence is that we often fail to migrate over users and consumers to the new components.

For example, if you are creating a new set of data products, make sure you take the time to migrate over the existing consumers—reports or ML models—of the lake or warehouse to them. An atomic step of migration includes adding new source-aligned, aggregate, or consumer-aligned data products, migrating the consumers over to the new data products, and retiring the tables, files, and pipelines of the lake and warehouse. The migration step is complete when all these steps happen or all revert if some don't complete. At the end of this atomic step, the architectural entropy is reduced.

Conversely, the atomic migration step is not complete if we don't migrate the consumers after creating new data products or if we don't retire the existing pipelines and lake files. Make sure your project scheduling and resource allocations are aligned with committing to *atomic steps of migration*.

Recap

Data mesh execution is part of a larger data strategy and in fact is a major component of the strategy. It needs business-oriented strategic initiatives, defining the hypothesis of how data generates value aligned with business objectives, to drive its execution.

ML and analytics-powered business use cases become the vehicles that execute identification and delivery of data products, adoption of data by domains, and establishment of governance and the platform.

Balancing between point solutions delivering a data-driven business outcome versus building a long-term shared platform across multiple use cases remains a challenge. Tools such as the evolutionary approach based on the long-term adoption roadmap and functions to measure fitness of the implementation according to its long-term objective help establish an equilibrium and guide the execution in an evolutionary fashion toward a mature state.

On rare occasions an organization has the opportunity to create a greenfield data mesh implementation. In the majority of cases, a brownfield execution must account for migration of existing architectures such as a data warehouse, lake, or lakehouse. In this case, migrating the old architecture and organization depends on executing atomic evolutionary steps that each migrate the data consumers and providers and everything in between the two toward the mesh.

These initial guidelines and approach should suffice to get you started while you learn and refine the process along the way.

What remains is a few notes on how to organize your teams and evolve the culture of an organization during this evolutionary execution, which I cover in the last chapter of this book, Chapter 16. See you there.

Organization and Culture

Culture eats strategy for breakfast.
—Peter Drucker

In Part I of the book, I introduced data mesh as "a sociotechnical approach to share, access, and manage analytical data in complex and large-scale environments—within or across organizations."

In this chapter I focus on the social side of this sociotechnical approach. I will elaborate on the changes that data mesh introduces to people's roles, responsibilities, motivations, and collective interactions in an organization.

I will cover a few of the key organizational design choices critical to the implementation of data mesh. I use Galbraith's Star Model (*https://oreil.ly/HWFpr*) to structure the organizational design choices around the five categories of *strategy*, *structure*, *processes*, *rewards*, and *people*. These categories are all interrelated and influence each other, and the sum of all of them results in the emergence of the organizational *culture*.

Figure 16-1 summarizes the Star Model applied to organizational elements of data mesh.

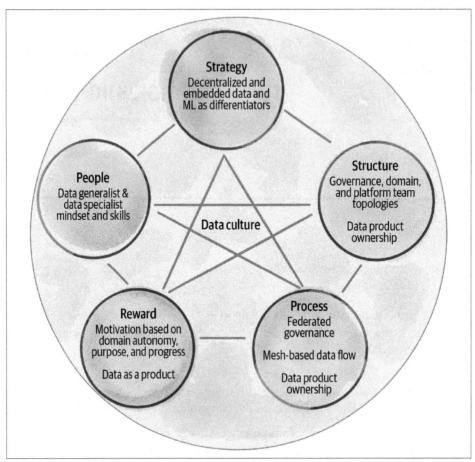

Figure 16-1. Data mesh organizational design decisions framed by Galbraith's Star Model

The components of the Star Model include:

Strategy

Data strategy frames and embodies data mesh. In Chapter 15 I covered how a data strategy aligns with the principles and components of data mesh to execute toward a decentralized data ownership that embeds data-driven value generated through ML and insights into each and every aspect of a business and its products and services.

Structure

In this chapter, I cover Team Topologies, including the distribution of power and decision making and the shape of the teams and roles within them introduced by data mesh.

Process

I summarize the key processes such as the global process of governance, peer-to-peer data sharing across the mesh, and identification and assignment of data products and their ownership.

Reward

I cover the motivations and rewards that align goals of teams and individuals with the overall data strategy, based on data mesh ways of working—autonomous teams delivering results and growing a new generation of data practitioners.

People

I will discuss the skills and mindsets of cross-functional teams to become data producers and consumers.

Culture

I will cover the core values that will drive organizational behavior aligned with data mesh principles.

In the rest of this chapter, I surface the *changes* that will occur for each of these categories as a result of a data mesh implementation.

First, let's look at the process of *change* itself.

Change

Whether you are starting a greenfield implementation, building a new data-driven organization, or brownfield evolving an existing one, you are creating *change*. Change in mindsets, skills, values, ways of working, and ways of being.

You need to decide how you are going to approach change. What I recommend is *movement-based change* (*https://oreil.ly/1Ma1r*). This approach to organizational change, introduced by Bryan Walker (*https://oreil.ly/pgDyV*), draws from *movement research*.[1] Its core finding proves that social movements start small and show early powerful wins to demonstrate the result and efficacy of change. These early wins help gain momentum toward large-scale change.

In Chapter 15, I introduced a movement-based execution framework ("Data Mesh Execution Framework" on page 279) that tied the implementation of components of data mesh directly to strategic initiatives and delivering data-oriented results, in the form of intelligent solutions and applications. This iterative and business-driven execution framework is a great vehicle to incrementally move organizational structure, processes, and motivations. The early results and wins demonstrated by a small

---

1 David A. Snow and Sarah A. Soule, *A Primer on Social Movements*, (New York: W.W. Norton & Company, 2009).

number of *innovator adopters* in the organization create buy-in and inspiration for an organization-wide change that scales through an evolutionary roadmap ("Evolutionary Execution" on page 286).

Since the early execution iterations and wins become the beacons for change (*https://oreil.ly/N6Oyh*), it's important to select them with qualifying criteria aligned with the organizational change objectives at the time.

For example, if establishing data product ownership by the cross-functional domain team is the objective, the *selection* of business initiatives must align with achieving this objective. Early business initiatives involve domain teams that are most conducive to this change and can be the beacons for others. For example, a domain with intrinsic needs for applying insights and ML to their function, e.g., the playlists team, is a good candidate. Such early teams have most of the skills needed to make the transformation and become the early creators of data products. Look for easier, quicker wins early on and find the most aligned adopters first.

Figure 16-2 demonstrates applying the selection criteria and an end-to-end execution of use cases to implement the data mesh technical components and also evolve the organization iteratively.

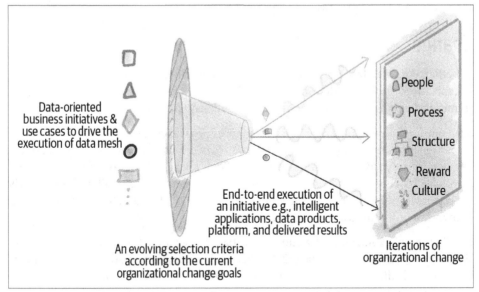

Figure 16-2. End-to-end execution of data-oriented initiatives create the context to iteratively make organizational change

A great side effect of this approach is that the teams and people who are directly impacted by the change are engaged in the process of creating change and delivering results. They can refine the change based on their learnings through the execution.

Keep in mind that change happens within the context of the phase data mesh evolution ("A multiphase evolution model" on page 286), during the *explore, expand,* and *extract* phases. What changes and to what extent evolves during these phases. For example, for early business initiatives and iterations of change, the teams involved in the change work as one group. The first data mesh initiative likely has the members of the platform team and the domain(s) involved work together more closely with synchronous tasks and collaborations. As the evolution moves to later phases, *expand* and *extract,* the teams work autonomously with less synchronous dependencies and communications.

While data mesh's movement-based organizational change gives you a starting point, there is a lot more to cultivating, enabling, and creating change. That is outside of the scope of this book: your organization must commit to discovering the art and science of the process that will *persuasively*[2] drive cultural and organizational change, from preparing the ground prior to the execution to managing people's emotions throughout. The organization needs to have a *top-down continuous and clear executive communication of the vision* on becoming a decentralized data-driven organization, and a *bottom-up enablement* through technology, incentives, and education. Everyone involved must set and track the *hard*[3] measures of change ("Guided evolution with fitness functions" on page 294) and the *soft* ones that follow employees' satisfaction, behavior, attitude, and capabilities.

The first step to drive change—the first initiative and the first teams to change—often feels like too much to overcome. Start small, start with teams who will have the least amount of headwind to change, get some wins, and pave the path.

Culture

Culture represents the language, values, beliefs, and norms that an organization embodies. Today, many organizations *value* the *volume* of data they are capturing. They *believe* that *data collection centrally* can deliver value. The *norm* is to *externalize* data responsibilities to someone else, the centralized data team. Concepts such as *data pipeline, canonical models,* and *single source of truth* are ubiquitously present in the *language.* Such a culture is at odds with data mesh and needs to evolve.

While changes to structure, process, rewards, and other organizational design elements have an impact on the culture, the core element I like us to focus on here is *the values.* Out of all the elements of the culture, values are the deepest manifestation of the culture, and not surprisingly the language and symbols are the most superficial.

---

2 David A. Garvin and Michael Roberto, "Change Through Persuasion" (*https://oreil.ly/FGcch*), *Harvard Business Review* (Brighton, MA: Harvard Business Publishing, 2005).

3 Michael Beer and Nitin Nohria, eds., *Breaking the Code of Change,* (Brighton, MA: Harvard Business Publishing, 2000).

For example, as of this writing, the language of "data product" has been widely adopted by the industry, while the manifestations of its core values widely vary from what is presented in this book.

According to Daphna Oyserman (*https://oreil.ly/geeBc*), professor of psychology, values are internalized cognitive structures that guide choices. They evoke a sense of what is wrong and what is right. They establish a sense of priorities and meaning.[4] Ultimately, values drive behavior and predict actions.

Defining and cultivating data mesh values within the context of your organization is an important step in establishing your data culture. These values are then lived through the actions and decisions teams and individuals make.

Values

Here are some of the core values of data-mesh-native organizations, summarized in Figure 16-3. If an organization adopts data mesh in its entirety, these values are shared by all the teams and are expected from each other. These values are uncompromisable. They drive action. You can use these as a starting point and contextualize them to your organization.

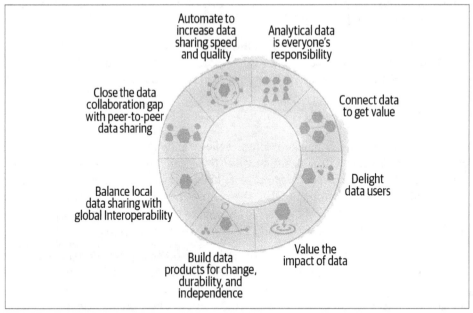

Figure 16-3. Values underpinning a data mesh culture

---

4 Daphna Oyserman, "Values: Psychological Perspectives" (*https://oreil.ly/lvUrS*), *International Encyclopedia of the Social & Behavioral Sciences*, (2001), 16150–16153.

Analytical data is everyone's responsibility

Domain-oriented data ownership promotes a sense of responsibility in providing or consuming analytical data in every cross-functional team and across the business. Whether these teams are enabling the business with digital technologies and services, building new products, or selling or marketing them, they are composed of cross-functional disciplines that are capable of using and sharing analytical data.

Connect data across the boundaries to get value

The premise of data mesh in support of scaling data usage is to enable connectivity of data across a mesh. The nodes on the mesh are connected across organizational boundaries, within and outside. This is in contrast to collecting data in a lake or warehouse. The connectivity is established on multiple levels: input and output ports that establish data sharing and lineage; data semantic and syntax sharing through schema linking; and data join and correlation through data linking and global identifiers. Valuing data connectivity fosters interoperability at scale, which leads to generation of insight over a large volume of diverse data.

Delight data users

Satisfy data users, earn their trust, and accelerate their analytical application development with data products. This value focuses on the purpose of data products. It places data users and their experience at the center. It drives actions that put emphasis on the impact of data products on data users in rapid development of analytics and ML applications with high levels of trust and confidence in the data.

Value the impact of data

What we value and measure as success drives how we behave and manage our resources. Data mesh focuses on the impact of the data and not its volumes. It values data usability, data satisfaction, data availability, and data quality over the volume of the data. Of course, in many cases volume contributes to impact, particularly in the case of ML where more is more, yet it's secondary to usability.

Build data products for change, durability, and independence

Constant change, independence, and data durability across a long period of time are the main characteristics of data products. For example, the data product design consideration to embed the runtime data transformation to mutate and generate a continuous stream of point-in-time data is necessary to accommodate continuous *change*. Data, by default, evolves over time. The design consideration to include the data and the policies that govern the data as one unit is necessary for data products to achieve a high degree of *independence* and self-sufficiency. The design decision to store data as time-variant information with long-term retention is necessary for *data durability*. Analytical use cases need access to data over a long period of time.

Balance local data sharing with global interoperability

DataBold Textbalancing local sharing with global interoperability mesh embraces local autonomy and diversity of the domains in sharing and using data. This autonomy is balanced with the global interoperability that enables mesh-level data discovery, connectivity, and conformance. Global interoperability is managed through the federated governance operating model and enabled by automated policies embedded in each and every data product.

This value drives actions to continuously find the balance between domain-level local optimization and mesh-level global optimization.

Close the data collaboration gap with peer-to-peer data sharing

Data mesh removes organizational and architectural gaps between data providers and consumers, connecting them directly through data shared as a product. Platform discovery capabilities and computational governance for granting access to data independently without intermediaries decrease such a gap and ultimately lead to frictionless access to data. This promotes a data- and experiment-driven culture.

Automate to increase data sharing speed and quality

Platform services automate and streamline data sharing workflows and continuously improve the quality of data. The platform teams continuously seek to find new and improved ways to utilize automation in removing friction in data sharing and optimize the experience of data providers and consumers.

Reward

How people are motivated and rewarded is another element of organization design.

One of the oppositions that I often hear about data mesh is that organizations struggle to get their application or product teams to care enough about the analytical data to put effort into building ETLs and data pipelines. I completely agree with this statement. If I were a developer in a domain team, let's say building the "Music player" application, I would not be motivated to build a bunch of ETL jobs to get data out of my database application and dump it somewhere else for use cases I don't understand. This is neither motivating nor aligned with the data mesh approach.

In the past, we have patched this problem by building data teams downstream from application teams to address data quality and modeling by building intermediary pipelines. This is not fixing the root cause. It simply creates accidental complexity. Data mesh addresses the root cause—drive and motivation.

Intrinsic Motivations

The data mesh approach builds on how people are intrinsically motivated. Daniel Pink (*https://oreil.ly/t2mry*), in his book *Drive: The Surprising Truth About What Motivates Us*,[5] emphasizes that modern businesses must foster the type of behavior and activities that have intrinsic reward and inherent satisfaction. He calls this *Type I* behavior, which leads to stronger performance and greater health and overall well-being. He then describes the three fundamental elements of motivation that lead to Type I behavior: *autonomy, mastery, and purpose.*

These intrinsic motivations are aligned with data mesh principles:

Autonomy of tech-business-aligned domains in ownership of data
> Domain teams are both accountable and have autonomy in defining and sharing their data for analytics use cases. They have autonomy in utilizing their data in ML and analytics to create data-driven value. This autonomy is supported by the governance operating model and the platform services.

Technologists' mastery in managing, sharing, and using analytical data
> Data mesh expands the mastery of working with data to generalist technologists, beyond an isolated group of data specialists. Skill acquisition to work with data is a positive motivator for developers. The platform enables new pathways for them to gain mastery in data and analytics.

Finding purpose in sharing data as a product directly to consumers
> Cross-functional teams serve their data directly to data consumers and are in control of providing what the consumers actually need. They measure and track the success of their data product based on the satisfaction of consumers and growth of adoption. More importantly, cross-functional teams find a higher purpose in managing data by advancing their applications and business with embedded ML.

The organizations evolving toward data mesh endorse and amplify these intrinsic motivations.

Extrinsic Motivations

It is very likely that a company executing data mesh has a reward system to extrinsically motivate their employees—bonuses, incentive plans, ranking, promotions, working conditions, etc.

I have commonly seen that organizations in the process of data mesh transformation link their extrinsic incentives, e.g., end-of-the-year bonuses, with the goals of

---

5 Daniel H. Pink, *Drive: The Surprising Truth About What Motivates Us*, (New York: Riverhead Books, 2011).

their data mesh execution. A troublesome example that I have seen is linking the end-of-the-year bonuses to the number of data products. This leads to a mad rush of creating data products right before the end-of-the-year review. It is counterproductive to the goal of the mission—to get value from data through data product sharing and connectivity across the organization and beyond. Often this rush results in additional effort later to revert the incurred tech debt.

My personal suggestion is to divorce backward-looking assessments such as employee performance review, rewards, etc. from forward-looking objectives and their measurements—e.g., the goals of data mesh execution. Focus the teams on forward-looking goals and incentivize them by showing how their objectives relate to the larger strategy's vision and the company's top priorities.

The forward-looking objectives can be expressed and measured as objectives and key results[6] (OKRs). OKRs can be a timely and relevant subset of measurable functions that I introduced in Chapter 15 ("Guided evolution with fitness functions" on page 294). Achieving these objectives collectively moves the evolution of a data mesh implementation toward its goals.

Here are a few examples for team or individual OKRs:

Growth of domains' data product usage
> This objective can be measured through *on the mesh* and *off the mesh growth rate*—the number of downstream data products that actively utilize the domain's data products, and the number of end consumer analytical applications off the mesh that directly use the data for insight generation.

Increased confidence and trust in data
> This can be assessed by a set of *target measurements* over a *period of time*, for example, for a data product with a completeness SLO of 95% over a day. Completeness is just one of the many SLOs averaged to measure key results.

Structure

When we think about organizational design, structure is often the first thing that gets attention. Organizational structure determines these dimensions, among others:

- Placement of decision-making power: centralized or decentralized
- Topologies of teams and departments: axis around which teams and departments are formed
- Shape of teams: flat or hierarchical

---

6 John Doerr, *Measure What Matters: OKRs*, (London: Portfolio Penguin, 2018).

Data mesh does not dictate the organizational structure from scratch. It makes some assumptions about the existing organizational structure and builds upon that.

Organization Structure Assumptions

Data mesh builds upon an organizational design influenced by domain-driven design. In such organizations, the architectural decomposition of solutions and systems is aligned with the division of the business functions and technical teams. If you are new to the concept of domain-driven design, for the purpose of this chapter, I highly recommend reading *Implementing Domain-Driven Design,*[7] particularly the chapter titled "Domains, Subdomains, and Bounded Contexts."

Figure 16-4 shows a portion of the domain-oriented organizational structure for Daff.

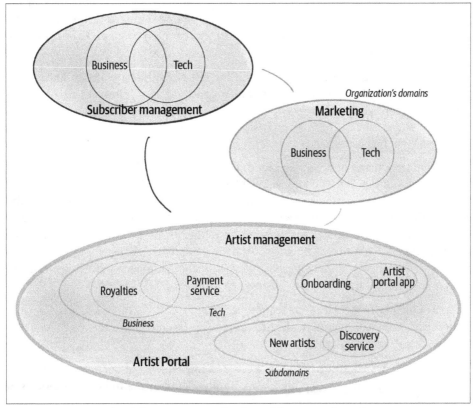

Figure 16-4. Example of domain-oriented tech-and-business-aligned organization

---

7 Vaughn Vernon, *Implementing Domain-Driven Design*, (Upper Saddle River, NJ: Addison-Wesley, 2013).

Assume that Daff is a domain-oriented organization. It has business teams who focus on different business domains of Daff including **artist management, marketing, subscriber management**, etc. Let's look at the business domain **artist management**. The purpose of this business domain is to engage and onboard more artists, facilitate sharing their content, pay their rewards and royalties, and continuously improve how artists get known, promoted, and connected with their audience globally. The success of an artist and their satisfaction with the platform is of priority for this business domain. As you can see, this domain can have multiple subdomains, unique and distinct areas of operation such as **artist payment, artist onboarding, new artist discovery**, and so on. In a domain-oriented organization, there are dedicated technical teams working closely with the **managing artists** business subdomains to provide digital services, applications, and tools. For example, **artist portal, artist payment services**, and **artist discovery service** are technical systems maintained to run the business of **artist management**. The alignment of longstanding technology teams working in close collaboration with their business counterparts is a key attribute of such an organization.

If you recall, to pass the data mesh readiness test ("Should You Adopt Data Mesh Today?" on page 271), you identified your organization as a domain-oriented one. This assumption creates a baseline to build data mesh Team Topologies.

Data Mesh Team Topologies

There is great synergy between data mesh team structure and interaction models and the work of Matthew Skelton and Manuel Pais on organizational design, called Team Topologies.[8] Team Topologies is "a model for organizational design that provides a key technology-agnostic mechanism for modern software-intensive enterprises to sense when a change in strategy is required (either from a business or technology point of view)." Continuous sensing of the environmental changes and adapting to them is well-aligned with data mesh's organizational outcome of embracing change in a complex, volatile, and uncertain business environment.

Team Topologies recognizes four team types (*platform, stream-aligned, enabling*, and *complicated subsystem* teams) with three core team interaction modes (*collaboration, X-as-a-service*, and *facilitating*).

Figure 16-5 shows an example of the teams and interactions of data mesh, expressed in Team Topologies terms, at a high level; it only identifies the interaction models of the logical teams at a point in time.

Domain data product teams, responsible for the end-to-end delivery of data products, are considered *stream-aligned* teams. They share their data products *as-a-service*

---

8 Skelton and Pais, *Team Topologies*.

with other teams. The data mesh platform teams provide their platform capabilities *as-a-service* to the data product teams. The governance teams partly act as *enabling* teams supporting both platform and data product teams. The governance teams, at times, work in *collaboration* with the platform team.

 The visual language of teams and interaction modes used in this chapter is an adaptation of the book shapes (*https://oreil.ly/oqLMY*) used in the Team Topologies concept. The image labels clarify the intent of the shape.

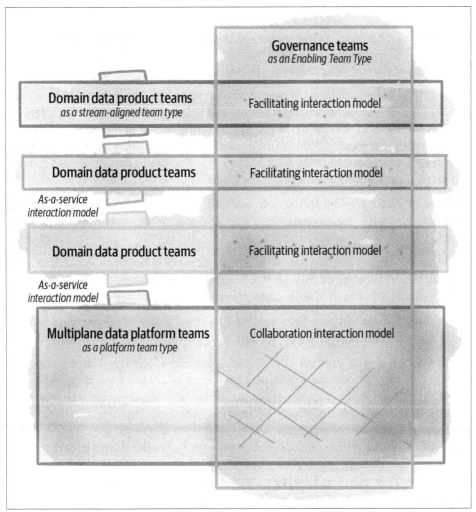

Figure 16-5. Example of a data mesh high-level representation of Team Topologies

The definition of *team*, based on Team Topologies, is a stable, long-lived group of people working together day by day (side by side) to achieve a common goal.

I will use the term *logical team* or *group* in cases where the definition is looser than a *team*. For example, in the case of governance, policymaking is done by a group of data product owners, subject matter experts (SMEs), etc., who come together to formulate policies, though the members of this group belong to different teams on a day-to-day basis. Hence, I call them a *group* and not a team.

The phrase *teams*, in the plural form, may be used to include both a team or a group, or both.

Let's look closely at each of these teams and their primary interaction modes.

Domain data product teams as stream-aligned teams

According to Team Topologies, a stream-aligned team is the primary team type in an organization. It is responsible for an end-to-end delivery of a single product, service, set of features, etc. In the case of data mesh, the (cross-functional) domain teams have one or multiple stream-aligned teams including the *application development teams* (*app dev* for short) as well as the *data product* delivery teams (*data product* for short). A *domain team* is a logical team, a team of teams.

Delivery of a data product focuses on an end-to-end continuous flow of designing, modeling, cleansing, building, testing, serving, monitoring, and evolving domain-oriented data.

The number of data product teams may vary depending on the complexity of the domain and its number of data products. Ideally, a small team is responsible for a data product. Each data product has an independent flow and delivery life cycle.

Data product teams will have roles such as data product developer and data product owner that I will discuss in the next section.

A source-aligned data product is *paired* with its source app dev team. They work together on a regular and more frequent basis than is expected from any other two teams. They have more communication to decide how the data product represents the analytical view of its collaborating app's internal data. The two teams may have bursts of *collaboration* to explicitly work together in a specific area. For example, the **podcast player** app dev team collaborates with the **podcast events** data product team to define how the application's operational data will be made available to the *collaborating data quantum* ("Data Product Data Sharing Interactions" on page 158). Collaboration interactions must be short lived as they are costly. The teams should find ways to limit the amount of collaboration effort. For example, defining a contract for the app dev team to expose their operational domain events reduces the collaboration overhead for the source-aligned data product team in understanding, processing, and converting these domain events to an analytical data product.

Figure 16-6 shows the data product teams as stream-aligned teams and their interactions with app dev and other data product teams.

Figure 16-6. Example of data product teams as stream-aligned teams

Data product teams use platform services through the platform planes' APIs, *as-a-service*, demonstrated earlier in Figure 16-5. I will discuss the data product team's interaction with the governance teams later in this chapter.

Data platform teams as platform teams

According to Team Topologies, the platform team type's purpose is to enable stream-aligned teams to deliver their work with substantial autonomy. This is aligned with the purpose of the data mesh's multiplane data platform ("Design a Platform Driven by User Journeys" on page 174).

The data platform team is a logical team made up of many teams with a fractal topology. For example, the data platform (logical) team can have multiple stream-aligned teams, each focusing on an end-to-end delivery of a particular self-serve platform capability of a specific plane, such as *data product testing framework, data product scheduler*, etc. There could also be teams who act as a platform team internally, providing capabilities as-a-service to other teams. For example, the utility plane logical team provides infrastructure provisioning services to other planes' teams and acts as a platform team.

Figure 16-7 shows an example of the data platform teams and their interaction modes at a point in time. In this example, the data platform team has multiple streams, one focusing on the data product experience plane and others focusing on different capabilities of the utility and mesh experience plane services. This is a snapshot in time that shows the occurrence of collaboration between two of the streams.

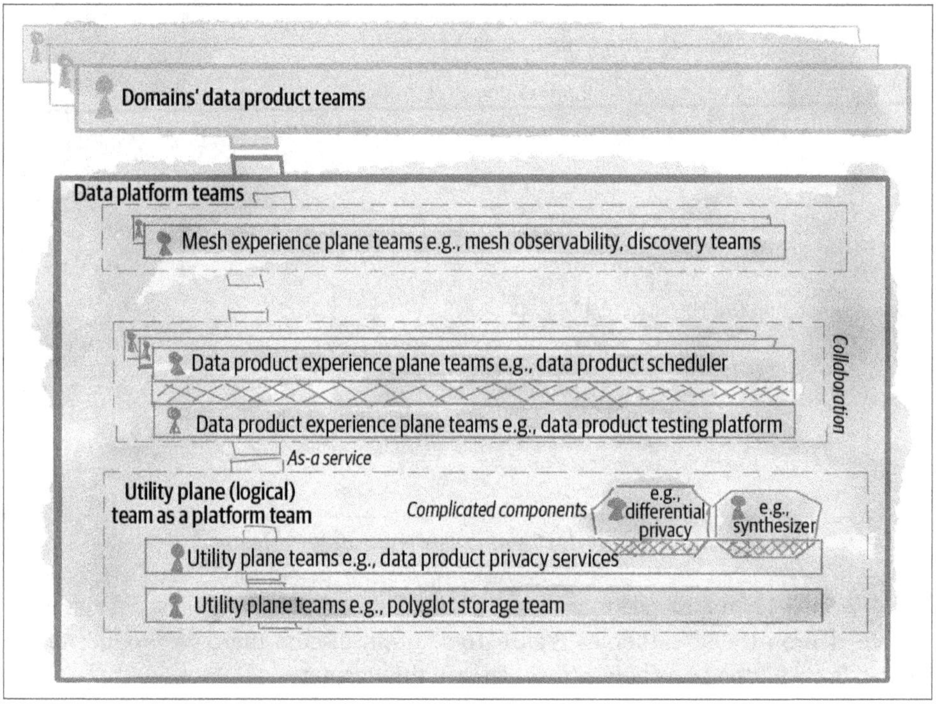

Figure 16-7. Example of data platform teams

How exactly a platform team divides itself into one or multiple teams depends on the scale, complexity, and revisions of the platform in an organization. The platform team may start as one team and over time break into multiple teams as the list of platform services grows. It's important to regularly assess and adjust the boundaries between the teams within the data platform itself.

The data platform teams have two main interaction modes, *x-as-a-service* and *collaborations*. For example, a data platform team can have a temporary collaboration interaction with a data product team during the design and inception of new platform features to understand their needs and improve their user experience. The objective is to get to the level of maturity that the interactions remain as x-as-a-service to reduce the friction of using the platform.

Given the complexity of the platform, there will likely be multiple *complicated subsystem teams* with specialist knowledge of a particular area. According to Team Topologies, "A complicated-subsystem team is responsible for building and maintaining a part of the system that depends heavily on specialist knowledge, to the extent that most team members must be specialists in that area of knowledge in order to understand and make changes."[9]

For example, the implementation of encryption algorithms, data synthesization, and anomaly detection all require deep specialized knowledge. Unless the platform utilizes vendor-supplied services for these features, there will be specialized component teams building components that the platform can then include in its services. There are temporary collaboration interactions between complicated subsystem teams and other data platform teams to design or integrate the subsystem.

The goal should be to minimize the number of complicated subsystems since they can easily become bottlenecks, instead embedding the specialization needed so the teams become self-sufficient. The interaction mode between these complicated subsystem teams and the platform teams is collaborative.

I cover the data platform team's interaction with the governance group in the next section.

Federated governance teams as enabling teams

The key role of federated governance teams is to facilitate decision making around global policies. These policies then get implemented computationally by the platform and adopted by the domain data product teams. Chapter 5 introduced the operating model of governance.

In addition to establishing policies, the governance group brings subject matter experts together who *enable* the data product teams. According to Team Topologies, an enabling team helps stream-aligned teams to establish practices, provide informed guidelines, develop their capabilities, and close knowledge gaps, while focusing on their main responsibility of delivering their stream's end-to-end outcome.

Figure 16-8 shows an example of governance broken into multiple groups and their interactions with data product and platform teams. In this example, I'm classifying the breakdown as groups—a looser construct than a team. The members of these groups come together to perform a specific task, for example deciding on a global policy, but they don't work together on a day-to-day basis in a long-standing team.

---

9 Skelton and Pais, *Team Topologies*, Kindle Locations 1801–1803.

At the time of this writing, the optimal model for governance groups is an area of exploration. Ultimately, the objective is to avoid creating governance teams that become bottlenecks.

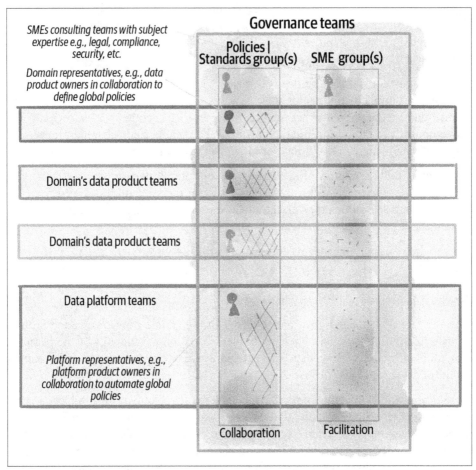

Figure 16-8. Example of data governance groups and their interactions

In this example, a global policies and standards group composed of domain representatives, such as data product owners and platform representatives, such as platform product owners, and SMEs, work collaboratively to identify and define a small set of global policies. The platform collaborates with this group in automating the policies.

A group of SMEs such as legal, security, and compliance continue to consult the data product teams.

Discover Data Product Boundaries

Boundaries of data products directly define the boundaries of the teams. One of the questions I often get asked is how to identify data products boundaries? What data needs to go into one data product versus another? What is the right granularity for a data product?

These questions are important and underpin the allocation of the data product teams and their long-term responsibilities. Hence, I answer them here in relation to the design decisions for an organization's structure. The answer to these questions is not an exact science and more importantly would change over time as the organization evolves its data mesh implementation.

If you consider some of the principles that underpin a data product, you will arrive at a set of heuristics to test whether the boundaries you have selected for your data products are the right ones for the moment or not. In this section I introduce a few of these heuristics.

Before going ahead, a quick reminder that however you assess and identify the boundaries of data products, what good boundaries look like will change over time. That would depend on which phase of the data mesh evolution ("A multiphase evolution model" on page 286) you are in, the level of operational maturity to handle a large number of data products, the complexity of the mesh, the available capabilities of the platform, and the hard constraints that the underlying vendor-provided technologies may impose at any point in time. Plan and design for continuous improvement and change, and not for a static and perfect design.

Start with the existing business domains and subdomains

Is the data product aligned with a business domain? Or is the data product manufactured based on theoretical modeling? Does it match business reality and truth?

Data products are owned, sourced, and consumed by the business-tech-aligned domains. This is a fundamental organizational assumption of data mesh. Discovering business domains drives creation and ownership of data products. Start with identifying the business domains to discover what data products they share or need.

You may ask, how do I identify the business domains? Well, you don't need to do much; they already exist. They represent how the business divides its resources, responsibilities, outcome, and knowledge. For example, Figure 16-4 is an example of Daff business domains.

Looking at these domains and their subdomains is a starting point to find the rough boundaries between data products. There are cases where a data product doesn't squarely line up with one domain, and it's an aggregate of multiple domains, in which case either a new domain is established or an existing domain with a stronger influence on the life cycle and design of the data product will take the ownership of it.

Data products need long-term ownership

Is the data product conducive to long-term ownership? Does anyone care about this domain enough to own it?

Data products are long-standing artifacts with long-term ownership. They are not artifacts built for a particular project and then forgotten by the original project developers. They are expected to evolve over time depending on the changing and new usages.

If the data product you are identifying does not have such longevity, it is not a data product. It may be a dataset inside a specific application database built for a particular project.

Data products must have independent life cycles

Does the data product have high cohesion for ease of use and atomic integrity? Does all the data the data product serves have the same life cycle? Or does the data product compile multiple datasets that each change independently based on different processes and triggers?

I suggest designing data products in a way that each holds data with the same life cycle—create, update, delete—based on a single and well-defined process. Applying loose coupling and high cohesion principles to define what datasets should or should not belong to a data product assures the integrity and usability of data. The user of a data product should be able to easily understand the logical decision behind combining various datasets into a domain data product. Each data product should independently drive value and meaning—without data users always needing to join it with other data products to get to something meaningful.

For example, consider the **listener profiles** aggregate data product. It serves the listeners' personal information, as well as a few derived characteristics such as music profiles and the cohorts they belong to. The **listener profiles** can change based on multiple inputs such as the **registration** process, **subscription changes,** or changes to their **listenership behavior** or **location**. Despite having different triggers, all these triggers change one aggregate entity, the **listener profiles,** with a single transformation logic. Of course, it's also OK to break this data product further to separate data products, e.g., **listener personal information** and **listener profiles** to get a more independent life cycle. The former changes because of registrations, and the latter changes because of listening behavior. I think both of these models are acceptable. I start with a less granular data product, while respecting the cohesion of the data life cycle.

In contrast, if the data product serves two completely different types of data that each change independently with different life cycles, under two aggregate roots,[10] then the boundary needs to be refined to create two different data products. A pathological example is a data product called **everything we know about listeners** that serves listeners playlists, their devices, their profiles, etc., all in one data product. Each of these outputs can change independently; hence, they must be converted to different data products.

Data products are independently meaningful

Does the data product provide meaningful data independently? Do all your data product users need to join and connect the data product with others to use it?

Traditional data warehousing uses database normalization techniques with fact tables to join many different dimension tables that each keep data about an entity. This allows a highly flexible query system to cross-correlate data across many dimensions. This high-effort modeling is time-consuming and can cover only a subset of use cases.

Data products on the mesh do not intend to design one perfect model optimized for all possible queries. Data products on the mesh optimize for minimal modeling and maximum reusability, and there is composition of fit-for-purpose data products only if needed. Hence, they attempt to provide value—meaningful data—independently. They replicate information from other data products if needed to avoid unnecessary joins. This does not replace cross-data-product joins but makes sure in the majority of scenarios the data product can be useful independently.

Data products boundary Goldilocks zone

The Goldilocks zone for the boundary of a data product—its granularity, the data it serves, and the transformation it executes—is at the intersection of *ease of usability*, *ease of maintenance*, and *business relevance*.

The data product output must be usable on its own and deliver value and meaning to its users. If the data product is bloated, encoding too many facets that can independently change, and if it's hard to understand why and how it changes, it's time to break it down to simpler data products.

The data product transformation logic complexity should not inhibit its maintainability. It must be easily understood, tested, and maintained. If the transformation of a data product turns into a complex pipeline with a high rate of change fail ratio, it

---

10 "Aggregate (*https://oreil.ly/P5Awy*) is a cluster of domain objects that can be treated as a single unit. An aggregate will have one of its component objects be the aggregate root."

is time to revisit the boundary of it. It's perhaps time to decouple it into independent data products.

If the data product does not resemble the reality of the business and has morphed through aggregation and transformation far from the original business context, it may have drifted into the land of perfect modeling. In this faraway land, maintenance cost is increased, and data products are more difficult to understand and use. It's time to revisit the reasons behind complex transformation and revert back to the real-world context.

Data products without users don't exist

Is the data product used by anyone? Is it providing data for any reports, training any ML model, or feeding downstream data products? Or is the data product created for hypothetical use cases that might be needed one day in the future?

There is a temptation for the people who concern themselves with data to decide up front what data products the organization might need one day. Perhaps fear of missing out drives the creation of such hypothetical data products. I agree that the sooner we capture the reality of business digitally, the easier it will be to give future use cases the opportunity to derive insight from the past. However, the cost of this up-front investment and lack of knowledge in what we actually need to capture do not outweigh the benefits. So instead, I suggest following the business-driven ("Business-Driven Execution" on page 280) execution approach I introduced in Chapter 15 to discover the use cases first and then rapidly start building the required data products.

People

Organizational design decisions concerned with *people* include their roles, their capabilities, development and training, and recruitment. In this section I'm going to only address the key distinctive areas that data mesh impacts—new and changing roles and responsibilities and new development pathways to generate the talent, skills, and mindsets necessary to implement data mesh.

First, let's have a quick look at the changing or new roles.

Roles

The introduction of the principle of data as a product and domain ownership introduces new roles within each domain team such as data product owners who facilitate the prioritization of data products and their features.

The self-serve data platform puts an emphasis on the role of platform product owners, who facilitate the platform capabilities offered as internal technical products.

The federation of governance decision making to domains changes the existing governance roles such as data governance officer, data stewards, and data custodians.

Ultimately, the decentralization of data ownership to cross-functional domain-oriented teams shifts the responsibilities and the role of the organization's head of data, e.g., chief of data and analytics.

The data product owner role

Data product owners work within a particular domain and are accountable for the domain's data products. Depending on the number and complexity of the subdomains and the data products, there could be one or multiple data product owners. Data product owners facilitate making decisions around the vision and the roadmap for the data products, concern themselves with the continuous measurement and communication of their data consumers' satisfaction, and help the data product team improve the quality and richness of their data. They manage and communicate the life cycle of the domain data products, when to change, revise, and retire data and schemas. They strike a balance between the competing needs of their data consumers.

Data product owners define, continuously monitor, and refine the success criteria and business-aligned KPIs of their data products—a set of objective metrics that measures the performance and success of their data products. They use these metrics to get observability into the state of their data products and help the team improve the data product.

Data products' success, like any other product, is aligned with the satisfaction of the data consumers. For example, data consumer satisfaction can be measured through net promoter score—the degree by which the consumers recommend the data products to others, the decreased lead time for data product consumers to discover and use the data product successfully, and the growth of users.

The domain data product developer

In order to build and operate the domains' data products, the app dev team's roles need to be extended to include data product developers. Data product developers work closely with their collaborating application developers in defining the domain data semantic and mapping data from the application context (data on the inside) to the data product context (analytical data on the outside). They build and maintain the transformation logic that generates the desired data as well as the usability traits and guarantees of their data products.

A wonderful side effect of such a cross-functional collaboration is cross pollination of different skill sets and the ability to cross-skill existing developers so they become data product developers.

The platform product owner

This role is not unique to the data mesh platform and is a must-have for any internal technical platform. The multiplane platform services are simply products, products that internal users, data product developers, and consumers use to do their job. The success of the platform services depends on ease of usability, satisfaction, and frankly the adoption of the platform services without force. The role of the platform product owner is to facilitate the prioritization of the platform services to design and build the experience of the users of the platform. They drive the inception activities that define how the platform services fit into the overall journey of a data product developer, consumer, the operation team, governance, etc. A platform product owner then works closely with the platform architect and the development team in refining how those experiences are built.

A platform product owner must have a deep knowledge of the users, in this case data developers, data product owners, etc. Often the platform product owner has been a power user in the past and has experienced, firsthand, the journeys of data producers or consumers. They have a reasonable understanding of the landscape of technologies that they will be using, building, or buying as part of the platform.

Product ownership skills such as user research, product validation, feedback collection, A/B testing, etc., are necessary.

Shifting role of the existing data governance office

Today, various data governance functions operate under the data governance office. The exact structure and roles vary from one organization to another.

Nevertheless, data mesh changes the roles within this office—data steward, data custodian, members of the data council, etc.

Here are a few examples of changes in the governance roles:

Today, data stewards operate in the central governance team and are in charge of managing, investigating, and resolving data quality issues for one or multiple domains. With data mesh, this role is shifted to the domains and becomes part of a domain, as a data product owner. People currently in this role can either shift to a domain's data product owner role or move to the platform as a specialist to help automate data quality testing, observability, and recovery.

Today, data custodians are often hands-on in charge of day-to-day work with data sources and maintaining the data. This role is deprecated and shifted to domains as data product developer role.

The data council, as the highest decision-making body with accountability for policies, also shifts to a federated model with representatives from domains.

These examples are a starting point to move toward automation and federation of governance, removing synchronous controls and bottlenecks and giving accountability to people who have the power to make changes.

Changing the role of chief data and analytics officer

Today, technology organizations are run by functional executives, such as a chief data and analytics officer (CDAO), chief technology officer, chief digital officer, etc. Traditionally, the role of CDAO has been concerned with all things data: accountable for the enterprise-wide creation, utilization, and governance of data to drive business value. Many of the CDAOs that I have worked with are responsible for building the data platform, harvesting and collecting the analytical data, and building many of the analytical solutions that business demands—dashboards and ML models. In short, many different responsibilities that require data specialization fall under the CDOA's functional organization.

Moving data from a specialized concern to a generalized one, distribution of the data responsibility to cross-functional domain teams, and diffusion of data expertise all influence a shift in the role of a CDAO to an *enablement* role, with close collaborative relationships with chief digital or technology officers. CDAOs will remain responsible for areas that are highly specialized. It's too early to say what highly specialized areas will evolve and what the role exactly would look like. Nevertheless, organizations must resolve the conflict between the decentralization of data accountability and the centralization of data accountability under a CDAO.

Skillset Development

Data mesh strategy requires the diffusion of minimum skill sets required for everyone involved in digital solution development—applications, services, products—to appreciate, understand, and use data. Removing the walls of organizational silos between the data specialists and everyone else is a catalyst for an organic cross-pollination of skills, language, and understanding.

While creating an organizational structure conducive to learning new skills by osmosis is a good starting point, organizations must invest in creating and executing an intentionally designed *data literacy* program across the board.

In addition to raising the water with increased data education, new career development pathways must be designed for people to step into the new roles and responsibilities that data mesh introduces.

Education drives democratization

Increasing participation of people in data sharing across the organization with different roles and levels of skills is a common goal of many organizations—referred to as data democratization. If you follow the root of the word "democratization," you arrive at "dēmos"—the people." Education increases people's awareness and their level of participation. In fact, research shows the level of people's education directly impacts the level of democracy at the societal scale,[11] but that is a conversation for another time.

A successful implementation of data mesh depends on participation in data sharing above and beyond what previous paradigms have expected. It assumes generalist technologists participate in providing the data and putting it into use. It assumes that product managers, application developers, and systems designers no longer externalize the knowledge and responsibility of data.

Data mesh does not expect people to become data specialists, but it does expect them to become experts in their own data. The platform lowers the degree of specialization required. It does expect collaborative cross-functional teams, and many generalists establish the language, mental model, appreciation, and empathy for data and data use cases. Similarly, it expects that data specialists work alongside and in-stream with software engineers to pick up software engineering's evergreen practices when managing, applying, or sharing data.

An organizational-wide data education program considers multiple dimensions. Here are a few dimensions to consider:

Everyone
> Everyone involved in either building, supporting, or managing digital solutions must have an awareness of what is good data and how it can be utilized. Learning about the application of ML—as generative applications, optimization solutions, recommendation systems, anomaly detection services—applied to the organization's specific industry increases creativity and the desire to participate. Everyone learns about data analysis and visualization. Data analysis is simply a new digital experience enhancing existing digital workflows. The expected outcome of this education is creating awareness, appreciation, empathy, and curiosity for data.

Executive and decision makers
> Executives must deeply understand why data mesh is relevant to the organization and know its underpinning principles. During the execution of data mesh, they will be faced with many critical decisions where they need to balance short-term tactical needs versus strategic ones. A deep understanding of the long-term effect of data mesh and its short-term deliverables can help them make the right call.

Generalist technologists
> Scaling the population of contributors to data sharing, either as data product developers or data users, requires mastery in a new set of tools. Technically, the

---

11 Eduardo Alemán and Yeaji Kim, "The Democratizing Effect of Education," *Research & Politics*, (2015) 2(4), doi:10.1177/2053168015613360.

developers need to be educated on the platform interfaces and services and the standards and policies that govern the data products. They need to understand and work within the framework of a continuous delivery of data products. Education on the platform and governance can be an ongoing enablement activity.

Data specialists

Many of the data specialists—data engineers or data scientists—will be joining the domain cross-functional team. They will work in a stream-aligned team that delivers an end-to-end outcome. They no longer work on one isolated step. This means tighter collaboration and integration using software engineering practices and technologies. The education program must help data specialists learn software engineering practices such as coding, testing, and continuous delivery.

Platform engineers

Data infrastructure engineers must get closer to computation and operational infrastructure—building and hosting applications—and computation infrastructure engineers need to understand the data infrastructure landscape better. Data mesh demands seamless integration of data and application platforms.

Flexible organizations require flexible people

Data mesh embraces a move from specialized and isolated teams to cross-functional and collaborative teams. It also depends on the two forcing functions—lowering the level of data specialization through the platform and raising the level of data literacy. This is to get the majority generalist technologist population to actively contribute to data products and solutions. Organizations must design career pathways to close the knowledge gap between these two groups.

Process

Previously I covered the structure of an organization under the influence of a data mesh implementation. Now let's look at the changes to its processes and functions.

Generally, processes fall into two categories, *vertical* and *horizontal*. The vertical processes flow decisions or information up and down the organizational hierarchy. For example, the decisions around budgeting often are centralized by gathering requests from all departments and centrally prioritized at the top. Horizontal processes, also called lateral processes, are designed around work streams for an end-to-end outcome across organizational boundaries. Most data mesh processes are horizontal. For example, the delivery of a new data product is a horizontal process.

So far you have encountered a few key processes involved in data mesh:

Data mesh execution
In Chapter 15, I discussed the overarching process of executing a data mesh implementation, aligned and driven by the larger data strategy, executed through evolutionary and incremental business-driven thin slices.

This is modeled after a transformation process that the Digital Transformation Game Plan[12] calls *thin slicing*, narrow and targeted change processes that cut through all aspects of the business and tech to identify necessary changes and impediments. This is a horizontal process.

Data value exchange
The mesh is a network of data providers and consumers that share data products as a unit of value exchange with minimal friction and interactions. The exchange is facilitated by the platform. I walked you through a couple of processes involved in Chapter 10: the data product developer journey and data product consumer journey. These are horizontal processes.

Global policy definitions
In Chapter 5, I discussed the approach to establishing global policies and standards by the federated governance group. This is a vertical process.

Data mesh dynamic equilibrium with feedback processes
In Chapter 5, I introduced removing process controls in favor of automated feedback loops to maintain the health—dynamic equilibrium—of the mesh. For example, introduce positive and negative feedback loops to reduce the number of duplicate and unwanted data products as an alternative to creating a central control in the data production creation process. These are horizontal processes.

Key Process Changes

Data mesh's endeavor to create a scale-out system of value generation and value exchange with data looks for every opportunity to remove bottlenecks, delays, and unsustainable manual tasks. It looks for opportunities to introduce elements such as feedback loops and levers, automate them, and reduce the need for centralized controls.

In short, if you follow the thread of removing bottlenecks, responding rapidly to change of data, and scaling out the system of data sharing, you will find many opportunities to improve the data sharing processes unique to your organization.

---

12 Gary O'Brien, Guo Xiao, and Mike Mason, *Digital Transformation Game Plan*, (Sebastopol, CA: O'Reilly, 2020).

Following are a few examples of process changes that occur under the influence of a data mesh execution.

Devolve organization decision-making structure to domains
> Many of the processes that traditionally involved the governance team, such as data modeling, guaranteeing data quality, verifying data security, etc., are delegated to the domain.

Automation
> Automating the traditional manual processes is a must to scale a data mesh implementation. Examples of such processes include access to data and verifying and certifying data quality.

Replace synchronization with automation or distributed consensus
> Processes that demand centralized synchronization inhibit scale and agility. Any time you find yourself faced with one of such processes, find other ways to achieve the same outcome in a distributed fashion.
>
> For example, you may decide that the process of identifying new data products and their owners is a decision that the collection of data product owners can make. You may even imagine this as a meeting of sorts to discuss and identify the data product team allocation. Such a meeting is a point of synchronization that can block the progress of the creation, change, or allocation of existing products at scale.
>
> Alternatively, this synchronous and manual process can be replaced with a set of global heuristics that a team can use to self-assess product ownership.[13] Introduction of automated feedback loops and leverage points prune out duplicate data products over time.[14]

Recap

What I would like you to take away from this chapter is that executing data mesh needs a multifaceted organizational change. Iteratively and along with the delivery of your data mesh thin slices, I encourage you to look at modifying all facets of organizational design decisions, summarized by Galbraith as *strategy, culture, reward, structure, people* and *process*. Deploy a movement-based organizational change (see "Change" on page 305), start small and move fast to show value, get buy-in, and gather momentum toward a sustainable and scaled change.

---

13 I discussed this as an example of a global policy in Chapter 5.

14 I discussed this in an example of feedback loops and leverage points in Chapter 5.

Define and communicate the cultural values (see "Values" on page 308) that foster actions and behavior that are aligned with a data mesh strategy. The good news is that there is an inherent alignment between humans' intrinsic motivations (see "Intrinsic Motivations" on page 311)—mastery, autonomy and purpose—and the tasks required to implement data mesh.

While the exact organizational structure would vary from one organization to another, use the templates I offered to design your teams and interaction modes based on data mesh Team Topologies (see "Data Mesh Team Topologies" on page 314). The boundary of data products will have a direct impact on your core teams, data product teams. Use the heuristics (see "Discover Data Product Boundaries" on page 321) that I introduced, refine them, and build new ones for your organization to create a system for teams to easily self-assess and decide independently.

Introducing new roles, or perhaps shifting existing ones (see "Roles" on page 324), will be one of the hardest changes you need to make. I briefly discussed some of the role changes. Be kind to people who are moving to new roles, from the comfort of the known to the unknown, particularly around existing governance and centralized data team structures.

I left you with a few key shifts in existing processes (see "Process" on page 329) such as removing organizational synchronization points and manual processes and devolving some of the decision-making hierarchies to achieve scale.

No matter what the changes are, nothing is constant. Continuously observe, evaluate, and change if your team structure, roles, and processes are still getting in the way of getting value from data at scale.

The only thing left is to congratulate you for getting to the end of this book and wish you luck and a whole lot of fun in your journey executing data mesh.

Index

experience planes (see data product experience plane; mesh experience plane)

explorability, data product architecture, 233-236, 241, 242

explore and bootstrap phase, evolution execution, 289, 290, 292, 293, 307

extract and sustain phase, evolution execution, 289, 291, 292, 294, 307

extracting versus publishing/serving/sharing data, 42

extrinsic motivations, for rewards, 311

F

facilitating team interaction mode, 78

FAIR data, 34

federated computational governance, 8, 11, 67-91
    applying computation to governance model, 83-86
    applying federation to governance model, 75-83
    evolution execution phases, 292-294
    fitness functions, 298
    logical architecture role, 146-147
    policies (see policies)
    systems thinking applied to, 69-75
    teams as enabling teams, 319, 326
    transitioning to, 86-88

federated team, 76, 77-78

feedback loops, 71-73, 109

fit-for-purpose data aggregates, 23

fit-for-purpose domain data, 24, 81

fitness functions, guided evolution with, 294-298

Forrester, Jay W., 74

foundation framework, shifting to data mesh, 65

Fowler, Martin, 6, 210

G

gap modeling, transitioning to federated computational governance, 88

garbage collection, feedback loop system as, 72

generalist technologists, 48, 53, 63, 65

global control port function, 216

global incentives, 82, 83

global interoperability, 71-74, 79, 310

global policies, 11, 81, 85

global standards, 68, 79, 80

globally unique identifiers, for data products, 250

governance, data (see data governance)

H

harvested framework, evolving, 65

human element of data composition, 251

hyperlinks, relationship defined by, 248

I

identity standards for access control, 261

immutable data, 206-208, 216

incentives, applying federation to governance, 76, 82-83

inception and exploration of data product
    consumer journey, 188
    developer journey, 177-178

incidental complexities, reducing with data mesh, 111, 208

inflection points in shift to data mesh
    data architecture before the shift, 121-136
        characteristics of analytical data architecture, 126-136
        evolution of analytical data architectures, 121-126
    introductory example, xxvi-xxxvi
    outcomes after the shift, 105-117
        data mesh goals summary, 117
        increasing ratio of value from data to investment, 115-117
        responding to change in complex business, 106-111
        sustaining agility in face of growth, 111-115
    strategic organizational, 95-103
        expectations of data, examples of, 96-98
        great divide of data, 98-99
        navigating complexity, uncertainty, volatility, 101
        plateau of return, approaching, 102
        scaling in terms of volume, velocity and variety, 100

infrastructural perspective
    in data mesh goals, 5
    data platform infrastructure plane, 162, 172, 173
    dependencies, 152
    domain agnosticism of underlying infrastructure, 54, 223

W

About the Author

Zhamak Dehghani is a director of technology at Thoughtworks, focusing on distributed systems and data architecture in the enterprise. She's a member of multiple technology advisory boards including Thoughtworks. Zhamak is an advocate for the decentralization of all things, including architecture, data, and ultimately power. She is the founder of data mesh.

Colophon

The animal on the cover of *Data Mesh* is a great snipe (*Gallinago media*), the fastest migratory bird known to humans. Great snipes breed in northeastern Europe and migrate to sub-Saharan Africa. Researchers have recorded great snipes flying 4,200 miles at up to 60 mph without stopping.

A typical great snipe wingspan is 17–20 inches. They normally weigh under 7 ounces. The great snipe's plumage is mottled brown, an effective camouflage for the grasslands, marshes, and meadows they inhabit, with a dark stripe across their eyes. The beak is long for foraging in mud and wetlands for worms and insects.

The great snipe population is Near Threatened, according to the IUCN Red List. Many of the animals on O'Reilly's covers are endangered; all of them are important to the world.

The cover illustration is by Karen Montgomery, based on a black-and-white engraving from *British Birds*. The cover fonts are Gilroy Semibold and Guardian Sans. The text font is Adobe Minion Pro; the heading font is Adobe Myriad Condensed; and the code font is Dalton Maag's Ubuntu Mono.

Printed in the USA
CPSIA information can be obtained
at www.ICGtesting.com
JSHW051308241123
52664JS00009B/87